The
East of
England

The East of England

AN ARTIST'S JOURNEY THROUGH ENGLISH LANDSCAPES

SYDNEY R. JONES

SENATE

The East of England

First published in 1954 as *England East* by
The Studio Publications, London & New York

This edition published in 1998 by Senate,
an imprint of Tiger Books International PLC,
26A York Street, Twickenham,
Middlesex TW1 3LJ, United Kingdom

1 3 5 7 9 10 8 6 4 2

ISBN 1 85958 525 6

Printed and bound in the UK by
Cox & Wyman, Reading, England

CONTENTS

PREFACE

This book is the last of three volumes with which I promised to amuse or annoy my readers by presenting selections from my drawings and notes gleaned throughout England during a good many years. The contents include visible scenes made by nature and man, parts of the English heritage that is now being extensively destroyed. Departed invisible people also are resuscitated. Once alive on two legs and since for ever silent, their static works and memorials survive to recall them. At various places therefore I have remembered words written by Sir Thomas Browne as he progressed through uncomfortable times of revolution such as we now enjoy. Even while Cromwellians rampaged, the pious antiquary of Norwich could still declare

> Man is a noble animal, splendid in ashes, and pompous in the grave.

Diversity of scenery, architecture, historical points, and local peculiarities spread over England's area dictate many pitfalls for planners who attempt to divide the country into convenient sections for particular consideration. Classification may be determined by county boundaries, alphabetical sequence, geological formations, physical features; but whatever solution is tried terrors always await the topographical recorder. Essex for example largely belongs to London; Norfolk juts into the Fens. Alnwick, Northumberland, and Amersham, Bucks, both alphabetically A, are a long way from each other. Geology leads to strange mix-ups in the earth's structure, landscape character, or architectural expression. To obtain logical order might be likened to solving a complicated jig-saw puzzle. Faced with these intricacies makers of books on the English scene generally have solved the problem by sweeping upward through roughly parallel divisions, starting from the South Coast, reaching the Midlands, ending at the North. My scheme also includes the whole of the ground but in a different way. An imaginary central vertical alignment from the Thames to the Tweed separates this present *England East* from the *England West* of my previous volume, and south of the Thames belongs to the first book of this trio, *England South*. The eastern and western regions, thus delineated, each have the advantage of offering perambulations through many varieties of countryside from south to north. The plan, which seemed convenient, actually originated with my publisher, Mr. Frank A. Mercer. Of course the scheme invites objections—nobody can please everybody. Possibly the artists who live in the Constable Country or the grand farmers of East Anglia may not appreciate being mixed with the coalminers of Durham or the Northumbrian Percys settled in my *England East*. For good or ill I have done my best and with this volume bring to an end these adventures in books.

S. R. J.

1. INTRODUCTION

LONDON BORDERS TO THE TWEED

At *The Studio* offices in London, where good books come from, the lights of the institution asked what I proposed to do about my final effort on England. Meekly I suggested a few main directions for attacking the scenery and natives in *England East*. Of course, they said, you will include Sandringham, the royal home, something relating to mighty names like de Vere, Cecil, and Nevill, every type of landscape, all the cathedrals, castles and pubs, all the big houses awaiting doom from doses of Death Duties and Income Tax, the innumerable old villages and historic towns now being swamped by council dwellings, prefabs, community centres, cooling towers, and similar objects which prove that the old country advances in the rhythm of forward movement.

"When my father Geoffrey and I lived at Old Bridge House in Kelvedon," said Rathbone Holme, "we sailed on the Blackwater, visited Layer Marney Hall, and thought Coggeshall wonderful with Paycocke's House, the *Woolpack*, the brick chapel and bridge. These places really ought to be illustrated."

"And certainly Norwich, *my family home*," murmured Kathleen Frost.

"Absolutely imperative," I answered, gallantly adding, "*Your* signs of lineage never could be left out."

"Though Kent bred me," Frank Mercer remarked, "the Mercers were mercers wool-gathering all over East Anglia from the reign of Edward III. You might look up and note some of their quarters, say at Worstead, Aylsham, Kersey, or Lavenham."

"Naturally," I responded, "anybody is proud to air a long woolly pedigree—but don't forget that all of us claim descent from Adam, Eve, and the monkeys."

The pretty girl who types soon entered with letters for signatures. Apparently overhearing the conversation, she whispered under her breath, "Widford and Mackery End in Hertfordshire. I adore Charles Lamb!"

Later the door opened to admit a young sylph presenting cups of tea without victuals to cheer our deliberations. Possibly deploring an absence of Yorkshire girdle cakes, she said almost inaudibly, "Appleton-le-Moors! My great-aunt there is such a good cook." Behind the open door an imp waited to deliver blockmakers' proofs. Fresh in the conquest of London from Barnard Castle, he was distinctly heard entertaining somebody with the superior glories of Caldron Snout and High Force. The telephone then rang. Eavesdropping I gathered it was a request for space in the pages of *The Studio* magazine for an appeal to help keep either York Minster, The Cheviot, or Hadrian's Wall from falling down, though my secret listening did not inform me which particular monument needed assistance.

When the conversation ceased and we again got down to our subject it was agreed that surely enough geographical points had just been mentioned in a very short time to start a very big book.

"And remember," I said, "one volume would hardly do. This I know after a lifetime of sketching the countryside, old houses, cathedrals, castles, villages, and towns, noting the changes in scenery, and finding so many sights illuminating England's old tale. Continually you are reminded of kings, queens, feudal families, monasticism, medieval guilds, market charters, the great early wool trade, champion husbandry, enclosures, farming evolutions, and all the things that once mattered very much in moulding native instincts and social history. It's really exciting. Every plot and picture tells a story and also the truth."

"Like a pill advertisement?" here was rudely interposed.

"Or the Durham coalfield!" I retorted.

Scorning the interlude, I continued, "we can only attempt general impressions, local and regional, mere bits of the whole panorama. Of course lots of old buildings must come in, because architecture, both monumental and homely, tells better than anything else what people thought, how they looked on life, the sort of things they really wanted and therefore got. Vivid survivals will prove that once upon a time an aristocracy of thought and culture created true and great national styles in building. Samples of weathered homes will indicate how and where lived the family stocks who struck roots into the soil. Innumerable big and little effects made long ago by local craftsmen for ordinary folk in towns and villages may further help to remind us of the good looks and the beauty that jewelled England's landscapes and counties."

"And this," I concluded, "is my brief scheme for perambulating. Start along the Chiltern Hills to Hertfordshire, look towards London, cross Essex to the River Stour and old wool towns in Suffolk and Norfolk. A drop from the East Anglian heights will mean Fen levels, Boston, Ely's loveliness, Cambridge Colleges. Next I'll go down the Great Ouse, then up to the Midland stone and the church spires pointing all the way to Peterborough and Grantham, and follow on to Leicestershire grasslands and wolds, Nottinghamshire trees, Trent vale, Lincoln's superb hill. Northward will lead me to Yorkshire's varied scenery, glories in York city, mountains and fast rivers, incomparable Durham, and an ending at the Roman Wall, Border strongholds, Holy Island."

"Add the trimmings and this might do," my listeners said.

"Right," I replied, "I'll go back to my hut near the Chilterns and start from there."

IN THE SPIRE COUNTRY. *Middleton Cheney.*

FENLAND TOWN IN ENGLISH HOLLAND. *Boston.*

YORKSHIRE COAST AND PANTILE ROOFS. *Whitby.*

CHILTERN SCENE. *Turville.*

2. NORTH OF THE LOWER THAMES

BUCKINGHAMSHIRE, BEDFORDSHIRE, HERTFORDSHIRE, ESSEX

Chiltern Hills and the central mass of chalk lead down to the clays and sands of the Thames valley and Essex. Here ready for our pleasure are expansive views from the northern scarps, combes, downlands, Chiltern beech woods, green miles and golden corn in Hertfordshire, Epping and Hatfield oaks to recall ancient forests, the quiet Essex countryside, a broken coastline bounded by wide flats. Prehistoric earthworks, the Icknield Way, Roman roads, remains at St. Albans and Colchester, routes used by the Danes, and medieval tracks all prove that the area was much travelled onward from earliest times. The district in every part holds reminders of historical places and people, while spreading suburbs, far-flung from London, have brought new sights. Traditional architecture developed notably in splendid brickwork, flint, external plaster-work in the chalk regions, timbering for town and rural homes. The mighty of the land settled down at establishments associated with famous names; many in number, they include Chequers Court, Hatfield House, Audley End, Layer Marney Hall, Castle Hedingham. Humbler folk built houses and cottages good to look at, and left village effects of particular charm.

CHILTERN AND CHALK COUNTRY

Any fine day from my home in the Thames valley I can see the darkly wooded scarps of the Chilterns reared in long bold lines above lower slopes, hillocks, and the wide plateau patchworked with fields for growing wheat, oats, barley, and rye. It is a graceful scene, not dramatically set out, one of the kind that you never tire of looking over. Broad expanses of natural forms, trim shapeliness of cultivation, and the band of hills beyond are full of landscape variety. Sunlight and shadow, clear days and misty atmospheres bring never-ending gradations in tone and colour. As the year spins round nature's palette paints the changing seasons, vivid greens and chalky browns in spring, summer's fullness, autumn's golden tints of grain, stubble, and beech, delicate films of white when the snow flakes down and sombre tints of woods, trees, and hedgerows accentuate surface outlines and patterns. Curiously the effects often remind me of pictures by Hobbema or Jacob Ruisdael, even though these painters were Dutchmen and the Chiltern canvases are out-and-out real English. And if the planes from Benson aerodrome circle and swoop overhead, like vultures born of an unstable and explosive epoch, the ground shapes below them keep the placid look of permanence and ageless continuity. The hills have stood for millions of years, their name is of prehistoric origin, the ancient ways running north-east to Norfolk are ancestors of road travel, the cornlands where combine-harvesters now reap have yielded since man first began to till English soil.

I have indicated this scene because it is typical of the landscapes that are visible to travellers as they cross the Oxfordshire or Aylesbury Vales, follow Watling Street, or proceed through mid-Bedfordshire when bound south-east from the Midlands. Whichever way you may come, there ahead are the Chiltern Hills extended in well-defined escarpments, outlined with woods or piled in elemental and bare ramparts. They bar the way, demand to be climbed, bring the consciousness of facing a barrier, a pulse line, that from time immemorial divided the Midlands from the South. Certainly long ago the native Britons and the Romans cut through (notably with Watling Street) as the coaches and railroads did much later; but even to-day the southern hills conquer, for no railways penetrate them between Princes Risborough and the Thames. In that region, only 25 miles from London's outskirts, you can be as lonely as you wish and feel completely remote from the twentieth century.

Continuing the west-to-east elevations made by the downs in Berkshire, the Chilterns mount up from the Thames. Rising to Nuffield at the head of Grim's Ditch—an earthwork dug by ancient folk—the hills begin the command of vista and distance that is their especial prerogative onward from county to county. They thrust headlands into the plain, shape deep combes, gain in height, top Shirburn, Bald and Beacon Hills, continually offer great panoramas spread to the west and the north, keep the thick covering of woods above Crowell, Chinnor, and to Wain Hill at the Buckinghamshire border, where more particularly our travels for this volume begin. Thence, cornering round Bledlow Cross, the line goes eastward. It sends curve, warren, and inlet down to the cornfields, sets back round the gaps at Risborough, Wendover, and Tring. The high lands, often defining the places of forgotten people by tumuli and earth markings, jut arms out to spur and promontory ever in command of the great plain patterned by human labours of centuries. Whiteleaf, Cymbeline's Mount and Coombe Hill, Aston Hill, Ivinghoe Beacon, Barton Hills, and point after point afford visions over seeming limitless acres and northern distances; shaped in eons before the dawn of history, they stand like sentinel cliffs of old time keeping watch over the oceans of memories.

Detached from the main Chilterns by Hitchin and the Hiz valley the uplands lead on through north Hertfordshire. Here the rhythm is changed. Accents are less pronounced. Earthworks and burial mounds still denote a former presence of the ancients, Ermine Street crosses the rolling hills, and a broken way beyond Clothall's fascinating little church tells how the Romans went from Baldock to Braughing. But times not so remote are more conspicuously suggested by the charming villages set on the hillsides and hollows. They have about them a look of peaceful long settlement, a fragrant air of the years before horses, latten bells, candlelight, and the merry-making of honest rural folk faded into the mists of now mythical old-fashioned England. Weston, Wallington, Therfield, Barkway, and more quiet and picturesque places show their white-faced walls and thatched roofs in most engaging fashion among the undulating fields, hedgerows, and patches of woods. The higher ridges from Weston Hills to Periwinkle Hill (here a Roman left a statue of Mars) overlook the north; they send out feelers towards Ashwell and Royston, and long views open out across the levels watered by many brooks and the young Cam stream winding to Cambridge. Making final bows to Hertfordshire, the hills project their pretty ups and downs to meet the East Anglian heights.

Everybody acquainted with the countryside knows that these stretches of upland from the Thames to the end of Hertfordshire are due to the *massif* of chalk, the long formation spread in a well-defined belt from the Dorset coast to the Wash in Norfolk. Over the Chiltern section it slightly varies in width, generally measures from 15 to 18 miles across, and the hills, barely middle-aged in the reckoning of the old world's time, geologists calculate have been upstanding for about a hundred million years. Bordering the northern flank of the chalk is the Upper Greensand strip, approximately 3 to 5 miles wide, and this in places leads down to the Lower Greensand. Though geological particulars can make dull reading, the effects influenced by the construction of the earth often turn out to be very exciting. Here for instance the age and construction of the

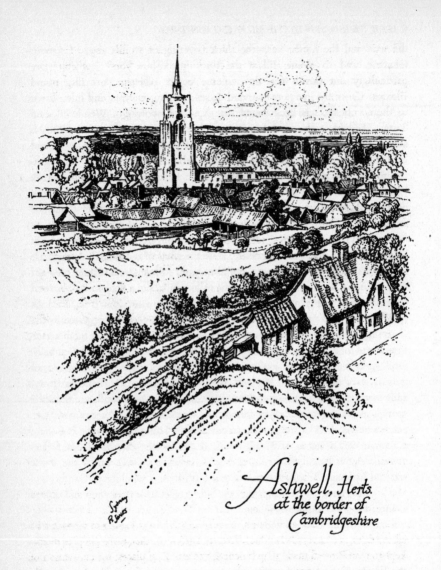

Ashwell, Herts.
at the border of
Cambridgeshire

formations in this Chiltern country, chalk sprinkled with flints and the accompanying beds of greensand and gault, accounted for a good deal more than affording materials for building houses, cottages, and churches. In primeval Britain, then thick with forests and tangled undergrowth, impassable across vales and marshes, the chalk offered the easiest going when men first began to travel. It had the best drained and least impeded land surfaces. So from the dawn of man's known periods these hills bore on their backs the interminable comings and goings, the foot-padding and cavalcades of centuries. Prompted by the knowledge that a mere scratching of the turf revealed the white chalk, unknown people for unknown purposes cut out devices on the hillsides. The inspiration for executing these feats will probably remain a mystery, but Bledlow Cross on Wain Hill and Whiteleaf Cross above Princes Risborough still show in white against green from near and far, just as the curious animal cut on White Horse Hill continues to be a landmark over the wide Berkshire vale. There are the numerous banked earthworks and forts dominating the heights from western Buckinghamshire to Maiden Bower, near Dunstable, and Ravensburgh Castle in Hexton parish, Hertfordshire; now points for stimulating discoveries and affording great views over the plain, they prove that prehistoric natives valued the hills for residence and security. Where some of those natives concluded their labours and finally retired underground is obvious to inquisitive eyes by the frequent green mounds and rumpled earth of the round barrows and tumuli. Primitive people, as they cleared woodland and scrub, ventured downhill, found the greensand where the crops grew best. From the lower chalk the springs broke out, sent the water along to sheltered spots, obviously good places for settlement. Their descendants, the chain of pretty villages and hamlets linked through Lewknor, Horsenden, Little Kimble, Drayton Beauchamp, and away to the east, yet are found most thickly clustered where the streams flow, watercress grows, and the productive soil yields the corn.

There are of course other subjects for speculation arising from geological phenomena. The actual shape and make of the hills and their surface markings send the mind wandering through abysmal time, bring a feeling of contact with all the ages of history. Neolithic, Bronze Age, and other early peoples mostly kept to the tops and made strip lynchets, yet visible in places, for cultivation on the slopes. Similar positions in later times accounted for noble domains, the landed estates of Great Hampden, Ashridge, Tring and more parks, and Chequers Court, an Elizabethan home standing high on a Domesday site, now a hiding-place for Prime Ministers during weekends. Whipsnade's 700-feet elevation doubtless accommodated prehistoric reptiles at the very spot where the motor coaches halt, and deposit the human species to inspect zoological wild beasts at large. The secluded aspects of wooded uplands and combes in the Chiltern Hundreds explain why the district in past times attracted outlaws, vagabonds, rogues, religious fugitives, and more recently exploded politicians, all in their generations in search of quiet and peace, amplified by the convenience of beautiful natural formation. "Here if you beat a bush, it's odds you'll start a thief," wrote Drayton in the seventeenth century. Records tell that the Stewards of the Hundreds once had busy occupations in their arduous jobs of chasing and rounding up footpads and robbers; their successors nowadays, retired M.P.s, find not much to do and usually spend the time by going into hiding themselves.

Though the woodman slaughters, real estate is planted with bricks and mortar, urban picnickers bestow their leavings of waste paper and empty bottles, a good deal of the Chiltern loveliness remains unsullied. Fuller and more varied than in much of our chalk country, here this characteristic type of English scenery is at its best. Along the northern heights marshalled in a long wavy line, boldly advanced, or set back, the profiles of hill and combe have the distinctive perfections of their origin, the swell and curve slowly made millions of years ago by deposits accumulated when the great waters covered the face of the land. Predominant on these smooth rounded contours are the woods, the famous and glorious woods of the Chilterns. Ranked along skylines and densely covering upper slopes, the beeches unlimited and mixed trees jut in and out with bosky shapes to embroider the lower woodland borders. Clumps and thickets, the hawthorns and the hollies join in the riot of nature's harmony. Wild box is prolific here and there (especially round Coombe and Pulpit Hills), and the junipers, the aborigines, darkly speckle many hillsides, as much as to say, "We've been here longest and mean to stay." Up on bracing open spaces rough grass sings in the breeze and stretches of springy turf plainly tell who trimmed them so fine—the rabbits, conquerors that play havoc above and below ground, throw up nodules of chalk, and multiply like present human generations. All the year round there are fresh sights for the eye and memory, quiet too in the solitudes, and for music the wind and the birds, singing thrushes, laughing woodpeckers, notes of the noisy magpies. Bluebells, nowhere found better, send out myriads of corollas that shimmer in azure and dispel delicate transparent haze. The rampant ragwort advances with flaming colours. Beeches shower down carpets of russet and gold, and their trunks and branches, tinted pale green and silver, never look lovelier than in winter sunshine. So the pageants of the trees, plants, and wild flowers, the prodigality of growth and maturity come and go season by season. Always in clear weather on the heights the great views over the vale and far-flung distance contrast with the near at hand; wooded, tree-dotted, and bare hills, curves swelling down to the plain, and the expansive lowlands emphasize the diversity of natural design trimmed and developed by the diligence of man.

Of all the effects dictated or influenced by the hills the Icknield Way always appeals to me as the greatest fact of the Chilterns. Originally traced by feet and hoofs, the old road ranks amongst the most ancient works made in England. Its very permanence grips, imparts meanings. In scenery it is vivid and for the imagination stimulating. This prehistoric relic served in man's dawning times, Romans made improvements in parts to suit their purposes of conquest, it carried west-to-east traffic through the Dark, Middle and later ages, by-passed the Industrial Revolution and the railways, and to-day it remains primitive, green-faced, and white, or macadamized, tarred, and motor-ridden, triumphant through and over Time. Walking on Icknield ways trodden by Bronze Age folk or speeding along over Roman foundations can bring a sense of feeling the pulse-beats of centuries. From the course and beyond lower slopes full land-scapes stretch away to far northern distances. They spread out like open pages of old illuminated manuscript jewelled with parchment tints of ripening corn and harvested fields, pastures and woods, church towers, villages and country towns, the pointers of settlement and history formed and matured while travellers unceasingly passed to and fro along the Icknield Way.

On a previous page I have mentioned that the chalk hills offered the driest and easiest trackways for communications in a primeval England much entangled with forests, undergrowth, and swamps. Not by accident therefore did primitive men first blaze this route. Oldest of all, a very patriarch in road systems, the great ridge crossing kept to the crests of the hills. It pursued a dauntless course from the early religious and commercial settlements centred on Salisbury Plain and round Avebury, topped the downland heights of Wiltshire, Berkshire, the Chilterns, swept eastward to the ancient wheat-producing and agricultural districts that extended into Norfolk. Thus the route established a vital line for the flow of traffic, trade, and ideas between East Anglia, the mid-South and the West. Later, yet of immemorial antiquity, the Upper Icknield Way came up from the Thames at the river crossing between Goring and Streatley. Parallel to its first ancestor, it was skilfully laid out to hug the northern slopes below the chalk crests. Subsequently the Lower Icknield Way developed, said to be the work of King Cymbeline the Road-Maker. This provided for fair-weather travel bordering the vale. The Upper and Lower Ways met and united at their Ivinghoe junction. This trio in a system of west-east communications, father, son, and grandson, have all the attributes common to England's first ways of travel. Their ancestry gives the spell of antiquity and mystery. Exhilaration comes from the rare passages of scenery which they offer. They have endured for thousands of years and kept place on the ground. Still they carry burdens on hard tops for a hard scientific age or merely continue, little used and green-coated, seductive to walkers, mellowed with memories of life and times gone. Many centuries have endowed them with a character almost human. If, as we are led to believe, mankind has persisted since the episodes in the Garden of Eden, I have an idea that when the human race comes to an end and the earth's crust eventually disintegrates the old trackways and roads, the first things that men made, will be the last to go.

The patriarchal top route continues the great Ridge Way from Wiltshire and Berkshire. Clear of the Thames the way plainly sweeps along the Chiltern heights from Nuffield to Aston Hill, winds in archaic sylvan measures through the woods of Crowell, asserts its true green surface past grass-grown burial mounds of the forgotten dead. A bend through woodlands on Wain Hill points a detour past more tumuli at Lodge Hill for crossing the higher lands of the Risborough valley. Onward, where sections have fallen out of regular use, eagle eyes, speculation, and the aid of imagination are needed for discovering the connected trace. Flights of fancy are not necessary for finding the Lower Icknield Way from Pyrton and Lewknor to Ivinghoe. It has kept intact; if King Cymbeline really was its maker and happened to come to life again he would be surprised to see how well his road has lasted from century one A.D. to the motoring era.

But of the three routes the Upper Icknield Way, the middle one in position and age, remains in its long length premier in scenes, remembrances, and mental suggestion. When men ventured down from the ridges before records were made it took first place, developed to be the regal and pre-eminent way. It ran through history until the reign of Queen Victoria. Where Romanized, macadamized, and finally rendered hard in surface it speeds the twentieth century onward. It marked and still marks parish and county boundaries, facts which unquestionably prove antiquity, and to-day on secluded grassy stretches the idea of first purpose and continuity is hinted on reading the notices, "No wheeled traffic." Through an immense span of time the tracks were marched by tribal Britons, Romans, Mercians, Saxons, and Danes, men laden with tin on their shoulders, pack-horses carrying wool-tods and products of the home industries, drovers of sheep and cattle, soldiers, pilgrims, merchants, tradesmen, pedlars, all travelling eastward or westward in the pursuit of profit, peace, war, or holiness. Perhaps their phantoms continue, ghosts that it is nice to think hide by day and come out in the moonlight; may be they wander again to their prehistoric camps at Maiden Bower and Ravensburgh Castle, fight anew on the traditional battleground of Britons and Romans at Cymbeline's Mount, look with awe and wonder at the mysterious hillside crosses of Whiteleaf and Bledlow, or feeling the weight of years, stir their Bronze Age skeletons in the tumuli and come up above ground for airings! If a road can have a soul and retain life to tell its stories surely this is one of them.

Of the processions bound to and fro for travel and trade up and down the Icknield Way since how long ago Heaven only knows it is my good fortune to remember one man who I think was the very last link in the cavalcades. George Hoar by name, he might have sat very well for a portrait by Hogarth or Rowlandson. Tall, strongly built, face weatherbeaten and edged with whiskers from ears to chin, wearing a patterned cloth coat buttoned up to a cloth collar at the neck, trousers bagged to the knees and tight down to the ankles, the headpiece completed with a square-topped hard hat, he looked the very picture of what he was—a dealer in horses, donkeys, cattle, and sheep, a descendant from a father, grandfather, and an ancestry engaged in the same way of business. This son of the open air had a curiously tender feeling for all animals. He knew every turn, tree, and gradient on the antique route, all the shady places and wide green verges for resting and grazing his cattle and sheep. He told me many a tale of his journeys along the Ridge and Icknield Ways in all weathers, fair and foul. Sheep were gathered on the downs and at Ilsley fairs. Flocks of his charge, numbering two to three hundred and accompanied by a shepherd, a dog, a pony and cart, proceeded over the soft and friendly tracks fit for slow going. In three or four days they covered the distance, then branched to the country-town markets, principally at Thame and Aylesbury. Little imagination is needed to re-create the scenes, the leisurely pace, halts and moving on, the watchful shepherd, the pony-cart ready for any weaklings, nights in the open under the stars. Before George died in 1914 the trade had dwindled. The motors came, considered by the old dealer to be the very inventions of the Devil. He never set foot in one and if offered a lift always courteously declined with a, "No, thank you, sir. I would rather keep on my feet." The Icknield Way lost its traditional uses. Now the green track-ways are deserted. I often walk them without meeting the semblance of sheep, horses, cattle, or two-legged animals; and just as often I send an old-shaped thought to George, last relic of his race, now tending herds and flocks on other upper ways among the Elysian fields.

The most romantic and beautiful stretch of the Icknield Way begins at Ipsden in Oxfordshire. It winds through flinty fields within sight of Bepin's Hill, mount of St. Birinus the missionary who sent the message of Christianity throbbing along this busy route through Wessex in the seventh century. Continuing as a narrow lane the Way skirts the treasured village of Ewelme, and thence offers one of the most glorious walks on prehistoric foundations in England. Where the hostile ragwort advances to the woodside below entrenchments on Swyncombe Down, the green turf and white chalk for a footing, the tangled verges and hedgerows contrive a kind of bolt-hole for escape out of the twentieth century, a means of passage for disappearing into the depths of Old Time. Drovers, horses, sheep are there no more. Cultivated fields right and left, once tilled by Saxons, catch the spirit of to-day, with mechanized farm hands driving petrol horses. Soon Britwell House strikes an eighteenth-century note, marvellously situated on a ridge. Onward the track sets no limits for finding nature's luxuriance or for making fanciful excursions into ages long gone. Where garden flowers bloom across the meadow stand the gables and chimneys of the house formerly called Dame Alice Farm. With that name I like to link the great lady of the fifteenth century, Chaucer's grand-daughter Alice de la Pole, Duchess of Suffolk, whose gorgeous memorial lies near in Ewelme church. Past Watlington White Mark, the scenes below the hill ramparts grow lovelier and lovelier. Lights and shadows splash the woodland walk. Near leafage of beech and oak shape spy-holes for looking to the white masonry and castled towers of moated Shirburn gleaming among avenues of elm trees down by Cymbeline's road. Scorning a short close association with a modern antiquated product, the railway running to Princes Risborough, this way of real antiquity gradually mounts, majestically climbs the slopes, gains the lower heights. Swinging past combes and hanging woods it rises to command downlands, middle and distant plains. After a dozen most wonderful English miles the great moments come for rounding Wain Hill into Buckinghamshire.

Wain Hill's great moments belong to the quiet and retired sort. Their causes are the trees, shady paths, dicky-birds and breeze, harebell blue, old turf's green, October's brilliance of yellow, red and gold, prospects "ever bright and fair" from the top on clear sunny days. Live humanity is usually invisible. Below ground, also invisible, lie people who died a tremendous long time ago. Here is a meeting-place of all ages. Most venerable and highest up the Ridge Way plainly shows its pristine green surface. Passing burial mounds of ancients departed, it then curves through the wood. Close at hand is the mysterious Bledlow Cross cut on the hillside. Near by an energetic archæological digger found bones, a Bronze Age skeleton with a Saxon skeleton superimposed in a round tumulus—mere bones but certain clues to the antiquity of the Chiltern trackways. A sunken chalk path, doubtless used by Saxon and earlier cattle-drovers, steeply dives to the Ridge Way's offspring, the Upper Icknield Way. Downward again the path becomes a narrow lane. It skirts a thatched cottage of old pattern and bungalows new and horrid, crosses the railway line, ends at the Lower Icknield Way, probably aged 1,850 years and now ridden by tractors going to till the ancestral fields. This curious mixture indicating time's phases and changes from the top to the bottom of the hill gives an idea of passing through centuries; with such a thought I climbed up to make the drawing of Bledlow Cross illustrated on page 25.

Only after a scramble and a search did I find this Cross at close quarters, cut on a steep hill face at a clearing between the beech woods above the Icknield Way. Roughly thirty yards high and twenty-eight yards wide (these were my paced distances), the depth below the ground surface varies from one to three feet. It is neglected, badly needs a wash, brush-up, and a scouring. Obviously the position was deliberately and cleverly chosen. When first sharply cut in white chalk the symbol would be plainly seen from the near downlands or far away, just as the next and well-kept cross of Whiteleaf now is visible across the Aylesbury Vale or from Shotover near Oxford. But the facts of size and placing are as nothing when compared with the more thrilling aspects of the mouldy old relic. It sends the mind floundering among insoluble queries. Who did the cutting, when, for what purpose? Did it symbolize a primitive religious cult, victories over the Danes, pomposity and power, or was it merely left by a hairy cave-man who, like the humble unlettered, just made "his mark"? On such questions the Cross is inscrutable, gives no answers, therefore gains in fascination. The position, too, is a grand one. Finely elevated, backed by woods, it overlooks the coloured miles. Perched on the hillside making my drawing brought to my mental apparatus an eerie feeling. Nothing near and visible seemed to move. Nobody came throughout the day. Only magpies broke the silence. Clouds that rode across a blue sky belonged to the eternal. The ground, rank grass, junipers, and the chalk device told of the elemental. The solitude was complete. I might have been the first man on earth at the threshold of beginnings or the last one awaiting finality. Anybody in need of a change from life as it is might do worse than take a turn on Wain Hill, find the Cross and scour it, see the wonderful views from above by standing on the top of the Bronze Age *cum* Saxon skeletons, feel temporarily prehistoric, and forget all about fiduciary issues and atom bombs.

Immediately below the Cross and on the Icknield Way stands a house, modest, pleasant, faced with Georgian brickwork. Until 1912 it was the *Leather Bottle* inn. How long an inn has been there no man can say; it may have been started as a pull-up for Iron Age excursionists. Strange stories, rumours, perhaps spectres, I have heard are secreted here; tales of old wayfaring days when journeys were not only difficult but dangerous, when landlords had illicit connections with robbers and villains, when travellers well stocked with money-bags sought accommodation, obtained beds, but ate no breakfasts, because in the small hours they and their money mysteriously disappeared, never to be heard of again. Opposite the house a gate opens to a bridle-way. Enigmas, very likely hobgoblins lie concealed at the site of that gate. Horses do not like it. A rider told me that on reaching the point an animal is liable to get restive, prance, shy, refuse to pass. Such a commotion of course must signify something very dreadful, foul deeds, even murder, unrecorded tragedies on the Way—for the horse, we all know, is strongly endowed with the supernatural sense!

At our parting from Wain Hill the Way flashes one of those surprises that often reward discoverers of the countryside. As a great snake coiling, the track here changes direction, points eastward on rounding the hill. You follow the grassy bend from the defunct pub. Beeches rise in delicate beauty from the borders. A deep combe opens below, graced on one side by the Warren, lately robbed of its once exquisite wood clothing to satisfy money-grubbers. Onward —ah! then comes the surprise. In an exultant moment you behold a reality and a vision, a concentration of English landscape and all that it means, gloriously set out in the ordered confusion of feature and variety. Clear broad sweeps of hill, valley, and plain, the full richness of woods, meadows, and cornlands lead the eye to softer intermediate lights and shadows and the blue of distance far away. Beyond hedgerows and trees you sight Bledlow, Monks Risborough, and known villages of delight, farms and churches, hunting country. In the circuit of the view are the parklands of Hartwell and Waddesdon storied with the names of Louis XVIII and Rothschild, Aylesbury battlefield of 1642, ground travelled by Cromwell for reaching Dinton after Naseby, the strip of Bedfordshire from which Bunyan looked up and immortalized the Delectable Mountains. Imagination repeoples the scenes with many generations whose efforts transformed and refined the wide expanses while history was made. Whiteleaf Cross shines white above Princes Risborough, Pulpit Hill stands out, miles of Aylesbury Vale expand from west to east. Only vague suggestions am I able to give or illustrate of all that greets the seeker on reaching the memorable culmination of the Icknield Way's noblest stretch (34, 35).

Eastward the line of the Way shoots the big gap of Risborough at the Black Prince's old and new town, scales the hillsides below Whiteleaf. Soon *ichabod*. The glory departs, the primeval mantle fades. The Way has been smothered in an engineered hard road. It passes Ellesborough church where the embattled tower perched high on a mound commands everything—steep slopes, wooded bays, Beacon and Coombe Hills, Cymbeline's Mount, distances equal to those of uncharted dreamlands. Next comes Wendover, pretty in oldness and otherwise for newness, followed by a meeting with Akeman Street. Here we remember a few lines by Rupert Brooke, take the Roman road

By Tring and Lilley Hoo.

En route we meet the junction of the two Icknield Ways at Ivinghoe, see the dominant Beacon from which watchers on Sunday, 23rd October 1642, signalled news of the Edge Hill battle to London after the tidings had been flashed from the beacon tower on Burton Dassett hills forty miles away. From Dray's Ditches, between Luton and the earthworks of Ravensburgh Castle, to Punch's Cross and Ickleford near Hitchin the Way looks more like its antique self, only to lose countenance again on getting mixed up with the garden suburbia of Letchworth at the site of an ancient British settlement. Braced for the far eastern journey to Norfolk the bold modern line continues through Baldock and Royston, meeting Roman roads at each town, and sends the track past Ickleton to breach the ramparts of the Devil's Ditch outside Newmarket, a graveyard on the hoary route. Here the Roman general Ostorius began to

BLEDLOW CROSS and the *Vale of Aylesbury*.

AYLESBURY. *A town byway including the King's Head inn. The great Tudor window, made of wood in twenty lights, contains original heraldic glass.*

exterminate the Icenian Britons. Soon history knew their name no more. But their tribal route remained. First prehistoric and in remote ages known as the Icenhilde Way, it survived to be used by Romans and every subsequent generation down to the present. That is why it is so fascinating. To me it has brought many hours and days of pleasure and now causes me to detain my readers far too long on its tracks.

Below the Chilterns and the Icknield Way stretch friendly and charming landscapes. Places of old tenure and villages long settled lie amongst well wooded lands, arable fields and meadows. Good supplies of the new standardized homes, prim residences, the lunatic asylum at Stone, and other embellishments of progress prove that the district does not merely stagnate in the backwaters of old-time nostalgia.

The Vale of Aylesbury is rich, fertile, noted for good farming, well knitted together in gradations of scenery, neither too exposed nor yet too low down for living in comfort. Extended from the Vale of the White Horse at Slade End, near Wallingford, it generously continues two of England's grand vales stretched in a long dip from west to east. In addition to excellencies in cultivation the locality enjoys an admirable reputation for ducks. So great is their fame for first-class quality that the words "Aylesbury Duck" are used on menus all over England without respect for the pedigrees or natal origins of the birds so designated. Ten years ago when miles away from Bucks I became very friendly with ducks. They amused me quite near my own back door—for the antics of the duck rival those of the younger pig in giving free variety shows. Only too late did I learn from the breeder that he had supplied a number of these performers to my local hotel at which I ordered "Aylesbury Duck" promised by the menu. Too late it was to render obsequies. I had eaten half one of my friendly neighbours. A similar fate has overcome millions of true Aylesbury dwellers; such are the advantages and misfortunes of notoriety.

Not only the feathered tribe but two-legged beings without wings have appreciated the attractions of the wide Aylesbury Vale country. Apart from the artists who admired and painted the scenes (John Nash with *Aylesbury Plain* for example) and the poets who sung the praises (Rupert Brooke charmingly did so) all sorts of celebrated people doubtless found the prospects pleasing while they permanently resided or paid visits. Their habitations make the district a good one for finding and seeing numerous country houses, haunts with interesting associations and erected by their owners in past times of skilled building craftsmanship, light taxation, and before family coaches were ousted by the products of Messrs. Daimler, Morris, Austin, and Company. Three of the estates with names of the mighty attached dignify Waddesdon, Mentmore, and Hartwell. Conspicuous on a hill in a palatial domain Waddesdon Manor, a *château en Espagne,* distils a Frenchified airiness into the sweet English atmosphere of the vale. Here was accumulated the magnificent collection, now the Waddesdon Bequest possessed by the nation. Mentmore House, designed by Sir Joseph Paxton, hero of the Crystal Palace, gains from its hillside placing in glorious parklands, wonderfully impressive when seen in the approach from the south. Both mansions shine in the fame bestowed by the name of Rothschild, at Mentmore linked with the brilliance of Rosebery, the wise man who attached himself to the financiers. If the Rothschilds did not flourish in England until 1797 the years of Hartwell dig deep into the roots of time. The Domesday Survey scheduled the manor as *Herdeu-uelle.* The mansion stands in a beautiful park and its sale in 1938 ended a very long tenure of more than 350 years held by the distinguished family of Lee. They built the showy Elizabethan front with the entrance porch, and fortunate visitors may see within the remarkable staircase alive with many carved figures sprouting from newels. The park also is sprightly with King "Farmer George" attired as a Roman and other set-pieces of eighteenth-century statuary elegantly disposed against backgrounds of noble chestnuts, elms, and avenues. To these delicate shades Louis XVIII brought a royal name and memories. While Napoleon strode Europe the French king came here for a change of air; his retinue of many more than one hundred must have played giddy games of hide-and-seek in finding accommodation at their temporary Versailles. Another curiosity in the park is the church. This replaced an older one in 1753–56 and was built for Sir Henry Lee. Henry Keene, Surveyor of Westminster Abbey, who made the design apparently fancied the chapter house at York Minster with new effects added, notably two towers and elaborate fan vaulting made of—plaster! The result may appeal as an architectural joke, or be regarded as a minor masterpiece by enthusiasts for the fancy-dress Gothic of the Horace Walpole era.

From the group of other homes in this vale I mention Lower Winchendon Priory, suggesting the site of a monastic establishment completely gone. Its twisted chimneys, also cottages in the village, add prettiness to the pastoral windings of the River Thame. Lower downstream Notley Abbey, settled in the water-meadows, gives a picture of gables, high chimneys, a tower, and a big pigeon-house of long standing, only but faded glories of an abbey that was founded in the twelfth century and possessed broad lands in many counties. Further north a manor-house within a forecourt beyond gate piers calls us to Brill, a queer little townlet situated on a hilltop signposted by a windmill. Odd as ever the place seemed when I renewed its acquaintance recently, curiously planted among grassy disused sandpits where the *Sun* never sets—for that is the name of the inn. Former royal importance and a palace much favoured by Edward the Confessor and Norman kings are hardly suggested, and only earthworks near the church remind of incessant trouble caused to the Roundheads. Yet the spot repays finding for its oddity, views over the plain, and bracing air, attractions to which Master Benjamin Jowett escaped from the concentrated intellectualism of Balliol to write translations from the Greek. Two long miles below the hill is found a very satisfactory Boarstall Tower, satisfactory because the massive gatehouse makes a good picture in the moated fourteenth-century style. It survives from the strongly fortified castle that sent shocks to the Puritan revolutionaries until finally captured by Fairfax in 1646. Dorton House, in the opposite direction beyond Brill, retains a squirely look in spite of vicissitudes in ownership. A toning of the past nicely merges with the present. Circular-headed windows and dormers decorate three sides of the rear courtyard, behind them are Jacobean interiors and staircases, ample stabling suggests departed horses for hunting and chaises, and over the way the Norman church walling enclosed sleepers on Sundays in the long sermon days. Remains of Bernwood Forest account for the great beauty of the woodlands hereabout. Buried in the trees it is quite startling to find an imitative Temple of the Winds in a shaky condition, baths and cubicles similarly dilapidated, and a wellhouse over a chalybeate spring. These are the phantoms of Dorton Spa and pump-room. Erected by an enterprising landowner early in the nineteenth century after the rise of Bath had set the fashion for taking the waters, the woodland solitudes became gay and lively with bathers, revelry, dancing, and flirting at brilliant balls. Unfortunately neither a Beau Nash nor a John Wood appeared to develop the initial success. Meagre local accommodation offered by cottages, alehouses, a windmill at Brill, and the inaccessibility of location brought the capers to an end. The venture collapsed, leaving the birds and trees in sole possession. This Temple of the Winds, if not by now blown down, is quite difficult to discover in the sylvan depths. Only the spring has survived eclipse; it continues to emit liquid of a flavour so uncommonly nasty that sufferers of the ills of the flesh may prefer to endure their pains rather than drink the living waters.

Nearer to Aylesbury stands a house of rare quality and historical associations, Dinton Hall, which I illustrate on page 33. One end adjoins the churchyard and the later garden front overlooks meadows stretching to wide prospects beyond the Ford brook. Elizabethan and Jacobean features rise from earlier foundations. An entrance porch and colonnade, rows of gables, many chimneys clustered together, brickwork of soft mellow tints, and the play of sunlight and shadow on creeper-clad walls all pose perfectly for an English manorial home created in expansive years of leisure. Yet not always did tranquillity reign here. In Civil War times it was the home of the Maynes. One day Cromwell came, fresh from the slaughter at Naseby and thanking God for His help in the proceedings. The visitor left his victorious sword with his friend, Simon Mayne, who later was a Simon simple enough to sign the death warrant of King Charles. Mayne ended at the Tower, his body being buried at Dinton. His servant named Bigg, reported to have been the masked executioner of the King, retired to a cave near the village, where he lived and died as a hermit. The village matches the hall. It is delightful with avenues, chestnut trees, houses and cottages in charming plaster facings and timbered gables. Since Norman years little St. Michael has been grappling with a great wild beast in the carved tympanum above the notable south doorway of the church; the stocks and whipping-post on the green prove that the villagers did not always observe the conventions; and for a romantic touch the eighteenth century contributed sham castle ruins in the fashion of the period. Remembering the epitaph in the churchyard to old Henry Wootton,

> My landlord sends me word to quit,

we also quit Dinton for the county town of Buckinghamshire.

A dumpy spire on the thirteenth-century tower of the cruciform church beckons us into Aylesbury. Placed well up in the Vale the town looks bright, cheerful, busy, and bookmakers like myself, not vitally concerned with equestrianism, value the very good printing done there by Hazell, Watson & Viney. The place is ancient. It owned a dreadful long Saxon name and a lady patron saint christened Osyth who married a king and retired to a nunnery on her wedding day, particulars that need not trouble a sightseer for no signs of them exist. And if William the Conqueror demanded three green geese from this royal manor when he went that way in summer, the ducks we all know eventually predominated. That this was a Puritan stronghold is obvious. In the big market-square John Hampden stands finely posed in bronze, fierce, turbulent, sword drawn, ready to oppose anybody or anything. Contradictorily, and for evidence of backing the winner, the inhabitants erected the leaden clock lantern and spire on the top of the church tower to commemorate the return of Charles II. Later on, when elections really animated the good old days, bowls full of guineas and bowls filled with punch served useful purposes; three pieces out of one and a drink from the other bribed a vote until these happy sociable occasions were deemed corruptive practices and voluble gentlemen in Parliament ended the proceedings. Scenic backgrounds of these past times appealed to me in the two squares, quiet streets, curious narrow ways, and at ancient inns. The market-square, impressive for spaciousness, bordered by Vanbrugh's classic County Hall and hostelries of long service, evidently lost many degrees of picturesqueness while Victorians and their followers tampered with the buildings. More charming is the smaller square with the imposing and interesting church in the centre. Around, and in Church Street adjoining, the grouped architecture, an old grammar school, and capital Georgian homes suggest a placid elegant atmosphere. At the Prebendal House lived John Wilkes, M.P. for the town, celebrated for vigour, ugliness, wit, and

Sydney R Jones
Hertford

HERTFORD. *One of the watery backs in the castled town where three rivers meet.*

BRAUGHING. *A leaden Hertfordshire "needle" completes the fifteenth-century church tower. Fine gabled plaster houses stand in the village and neighbourhood. Roman objects have been found hereabouts.*

BARLEY. *Village street and The Fox and Hounds inn on the highway to Cambridge.*

STONE. *Derelict windmill, grinding days ended.*

DINTON HALL. *A Buckinghamshire house of historical and architectural interest in a delightful village. Here Cromwell visited Simon Mayne and left his sword after the battle of Naseby.*

THE ICKNIELD WAY. *The prehistoric track descends from Wain Hill to the*

Risborough gap. Whiteleaf Cross and Pulpit Hill rise beyond Princes Risborough.

Modelled detail on panel

HERTFORD. *Parge-work in Fore Street.*

WARE. *A quiet corner in the malting town remembered for John Gilpin's ride and once famed for the Great Bed of Ware, now in the Victoria and Albert Museum.*

AMWELL HILL *and the River Lea, beloved of Izaak Walton and the* *place of meeting for* Piscator *and* Venator.

WHEATHAMPSTEAD *and The Bull inn. "Within a gentle walk* *from Wheathampstead" stands Charles Lamb's "Mackery End, in* *Hertfordshire."*

HADHAM HALL. *Embattled towers of Elizabethan brickwork flank the entrance to the old home of the Capel family.*

WATER END. *Jacobean in date, probably the family home of Sarah Jennings, the celebrated and devoted wife of John Churchill, Duke of Marlborough.*

two ejections from the House of Commons in 1763 and 1768. For me one of the best tracks is to thread along a narrow cobbled alley from the market-square to the gables and long archway of the *King's Head*, an inn developed from a monastic hostel of the 1300's. To find the timber-framed window of twenty lights (26), original heraldic glazing coloured with royal armorial bearings of Henry VI and Prince Edward, and to sit inside the oak-beamed room can turn thoughts from mere refreshment and beds to the golden years of craftsmanship when Tudor builders showered over the land a rich extravagance of skill, material, and labour. While I contemplated this great window, massive oak posts, and the ceiling hardly changed since first pegged together, the only disturbing notion occurred from the suggestion that the Protector, arch destroyer of ancient buildings, may have sat just where I did. Fortunately Cromwell's ghost did not come out of the priest's hiding-hole like a huge death-watch beetle, nor did he climb the stairs to disturb my slumbers; I fell asleep peacefully and with a hope of meeting in dreamland Charles Rothschild, the benevolent giver of this inn to the National Trust.

Lastly of the Vale I mention its villages. Many of them are notably picturesque. They continue from the near Vale of the White Horse, where examples of England's most alluring villages lie. Effects bearing a similar family likeness, both around Aylesbury and far away to the east, brighten the scenes with houses and cottages built in combinations of timbering, brickwork, plaster, flint, and also stone, for here in Buckinghamshire the oolite meets the greensand and chalk. Haddenham is largely stone-built, and so is Long Crendon, a delightful spot full of good things known to Henry V's queen, manor-house builders, the late H. J. Massingham and clever artists. Ways lead on to pretty places of variegated old structures harmonizing with the richness of foliage, open greens, and shady lanes. Dinton aforementioned and Whitchurch vie with the best, but quite likely my windmill, sketched at Stone (33) many years ago, has given up the ghost. This village theme is carried onward by Cheddington, through Toddington, Silsoe, and Shillington in Bedfordshire, while Ashwell's high tower in Hertfordshire (page 16) signals a very long halt. Not only its fine Early English proportions, the lych-gate, and medieval beauty in the church demand admiration; this decayed market town has a wealth of overhanging gables, oak, parge decoration and light fronts in the streets. The Rhee stream (a source of the Cam) wells up from sparkling springs at a central hollow surrounded by ancestral ash trees. Widespread panoramas across and beyond Cambridgeshire are visible on climbing the chalk track and prehistoric banks used by the Romans. Down below, over the border in Cambridgeshire, Melbourn, Meldreth, Shepreth, Barrington, and a chain of attractive villages show plaster walls and thatching, colourings of white, cream, and brown brilliant among the orchards, buttercup fields, little streams, and watered gardens. The villages have led me a long way across this broad vale. But the Chiltern and chalk hills, marking the boundary, are always in view; they now remind me that it is time to mount up and explore beyond their shapely elevations.

OVER THE HILLS AND VALLEYS

South-east from the high Chiltern escarpments the inner ridges and hollows continue the subtle blends of rise, fall, and the distinctive unity of the Chiltern compositions. Here the groupings are closer, more intimate. Beech trees, monarchs of these fair lands, gleam in beauty. Ominous sights and sounds threaten in the directions of civilization's main arteries, the big roads and the railways aiming for Princes Risborough, Wendover, and Tring. Yet in between these tentacles there is freedom, quiet, remoteness. Lanes and byways, ridge walks and woodland paths yield all sorts of delectable sights. Often they lead to unexpected little settlements, the numerous "greens," "ends," and "bottoms" tucked away in clearings among the greenery. The groups of old homes, built in the local manner with brick, flint, plaster, and timber, served generations of natives who plied their craft of chair-making, turned wood with the primitive pole-lathe. Though graceful trees were killed in their prime to accommodate human bodies, an unkind fate that brought the trees low eventually descended on the chair-makers. Most of the workers in this indigenous craft fell victims in the conquest of machinery and mass production. High Wycombe town triumphed, became one of the greatest chair-producing centres in the world. Nevertheless it is still possible to enjoy minor excitements, to get a breath of an older and fresher way of life by finding stalwarts here and there carrying on, doing as their forefathers did, and continuing to fight a losing battle with beech and handmade chair-legs. Outside these workers' sheds and their huts in the woods are to be seen felled tree trunks, sawn logs ready for splitting with axe and beetle, and pole-lathes, so simple that they might have turned balusters for the Ark. To light on these scenes in woody recesses in this mechanized age is more than refreshing; out from the bushes at any moment Pan, yes, primeval Pan, might be expected to appear, playing on his pipe an Arcadian melody—and I have been told that some of the old bodgers were great lads with songs and fiddles.

Never thickly populated in times past, the inhabitants of this northern Chiltern country mostly congregated in small communities at scattered settlements and hamlets rather than in compact villages. These social arrangements consequently accounted for the frequency of the former and a comparative scarcity of the latter. Stokenchurch, 725 feet up on the Wycombe–Oxford road and long a centre of chair-making, stands for one of the highest (and noisiest) of the villages, while I name Turville and Aldbury for the two brightest attractions in the bunch. Radnage, behind Bledlow Ridge, might be reckoned a close rival. A Norman and later flint church, the rectory and clustered cottages sit serenely at the meeting of four close valleys; beech woods climbing up the ridge amplify the hillside curves and enrich the backing of this delicate scene. Turville we shall meet again shortly. Aldbury, sheltered below a wooded ridge east of Tring, lies snugly settled round its green, pond, and flint church tower. Thatched almshouses, cottages, and groupings happily made as the old villagers knew how to place them have been pictured hundreds of times by artists. When Mrs. Humphrey Ward settled down at her home called "Stocks House" to write Victorian novels and give the village a place in the pages of *Bessie Costrell* the stocks and whipping-post had ceased to function except as old-fashioned details in paintings and photographs. A favoured spot is this one, exactly balanced and related to the natural setting of meadows and wooded hill slopes; a place to find and not soon to leave, with a seat awaiting so invitingly under the shade of an elm beside the pond.

A mysterious protrusion, Grim's Ditch, shows itself in places as a kind of serpent in this Garden of Eden but badly segmented by the generations of Adam and Eve. Up from the Thames at Mongewell in Oxfordshire the broken trail of fosse and banking reappears in Park Wood near Bradenham. Running loosely parallel to antique neighbours, the hill escarpments and Icknield Way, the Ditch continues well marked from Lacy Green to Redland End and Great Hampden; it turns through Woodlands Park by Hunt's Green, rises over Cock's Hill and north of the British camp at Cholesbury, points across the hills above Northchurch, and ignominiously gets mixed up with roads and golfers at the end of Berkhamsted Common. Measuring about 35 miles from the Thames to Berkhamsted, it is a very long streak of antiquity, one of those primitive feats that can strike a modern mind as being prodigious for men who had hands, lusty arms, little in the way of tools, nothing like drills or bulldozers. The Ditch defies analysis. Nobody can say who made it or for what purpose. Perhaps that is why it is so seductive. Certainly time and nature's growth have tamed its twisting courses into lines of beauty. The best Buckinghamshire section swings a right angle from Great Hampden to Lacy Green. Better still, most romantic of all is the Oxfordshire piece that begins in Nettlebed Woods, skirts south of Nuffield church, makes a fascinating dive through Mongewell Woods, Foxberry Wood, across Icknield Way and so to the Thames. High banks, deep fosse, trees abundant, shade, quiet, grassy slopes to lie on, nobody about the livelong day—what more could a heart desire for peace in a peaceless age? You can start visions of British tribesmen forming a boundary earthwork, Celts bringing cattle along, Saxons marauding, anybody or anything in fact, while thrushes trill pure clear songs just as their ancestors did when men of whom nothing is known threw up the banking and made Grim's Ditch.

If the mystery of the Ditch may prove overpowering or the tough walking exhausting, relief and diversion are offered by varieties of scene and interest in the neighbourhood of the earthworks. The hills send limbs fanwise towards Hawridge, Chartridge, and Great Pednor's rose-covered manor-house, choice on a June day when I painted a picture of it. Southward from Little and Great Hampden is the network of steep slopes and tangled valleys around Prestwood (the Priest Wood of the Missenden monks), Bryant's Bottom and Speen, old grounds of the wood bodgers who supplied High Wycombe with chair-legs. Downs and commons behind the Ivinghoe and Pitstone Hills rumple and stretch in patches of green, gorse, and bracken to Ashridge Park, where magnificent trees kindly do their best to hide Wyatt's fantastic towers, battlements, and spiky outlines of Ashridge House; built along a 1,000 feet frontage for the Earl of Bridgewater, the palatial structure is a monument to the wealth made out of the Industrial Revolution early in the nineteenth century when mock romantic tendencies were fashionable and an aristocracy such as graced D'Israeli's novels ruled in state without suspecting their overthrow in the class warfare of a hundred years later. More to the east swelling undulations gather in their folds pretty villages, Lilley, Great Offley, King's and St. Paul's Walden, and more quiet and charming spots that invite discovery. Here and there in this district, and often painfully near, villas and bungalows splash and litter the landscapes, but freedom of height and slope, the graceful chalk forms, cosy valleys, beech woods ever in view, keep the Chiltern quality as fresh and vivid as the descents of the urbanites permit.

Below Grim's Ditch in Park Wood lies Bradenham. Here also was laid the mortal body of Isaac D'Israeli; known as "the bookworm," he is best remembered as father of famous Benjamin, novelist, twice Prime Minister, the brilliant romantic Radical with black ringlets, who turned Tory and first tried to woo the electors of High Wycombe attired in a laced shirt and pink-lined coat, adornments that failed to capture the seat. The manor-house occupied by father and son sits nicely behind gate piers and fine wrought ironwork. Its front, dignified and dormered in the eighteenth century, was fitted to a sixteenth-century original, visited in 1576 by Queen Elizabeth. Neighboured by a little flint church, curious for a Saxon font and early Norman south doorway, these ecclesiastic and manorial elements face the broad sloping green of the village. Nobody with an eye for the picturesque could be disappointed in Bradenham, and readers of *Endymion*, D'Israeli's last novel, will be pleased to find themselves looking at "Hurstley." A northward bound along the Ditch brings us to Great Hampden, reminiscent of another celebrity. Two small lodges opening to a noble avenue, the eighteenth-century mansion battlemented at the roof-line, and an adorable hamlet of Little Hampden distinguish a compact acreage of commons, bottoms, farms, trees, and beauty. The region often has been called

WIDFORD. "*On the green hill-top . . . by a slender,*
tapering length of spire, the grandame sleeps."
Charles Lamb

ST. ALBANS. *Within the outer environs of London there is no more fascinating town than this one. It offers historic streets, inns, houses, the Clock Tower and Abbey gatehouse, the second longest cathedral nave in Europe capped with a Roman brick tower, walls of the first Roman city, Verulamium, and the place of St. Alban's martyrdom.*

either a shrine or a grave of English liberty. Whether a shrine or a grave is a question on which, in the light of accumulated knowledge and experience, it is possible for people to hold opposite views three hundred years after the Puritan revolt and suppression began to inflame an economic rather than a spiritual basis for life. Hampdens settled in Buckinghamshire onward from the Conquest. The eighteenth-century Hampden House, ornately built of brick and stucco, incorporates an earlier family home. The liberty story of course originated with John Hampden, Cromwell's kinsman, who refused to pay the taxes and met his end while fighting Prince Rupert at Chalgrove in 1643. His memorial in the church attracts many pilgrims who themselves pay rates and taxes of such a size that John Hampden never envisaged when he objected to pay twenty shillings for Ship Money. Therefore it may be best to admire the scenery at Great Hampden, which at least remains free as the air and lovely, and forget about liberty or slavery with taxes.

Of this inner Chiltern country one little tract at the western end for me is the best of all. It lies between the Wycombe—Oxford road and the Thames. Complex hill forms run this way and that, swell down to magical bends and turns in a maze of valleys. Fields criss-cross the bottoms. Squared colourings of pasture and arable—they might be Heaven's patchwork quilts dropped down on earth—lead up slopes to meet the deep tones of silent woods. Wild campanula, orchis, snowflake, and their coy companions meekly show themselves, suggesting the stitch and texture of embroidery. Humanity's signs are unobtrusive. Nowise do they conflict with nature's harmonies tuned in endless variations of a fragrant and delicate theme. The few villages, shining flints and mellow bricks of cottages grouped here and there at commons and heaths, the farmhouses, barns, and ricks, at least convey the idea of small local communities developed from long settlement and still content to keep contacts with their native soil. If this little land of rare finery is not unknown to the knowing ones it remains tranquil, remote, intimate, offers the promise of fresh loveliness awaiting from hill to hill. Surprises are in store on dropping down from hanging woods to valleys, winding lanes, and hamlets.

The landscapes, true to the English tradition, are good as could be wished for. The big view from the bump above Fingest's Norman church shows the quality at its best. Far-flung shapings made by curved formations recede to the south, where distant woods on the far side of the Thames close the calm and balanced prospects. Slopes fall to the lowlands through which the valley road descends. Past beech and elm, farmhouses, green meadows, and light brown ploughed earth the route reaches Hambleden, a village whose many attractions are enlarged by a gabled manor-house of c. 1600, local remains of Romano-British homesteads in Viscount Hambleden's museum, and a riverside mill by the weirs set for a picture on a site recorded by Domesday surveyors. The

Sydney R. Jones

Chilterns & Hambleden valley from Fingest

Wormsley valley, higher up, is of the same rhythmic mould but more diminutive in scale. Almost shut in by hill faces from the wicked outer world, fresh, untroubled, a place for woodland sounds and silences, dells and wild flowers, it might be a preserve in Heaven's less congested areas. Hungryhill and Ibstone ridge give views into this perfect and self-contained valley; its heart can be explored along the few white-faced byways that seem to wind to nowhere in particular unless they lead to Wormsley House, the ancestral seat of guardianship for this paradise.

More than thirty years ago when I made my first approach to Turville from North End, I wrote in my notebook, "Long descent, great woods, beeches, hill slopes, tree-lined road one of the most beautiful in England." Recent times have not brought a spoiling, as anyone will discover who travels that way through the fair and gracious countryside. Turville at the bottom stages a bright climax (12). For romantic situation and what a Chiltern village should present it is almost without a peer among the hills, a place for prompting one to breathe a little prayer that the woodman may spare the axe and the planners will make no blue-prints but leave this village as centuries and traditions have made it. The very name has deep human roots planted ages ago when Anglo-Scandinavians settled upward from the Thames and named *Hameldun* for Hambleden, *Skiremot* for Skirmett, *Tingeherst* for Fingest, *Thyrefeld* for Turville. The church with Norman features duly arrived and its squat bulky tower has faced the green since 1450. Cottages and houses developed in the proper local style. Now they sit for pretty pictures in mixed arrangements of brick and flint, exposed timbers, white walls, roofs of thatch, and brownish tiles blended to golden tints. For many a long year the *Bull and Butcher* inn has presented a creamy and timbered face served by a doorway adorned with two winking lamps derived from the candle and oily nights. A decayed windmill perched on the ridge broods over past corn-grinding and home-made bread. The eighteenth-century Hall in the Park keeps green the memories of an English Lord

Chancellor (Lyndhurst) and a French general and statesman (Dumouriez); the Grange on the Heath looks just what it is, capital Georgian. All around in fine array stretch the fields, hills, and woods, seeming immutable, eternal, if we did not know of capers possible from Government controls and bureaucratic developments. At the moment Turville stands, complete with farmlands, animals, birds, a nice lot of people in nice old homes, and asks the question, "What more could be expected of a real English village?" It has a grim shade too. An empty stone coffin, six feet long, lies inside the church tower. When discovered under the nave in 1900 it contained not only one but two skeletons of a male and a female. The man's bones may have belonged to a thirteenth-century priest; those of a woman unknown had two round holes through the skull. There are people who say that the woman's cranium must mean violence and murder, with the body hidden in the earlier coffin. Nobody knows the facts, so Turville keeps its mystery unsolved.

This diversion on bones brings me to a last impression hereabout. The setting was wintry, the time Christmas, the place of my sojourning a house high and hidden among the woods. Picturesquely old-fashioned outside, it has within stone-arched fire-places and a curious circular staircase made of solid oak blocks fitted round a central wooden pillar. With supposed monkish traditions it is of course the haunt of a monkish ghost. A jolly Christmas Eve dinner proceeded and ended. Soon after eleven o'clock I looked out to a sky bright with the moon and stars. Frost crisped the still air. Snow had fallen. Whitened branches curved from beech trunks. The perfect scene might have been just right for old King Wenceslaus, mummers, a Victorian Christmas card, or the promise of peace, goodwill, and plum pudding. Indoors a huge log burned on the wide open hearth. The clock struck twelve. After "good-nights" from everybody to everybody I stepped up the circular staircase to bed. My room, large and with a communicating bathroom, was the haunted one. At an unknown hour I roused, spied the outlines of a figure creep through the bedroom doorway, go into the bathroom, then pass out and disappear. Half asleep, I faintly imagined this might be the ancient monk on night work and quickly lost consciousness again. When the servant brought morning tea I asked,

"Was anybody prowling about during the night?"

"Not that I am aware of, sir," he replied.

Downstairs at breakfast I related the night's remembrances to my host. Ridiculously for me he burst out laughing.

"It happened like this," he said. "In your bathroom there was a pair of shoes that I wanted. I crept along to get them, and very stealthily to be sure of not disturbing your slumbers."

So my Christmas ghost story completely exploded!

Outside the morning sunlight flashed on frosted snow and white fields, lit Gothic-shaped arches in the avenues, added glory to the winter finery of the woods. We walked along through the fairyland to Hambleden church for Christmas matins, sang "Once in Royal David's City"—which obviously is a very long way from the Chilterns of our present pilgrimage.

Not quite so far distant from Hambleden and its environs is the opposite chalk tract in the north-east corner of Hertfordshire. It vies with the western counterpart in beauty. The rural aspects that greet the eye, their rusticity and countryfield feeling almost in touch with the buffers of England's capital city, might be considered good sedatives for allaying headaches caused by this noisy streamlined age of progress. That at least was one of my impressions formed in the district when down from London on a bicycle. The wheels purred along, carrying me through charming happy scenes. The hills were there, continuations of the Chilterns, often scaling more than 400 feet up in the swing and curve of chalk landscape. High and low, on slopes and in valleys, I found village after village pictorially schemed in old-fashioned colours. Creamed walls, brown thatch, flower gardens, the immemorial and prevalent greenery of the Hertfordshire trees, all looked calm and long settled among the cornfields.

Not for great mansions in wide parklands is the district notable—these lie more to the west. Of castle remains I counted but two, a moated mound near the fine church at Anstey, and hidden amongst trees the little Norman keep of Benington, wrecked in 1176 by Henry II, the spoiler of the robber-barons. Halls and manor-houses are plentiful enough. Some have descended in the social scale, others manage to keep their status, and gardeners too for the lawns, roses, hollyhocks, and besoms. Glimpses of curved brick gables at Furneux Pelham, the eighteenth-century aspect of Wyddial Hall, Barkway manor-house and Brent Pelham Hall grouped with their churches, and sights of comfortable substantial homes dating from the reigns of Tudors, Stuarts, and the Georges give a squirely flavour to the scenes. Gables, clustered chimneys, sash windows. and classic entrances remind of landowners proud of old lineage, rich merchants who built on newly acquired acres, and other large and smaller fry who once ruled and sported in the local life. Many of them, long dead, are kept alive by stone memorials and brasses erected in the churches; for explorers among pedigrees and doubtful family likenesses I suggest introductions to FitzGeffrey at Sandon, Goulston at Wyddial, Shotbolt at Ardeley, Benstede at Benington, Brograve at Braughing, Leventhorpe at Albury.

But particularly hereabout it is the village pictures that reward the finding. The attractions are interesting, varied, home-bred. They range among cottages, inns, farm quarters prettily arranged, great barns finely beamed and generously thatched, and all sorts of contrivances devised when life ran smoothly, quietly (and otherwise) in self-contained communities. You may find a pigeon-house

CHESHAM. *In the valley of the River Chess.*

BISHOP'S STORTFORD. *The Boar's Head Hotel opposite St. Michael's church on Wind Hill.*

DYRHAM PARK. *The gateway traditionally claimed to be the triumphal arch erected by General Monck when King Charles entered London at the Restoration in 1660.*

RIDGE HILL. *One of the most rural stretches near London. This view shows South Mimms below the slopes. In the opposite direction a wide expanse of Hertfordshire includes the cathedral tower of St. Albans.*

at Sandon, a wooden lock-up by the blacksmith's forge at Barley, Cromer's windmill gone into retirement, a pump on the green for an accent in Westmill's picturesqueness. Cherry's Green, north of Puckeridge, gives a literary setting; the thatched cottage bequeathed to Charles Lamb by his godfather Field stands well cared for, may be visited; perhaps with a copy of *Elia* open at "My first play" you read the essayist's words,

When I journeyed down to take possession, and planted foot on my own ground, the stately habits of the donor descended upon me, and I strode (shall I confess the vanity?) with larger paces over my allotment of three-quarters of an acre, with its commodious mansion in the midst, with the feeling of an English freeholder that all betwixt sky and centre was my own.

Buntingford is the small central town of this village region, Stevenage, Baldock, and Hitchin being the outliers. All have wide main streets, lines of jolly old houses, inns galore that can be repeopled with postboys, ostlers, and all the flurry of the coaching days under the signs of an *Angel, Sun, Lion,* or a *Hart* white or red, while the new petrol coaches fly past. Full of interest still, doubtless the towns do not figure so romantically as they once did, and Stevenage (a stopping-place for Pepys, "dinner *5s. 6d.*") is doomed to be engulfed by a satellite town. Buntingford with its long High Street on the Roman way remains quaint, fascinating, sentimentally far removed in time and space from the wireless erections reared above Baldock. Combinations of gables, projecting upper storeys, deep archways, old hostelries, signs hanging from scrolls of decorative ironwork, all would serve very well if transported for scenery in *The Beggar's Opera.* This mention of Gay's play may recall to many of my readers the poster designed for it by Claud Lovat Fraser, together with the stream of lively and fanciful inventions that flowed like magic from that artist in the years of not so long ago. A son of Buntingford, gifted, valiant, he fought and worked until the last, bravely met death at the early age of thirty-one and lies here in his native churchyard. Beyond the town to the east spreads more of this enjoyable and little-known strip of Hertfordshire, marked at the northern tip by Barley with its funny inn sign of hunters and hounds chasing the fox across the road (32). Roads and lanes lead on past cornfields and high elms. They reach white faced villages and hamlets. A distant tapering spire calls to Bishop's Stortford almost at the county boundary.

TOWARDS LONDON

Bishop's Stortford is one link in a chain of towns at the southern edge of the chalk belt. It is continued by Ware, Hertford, Hatfield, St. Albans, Hemel Hempstead, Chesham, Amersham, High Wycombe. Around and beyond them expand tracts of perilous fighting country, battlegrounds war-stained by the forces of Urbanus and Silvanus engaged in conflicts with bricks, mortar, and cement versus trees and the good earth. In search of lanes, green field ways, and antique buildings we may light on suburbs, new factories, red danger lights, polished highways. In short, we are getting well within the orbit of London.

This piece of England, "London's Country," already the subject of books galore, is much too packed with historic and present meaning to fit into my limited space. My geographical strides through these peopled areas therefore must be slight, and my illustrations merely a few from many drawings made in localities so well known and popular. And if acute ecstasy may not come from contemplating expanding towns, new homes good and bad, pavements, perambulators, drainage works, or the Green Belt showing signs of turning red, as yet not all this countryside has succumbed to the conquering march of progress. There for the finding are wild flowers, solitude, joyousness along lanes and footpaths, the exuberance of nature's bounty to please the landscape purist. Fields still grow bushels of corn instead of bricks to the acre, pretty farmhouses and villages stand amongst them, and many parklands, particularly in Hertfordshire, locate noble and historic homes. Towns of long standing, yearly growing bigger, retain old bits and features, the semblances of their former selves. Capital grouping around the Georgian Guildhall at High Wycombe, Amersham's street with picturesque buildings and a seventeenth-century arcaded town hall, highways and byways meeting at the curfew clock tower in St. Albans, Hatfield, Hertford, and other towns in the neighbourhood give good accounts of how they used to look; if Izaak Walton again walked through Hoddesdon he would recognize bulging inn gables, Marmaduke Rawdon's towered house, and various particulars he must have noticed when bound for angling days below Amwell hill.

From our previous rambles through the delicious north Hertfordshire country we might have entered Bishop's Stortford at Windhill, there attracted by weighty timbers of the *Boar's Head* (49) facing the flint and pebble walls of St. Michael's church. Another way in, by the Roman road across Essex via Great Dunmow and Hatfield Forest, opens up the best first impression of this town set on two hills. Hockerill Street drops steeply to the River Stort. Roofs and buildings on the hill beyond pile up in bright confusion to the tower and spire of St. Michael's, itself a tall and predominant note in the prospect. Comprehensive, the panorama vividly presents a real country market-town, which indeed Bishop's Stortford is. Thriving, busy, much concerned with flour, cattle and pig foods, seeds and maltings, it is agog on market days (Thursdays) with stalls in the streets, cars, traps, girls on bicycles, altogether looking about 300 miles instead of 30 miles distant by rail from Liverpool Street. Fortunately for the souls of the Stortfordians the railway services to London maintain the fame of the Eastern Region, variously reckoned just medium or awful. The maltings are very important, both commercially and odorously. Patrons of alcoholic refreshments must find the smells from the kilns gratifying, cheap, and comforting; a most courteous booking-clerk at the railway station, in addition to giving me a ticket and much information on beery ingredients and processes, told me of the fragrance to cheer his mundane labours when the wind kindly blows from the west. Obviously the town is ancient. This is told by its name, derived from an immemorial ford over the Stort and the manor granted by William the Conqueror to Bishop Maurice of London. Lots of bishops followed and in Queen Mary's reign the infamous Bonner pursued his trade for the Lord by performing dreadful deeds in dungeons and burning martyrs at the stake. If the general views over the town promise more interest than closer inspection yields, a number of likeable sights have been left over from earlier times. True, the castle gardens are without a Conquest castle, for that was destroyed by King John, but plaster fronts, weathered roofs, and hoary inns can be spotted amongst profuse and dull adornments added in Victorian and more recent periods. The *Boar's Head* has a good companion in Bridge Street at the *Black Lion*, black with much oak overhanging downward from the gables and supported by a carved angle-post and moulded beams—quite a prize of its kind and darkly panelled inside. At St. Michael's church on Windhill we can find the lofty Perpendicular interior, choir woodwork, and a Norman font, all noteworthy, before pushing onward past the pretty Hertfordshire fields and trees to the Hadhams and Widford.

On crossing the level plateau from Stortford a lone arrowy point is seen strangely poised among the treetops. Soon the land sinks to the River Ash and then the point turns out to be a slender spire set on a grey church tower. Built in the fourteenth century by Bishop Braybrooke, it locates Much Hadham which with Little Hadham, the Hall, Ford, and Cross grace a short length of valley. An avenue of limes leading to the church full of rare handiwork, groups of timbered walls, overhanging storeys, and Jacobean brickwork, a deep dell shaded by tall trees, and the stream meandering along, make Much Hadham a place for pilgrimage and memories. Only 26 miles from London's centre, it may have changed since I stayed at the old *Bell* inn between the two wars; I do not know but for me there is always a mental picture of those gracious houses, clustered cottages, roofs and chimneys, the church telling of many centuries, garden flowers and leafy settings all coloured in the warm glow of still summer days. Great folk knew the village. For centuries the Bishops of London had their country home at the Palace, an interesting farmhouse with the central hall divided when I last saw it; here was born Edmund Tudor, Earl of Richmond, father of Henry VII. The Elizabethan manor-house at Moor Place has been rebuilt since Bishops Ridley and Bonner went there, but the hall at Little Hadham (38), home of the Capels, remains splendid with brickwork, entrance turrets, and an Elizabethan long gallery, all once known to Lord Capel, the valiant and murdered Royalist. The rural quality of the scenery, farmhouses of Tudor and later patterns, and a fifteenth-century timbered porch, well preserved at the church give further distinction to this lesser Hadham village.

Lower down the Ash stream "a slender, tapering length of spire" calls us to Widford (43). "On the green hill-top," green with sloping fields and majestic elms, this is just the tranquil retreat for settling down in a summer shade by the farmhouse and old priory wall to open a well-fingered volume of *Elia*, of course at the pages titled *Blakesmoor in H——shire* or *Dream Children*. Around are the scenes of the essayist's happy childhood days, the nooks and corners in which he wondered and worshipped. Here were the home-places of Kitty Wheatley, Ben Carter, Margaret Gray at her spinning-wheel, Alice W——n the fair-haired maid, and all the kindly hearts, now still, that Lamb knew. Looking over the valley to the woods of Blakesware House you think of an earlier hall erected about 1640 by Sir Thomas Levensthorpe. Imagination pictures old "Blakesmoor." Fancy creates anew the busts of the Twelve Cæsars, fluttering tapestry, carved oaken panels, the haunted room in which old Mrs. Battle died, melancholy-looking yew trees, nectarines and peaches ripening on sunny walls, the fish-pond of the darting dace, and oh, so tenderly limned, grandmother Field, so religious, good, beloved and respected by everybody—all passed and gone, yet for ever living on the pages of Charles Lamb. Rousing from reverie you stroll to the churchyard gate, and near it find the grassy mound telling that Mary Field sleeps on amidst "the green plains of pleasant Hertford-shire."

Less than four miles away the Ash joins the River Lea. Feathery willows shimmer in the breeze, willow herb pinks the waterside, larks soar, wood-pigeons tune day-long murmuring from the higher trees; these were my accompaniments while sketching banks of pink flowers, tree trunks bent like ancient gnomes, the clear waters from the chalk hills. Here again the calm character and soft colouring of the landscape in sight of Amwell hill topped by the church tower (37) invite a wandering by the stream with another valued friend handy, *The Compleat Angler* open at *The Second Day* "in that meadow chequered with water-lilies and lady-smocks." The Lea and this valley, above all places, are linked with the memory of the contemplative hale old man, Izaak Walton. Needless is it to repeat how Sir Hugh Myddelton captured the water, sent it to Islington reservoir for the benefit of Londoners' insides, and caused the local poet Scott to warble,

> Amwell, perpetual be thy stream
> Nor e'er thy springs be less
> Which thousands drink who never dream
> Whence flows the boon they bless.

CHELMSFORD. *Classic, Gothic, and modern effects in the market town of the wireless age standing on the Roman road to Colchester. The Georgian Shire Hall was designed by John Johnson in 1790, St. Mary's church, now the Cathedral, rises to the fifteenth-century tower.*

55

WEATHERSFIELD. *Light walls and tiled roofs face the green near the big flint church tower with a copper spire.*

LEADEN RODING. *The Hall with old interior work, formerly a manor-house.*

These lines, copied in my notebook from Myddelton's monument on the island, seem to indicate that John Scott, a Quaker, was also a teetotaller, very unlike Sir Toby Belch who mentioned the place of our next halt by calling for "as many lies as will lie in thy sheet of paper, although the sheet were big enough for the bed of Ware in England"—that is to say, eleven feet long by eleven feet wide without allowing for tucking in.

Not just now do we enter Ware with John Gilpin, short of his hat and wig, nor can we speculate on how many sleepers, or wakers, tossed all together through long nights in the great bed. This remarkable work in Elizabethan cabinet-making, richly carved and seven feet high, rests in the Victoria and Albert Museum after spells at Ware House, the *Crown* and *Saracen's Head* hostelries, and later at the *Rye House* inn beside the Lea near Hoddesdon.

WARE

There I inspected it when deposited near the brick fragments of Rye House, a manorial building that gave a name to the plot for removing Charles II and brother James but ended with the removal of other heads in 1683. Ware town, whether from the approach or on close inspection, proves to be a jolly malting centre pictorially effective in kilns, cowls, and massed roofs (36), cobbled walks and peeps through archways. Narrow streets spiced here and there with an old-fashioned quaintness lead to the cruciform church, largely dating from the fourteenth and fifteenth centuries. The Bluecoat House keeps its air of 1686 though the Christ's Hospital children left it for Hertford in 1760,

57

and if Cowper needed adjuncts to bolster his larking the *Johnny Gilpin* inn and Gilpin House do it. At the Priory, changed a lot since Franciscans sat there in the 1300's, municipal gents now sit down or look out on lawns, gardens, big branching trees, and a weeping willow caressing the stream. Pretty as anything is the riverside walk. Across the water are vistas of back elevations, flowers blooming, coloured garden walls; summer-houses bulge this way and that, built by old cronies of years ago for their snoozes and spare tranquil hours untroubled by war's alarms or fears of Danes who floated past more than a thousand years ago to spoil the castle of *Herudsford*.

We too, though for peaceful aims, attack Hertford after a couple of miles' stalking from Ware, only to find the castle not very suitable for raising ecstatic emotions agitated by reminders of the burnings, bloodshed, and chivalry in the good old romantic days. After attentions from the Danes, a renewal by the Normans, a visit from King John of France as prisoner of the Black Prince, another visit by Bolingbroke for thinking out the indictment to get rid of Richard II, effectively used by Shakespeare in Act 4, Scene 1—in spite of these and other royal happenings the embattled and refronted remnant hardly lives up to past traditions. It presents an exterior not architecturally brilliant. The interior I think now accommodates the sort of people who concoct sundry inflictions and demands for paying rates with a kind of feudal autocracy. And if this very old town of Saxon kings does not appear to me so interesting as might be expected it is a good one to be in for a variety of purposes. The placid Lea, for instance, may suggest a very long time ago when Danish ships were left high and dry on the mud because King Alfred's men diverted the stream. Out on Corkbush Field you can think of 1647, Cromwell facing mutineers, and as Carlyle tells us, "one *is* shot, there and then. The name of him is Arnald, long memorable among the Levellers." But these are matters dead and gone. To-day only a sprinkling of the town's former picturesqueness remains for looking at while wandering. In St. Andrew's Street and elsewhere there are timbered and oldish buildings; gables and wood mullions at Lombard House overhang the Lea; a good staircase rises inside the *Salisbury Arms*; parge and modelled plaster decorate frontages in Fore Street (36); coloured Bluecoat boys and girls figure on the walls at Christ's Hospital. Most attractive to find are the odd jumbles of weather-boarding, brickwork, red roofs, malting cowls, trees and greenery, all repeated in liquid reflections along the hidden and winding backs at this meeting-place of three rivers (33).

Beyond the town these rivers come down through pastoral Hertfordshire studded with parklands and delicious rural scenes. Glorious are the county's famous elms; they enrich the near at hand and march far, far away, spreading their colourings, ever so lovely, across the plains to wooded distances. The Lea widens through the lordly Cecil domains and Capability Brown's lake in

Brocket Park. The stream babbles over the ford at Water End in one of the calmest spots under the sun, graced with the Jacobean house (38), thought to have been the family home of Sarah Jennings, Duchess of Marlborough. Up the river again, past old-fashioned Wheathampstead (37), we can follow the ways taken by Charles Lamb and Bridget Elia, there finding, as they did, the warm red brick house with gables curved and chimneys moulded, itself perpetual in that most delightful of essays, *Mackery End, in Hertfordshire*.

It is an obvious jaunt to leave Hertford for Hatfield. Here the home of the Cecils overshadows the ancient palace of the Bishops of Ely at which Queen Elizabeth I ended captivity when the news came that she was Queen of England. But the elaborate early seventeenth-century mansion, the church with its monuments, the Georgian houses, inns, and cottages of the pleasant old town are being hemmed in by building developments and industrialism. This fact reminds me that I am reaching the limits of my boundaries, that I can only mention or illustrate a few pointers from a host of places in a wide district still partly countrified or now becoming suburbanized in the outer environs of London. St. Alban's town (44) might have called us for hours to linger in historic streets, in French Row, at "Bleak House," in the Cathedral capped with a Roman brick tower, or to cross the Ver for a walk round the walls of *Verulamium*. We might have explored the prettiness of the Chess from Chesham (49) to Latimer and Chenies, the street of Amersham still charming in spite of the villas on the hill, the varied beauty of West Wycombe

West
Wycombe
and the park

Hedgerley

and the park safely kept by the National Trust. High Wycombe provides not only chairs but a notable wide street graced with the guildhall, good houses of early quality, the top of the *Red Lion* porch from which Disraeli made his first political speech, though nothing visible did I find to prove the solemn fact that the Moody and Sankey revivals depended on the town producing 19,200 chairs in a very short time. From west to north outlying the metropolis are the country sights enjoyed by wise Londoners—Hedgerley village and woodland paths; Denham's cottages around the fine Restoration Place; Penn Wood; the Quaker house of Jordans; church monuments at Harefield; an arched gateway to Dyrham Park (50) close to Telford's Holyhead Road. For the most countrified London Country that I know give me the seasons for wide views and bluebell woods along the grassy way from Ridge Hill (50) to North Mimms park and church. But these and many other scenes in the district must now be left only lightly indicated or not even mentioned; we are due in the next county.

ESSEX

Here, again, a big slice of this county is outside my present stretch. Only beyond houses, houses everywhere and the air of London, do the harvesters work and the nightingales sing in the true countryside. The low or slightly elevated expanses of the lower Thames borders are strangely mixed up in urban amenities and rural symptoms, clearly not for us to explore just at this moment. Mr. Bradshaw's most illuminating guide to the geography of England also reveals that the railway routes to the leafy glades of Epping, to the breezes and mud of Southend, and to Chelmsford, are each particularized as belonging to "London Suburban Service." And if we thus proceed to the last-named objective, or direct to it by following the parallel way from Aldgate Pump previously

WIVENHOE. *The riverside front of the Colne attracts with old-fashioned houses, small craft, a stone church tower and open lantern. Once flourishing as a member of the Cinque Port of Sandwich, the town sent a ship to fight the Spanish Armada.*

MALDON. *The strand where the fishing boats come in. St. Mary's church forms a lookout over the River Blackwater. Danes invaded 1,000 years ago: the centuries brought to the town three churches, Beeleigh Abbey, a Norman leper hospital, Moot Hall, ancient inns and picturesque streets.*

COLCHESTER. *Roman walls at Balkerne Hill. Below and beyond the King's Head inn are the remains of the Balkerne Gate, erected about 80 A.D. after the destruction of Camulodunum by Boadicea in the year 61.*

COLCHESTER. *East Stockwell Street, one of the medieval highways on Roman foundations. The sixteenth-century house (right) was restored in 1935.*

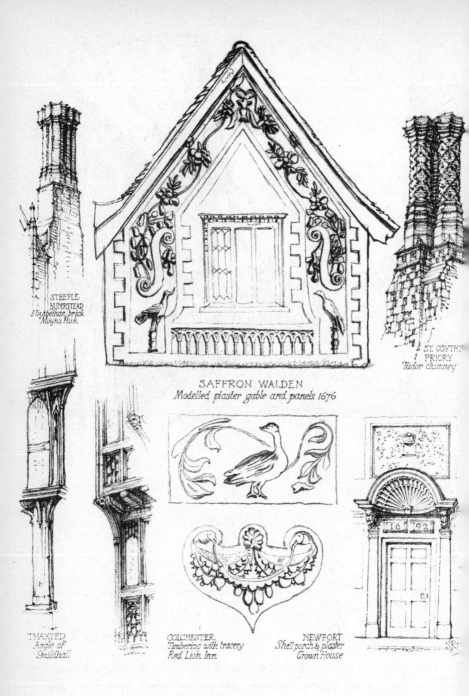

STEEPLE
BUMPSTEAD
Elizabethan brick
Moyns Park

ST. OSYTHS
PRIORY
Tudor chimney

SAFFRON WALDEN
Modelled plaster gable and panels 1676

THAXTED
Angle of
Guildhall

COLCHESTER
Timbering with tracery
Red Lion Inn

NEWPORT
Shell porch & plaster
Crown House

16 92

ESSEX DETAILS

travelled by Ancient Britons, Emperor Claudius, Queen Boadicea, and Mr. Pickwick, a variety of scenic effects can be admired on the route, straight ahead, to the right and the left. Not least conspicuous are the conglomerations of bricks and mortar, fit subjects for nightmares, that crowd far out from London. Eventually the air becomes fresher, buildings less crowded. Wooded and bumpy landscapes stretch eastward to Little Warley, Thorndon Hall, the village of Stock with a timber church spire. Westward and pretty lie South Weald, Noak Hill, natural beauty reigning in Hainhault Forest (where Elizabeth I sat under one of her many favoured oaks), and Havering-atte-Bower with a charming name to fix the site of an ancient royal palace fancied by kings and queens when bound for hunting days. Good rural country continues past Ingatestone's windmill and leads us into Chelmsford, approximately at the centre of Essex.

For many a long year this county has suffered the slings and arrows of calumny. Flat as a pancake, dull in scenery, generally uninteresting—these are its fallacious reputations and they die hard. Actual discoveries of facts rather than beliefs in fictions reveal quite different pictures. Flats exist in plenty, very flat flats. But there are lots of ups and downs, hills, patches of the highest ground in the three lower eastern counties. Grand trees and glades left from the old Essex woodlands belong to Epping, Hainhault, and Hatfield Forests. Greens, commons, thickets, and hedges blend with meadows and arable fields of rich fertile farms. Charming river valleys include those of the Roding, the Pant, the Colne, while the Stour of wide fame makes a northern boundary line. In choice surroundings stand pretty villages and hamlets, many of them more remote, quiet, and peaceful than any others to be found elsewhere within the same distance from London; a dozen or two within hail of Newport, Finchingfield, Castle Hedingham, and Steeple Bumpstead make one wonder whether fairer village scenes are visible anywhere. If the churches generally may not be very exceptional the two at Thaxted and Saffron Walden certainly rank high, and Greensted near Ongar holds a unique curiosity in wooden nave walls erected in pre-Conquest years. The splendid fragment of the enormous palace at Audley End, completed in 1616 for Lord Treasurer Howard and later acquired by Charles II, leads the way with the stately mansions. Most remarkable, however, both in numbers and traditional picturesqueness, are the moated halls, manor-houses, spacious farmhouses, and domestic buildings with notable craftwork wrought in timbering, brick, plaster, and great patterned chimneys (64). Such characteristics are well represented by the Tudor gables and Elizabethan brick-work of Moyns Park, Layer Marney's tall brick towers, the Tudor hall of Horham near Thaxted, at Paycockes, Coggeshall, one of England's richest timbered houses of a medieval merchant. In every rural locality, wherever you go, one, two, or many more of these weathered old structures delight the eye. They tell their tales of natives and ways long gone, and in town and country, streets, villages, and lanes historical points everywhere swing the story of England and its people onward from Roman and earlier times. Briefly these are some of my own impressions of Essex, which is commonly called flat. It is not my purpose to varnish the attractions but my eyes have taught me that the county is by no means flat, either for nature's sights, architecture, homely appeal, or human interest.

A good deal could be said in favour of the lowly flats that sweep across Essex to the broken coastline. Flat scenes in common with flat people appeal variously, depending on personal points of view, taste, likes and dislikes. Here they may be thought dull as the ditchwater of the marshes, creeks, and channels, or places of peculiar fascination in which the low landscape lines of extended prospects make high moving skies appear all the higher as the clouds shape and chase along. The play of soft atmospheres, delicate colour harmonies rather than strong contrasts are the rule, but light and life sparkle when the sun shines on the estuaries of the Colne, Blackwater, and Crouch where enthusiasts love to sail yachts and small craft. One typical evening effect I remember from watching at Abberton. Stunted tree forms showed darkly above rank grass bent in the breeze, a sunset glow reflected warm tints on pools of stagnant water, wreaths of mist formed and spread mystery over the low grounds away to Langenhoe Marsh and Mersea Island; then night soon fell to reign in its own deep mono-chrome. Pictorial possibilities abound. They are set among dykes, willows, and haunts of wildfowl, along the guts, channels, and windings of tidal creeks vastly used in smuggling days, at ancient sites once favoured by Romans and Norse-men. Tides in and tides running very far out add to the eerie character of the scenes in such solitudes as Wakering Stairs or the Saxon chapel of St. Peter's-on-the-Wall, built 1,300 years ago on the wall of the Roman Camp *Othona*, the great fortress of the Counts of the Saxon shore. Fisherfolk engaged with the oysters might fill pages of sketch-books, and whimsical locals to be met and talked with suggest originals discovered and conveyed unvarnished in print by W. W. Jacobs and Baring-Gould's tales of these salt marshes. Where the flats are broken by considerable heights wide-spread panoramas can be enjoyed. Danbury, 350 feet up, shows them broadly stretched over the estuaries and far distant miles from the early camp used by the Danes. Other expanses are visible from the uplands around Wickham Bishops and Great Braxted, while quite a Low Country-ish continental impression is obvious on looking from Fingringhoe to Wivenhoe and the lower Colne.

Wivenhoe and Maldon are the two interesting towns of this coastal region if we can forget the existence of Clacton, Frinton, and Walton-on-the-Naze, each replete with every attraction for the populace. A collection of odd and Georgian buildings closely neighboured by masts and all sorts of small craft straggled along the river front at Wivenhoe (61) suggest a canvas by one of the seventeenth-century Dutch artists. Narrow lanes leading to riverside houses, two aristocratic memorial brasses in the church, the big tower with a little open lantern on the top, and the frontage opposite elaborately decorated with parge-work ornamentation constitute other good points of this curious little town. Long ago it flourished with the busy life of a considerable port, sent a ship to fight the Spanish Armada; now it is best not to notice the horrible attacks of villas. A few miles downstream towards St. Osyth Marsh stands the Priory, a wonderful unity of ruined beauty and new life. Flint and stone, gables, patterned chimneys (64), Roman bricks, Norman arches, roses, and Lombardy poplars are gathered at the hallowed spot where the Danes seized the East Anglian king's daughter Osyth and murdered a saint. Maldon is a sea-flavoured town picturesquely set on a hill above the Blackwater. A good High Street shows hoary inns, Georgian brickwork, plaster houses, aged men who sit gossiping on churchyard walls, and native faces looking out from an extraordinary number of bay and bow windows. The moot hall, dating from the fifteenth century, is fronted with a large portico that props a roomy iron-railed balcony on which the mayor and corporation may show themselves on auspicious occasions supported by the arms of the borough, three fierce animals and a ship bravely heraldic. Right and left of the street winding passages lead to quaint corners and timbered gables. In Silver Street the *Blue Boar* sign invites a dive into a very ancient inn; the grey eighteenth-century brick front screens a courtyard with a black-and-white wing, thought to incorporate an earlier hall-dwelling of the de Veres, Earls of Oxford, owners of the Blue Boar crest. The peculiarity opposite, a triangular church tower, belongs to All Saints. It is also an American beacon, for in the churchyard lies buried George Washington's great-great-grandfather, Lawrence Washington, the parson of Purleigh, who was driven out of his living by the Parliamentarians on the charge of being "a malignant Royalist." This reminder impelled me a few miles southward to find and sketch Lawrence's embattled flint church tower, with the result of being mistaken at Purleigh for a good American, an honour I endeavoured to sustain without disclosing my ancestry. Back at Maldon the riverside intrigued me with the watery scene up and down the Blackwater, mud banks, gulls ever crying their weird notes; landward stood boatbuilders' sheds, the *Jolly Sailor* inn, St. Mary's Norman stonework and spired tower on the hill. While I made the illustration for page 61 the fishing-boats came in. A lithe clear-eyed man wearing long waders walked across the strand carrying a bag, the contents of which rattled.

"What have you got there?" I asked.

"Oysters," he replied.

"Worth a lot of money," I said.

"We don't get much, two shillings a hundred. After the oysters we go eeling.

But that's the same, the Dutch flood the market at low prices. Got to be away four nights next week. It's a hard life, fishing, out in all weathers, always in water, boats and everything always wet. We don't make old bones, rarely live over sixty. My father in the same line died at fifty."

He walked on to join his mate. I thought of oysters at 10s. a dozen on the previous night's menu in Colchester; it's an uneven world for rewards of fishermen, artists, and others who produce the goods.

On a previous page we arrived at Chelmsford. In my opinion this is not quite a sight-seeing town unless you happen to find interest in wireless masts, Marconi products, multiple stores, horrible noises and shapes invented by a scientific age, or county councillors concerned with planning and what they now term the "child bulge." Seekers wishing to acquire a cow, pig, sheep, goat, cock or hen will find all they want at the auctions held in the exhilarating market on a Friday. Splendid collections of tanned humanity then visible prove that Chelmsford is the centre for a wide agricultural district. When I asked one stalwart Corydon where he came from he replied, "Willingale Doe and Willingale Spain. They say two old willing gals built the two churches in one churchyard but I don't believe it."

"No," I said, "D'Ou was a man, a Norman, and the DeHispania family over from Spain got a mention in Domesday. They started your churches."

The most pictorial bit I found in High Street, here illustrated on page 55, and including the elegant Shire Hall of good proportions designed by John Johnson in 1790. To carry the Roman road over the River Can from Moulsham to High Street Johnson also schemed the graceful bridge dated 1789, now hemmed in by ugly buildings of the last and present centuries. The tower and flint-patterned porch of St. Mary's, the notable house of Guy Harlings with panelling and Tudor bits inside (formerly the home of the Provost), a courtyard at the *Spotted Dog*, the *Saracen* used by Anthony Trollope for writing sheets of copy, and willow walks in the meadows are among the relics that have defied sleek modernism in this old Essex county town.

Out of Chelmsford the Roman road leads through Witham, pretty for white walls and toned roofs at Chipping Hill. Kelvedon demands the next stop for its long street stored with picturesque old houses at a jumping-off point for Coggeshall and Layer Marney gatehouse. Onward, mentally changing the car for a chariot and trousers for togas, we mount the hill into Colchester. Here, instead of a few words and two drawings, a volume might be filled on the sights and phases of the town. There is magic in exploring its grounds, occupying the place of the ancient British capital ruled by King Cunobeline—Shakespeare's *Cymbeline*—and his son Caractacus. We tread over the site of the first Roman *Camulodunum*, wrecked by Boadicea in 61 A.D. Upstanding, visible, amazing, are remnants of the Roman city that rose in splendour from the ashes, flourished

GREAT BARDFIELD. *Next to Finchingfield in north Essex,*
one in a group of the county's prettiest villages.

BARTLOW. *A white village in the chalk country below*
the Bartlow Hills at the Cambridge-Essex border.

69

FULBOURN. Plaster walls and thatched roofs in reclaimed fenland near the Gog and Magog Hills.

for its little epoch, then faded. Saxon and Norman, Plantagenet and Tudor kings followed in succession. Each made Colchester a royal fortress. Eventually old-time war's alarms ended. The loyal stronghold, gallantly defended in a long siege, fell to Fairfax in 1648. In the ways of peace during the centuries Dutch and Flemish settlers introduced improvements in weaving, helped to make more than local fame for things called bays and says of silk and wool. The above particulars, though only fragmentary, point to a very full historical story connected with these Essex acres bordered by the River Colne. And of course the oysters never were forgotten. Legend tells that their flavour first lured Romans to invade Britain. Even now at the annual feasts in the Moot Hall civic dignitaries and distinguished guests celebrate the gastronomic charms of the natives.

To-day in this most Roman of English towns, one created on Roman found-ations and imperial dust, the weight and influence of ages long past are empha-sized by present realities. Outside appearances both kindle the imagination and dispense plenty of old-fashioned beauty. Only to walk along West and East Stockwell Streets (63), Trinity Street, and elsewhere is to realize how closely streets and byways have followed original alignments of the Roman rectangular town plan. The Conqueror's castle, now short of upper heights and angle towers, still makes a remarkable showing with the biggest keep in existence and largely built of Roman materials on the top of a Claudian temple. Saxons put up Holy Trinity tower, a present delight for archæologists. Benedictines turned flint and stone into the graceful gateway of St. John's Abbey. Roman bricks came in handy for the Austin Friars to erect St. Bartolph's Priory and complete a grand church, the spectacular ruins of which show how the Cromwellians ruthlessly spoiled it. Many good houses, overhanging, oaken, plastered, or brick-fronted, tell their tales of home life and where it was lived in the old days. Facing the massive castle and particularly elegant is Holly Trees Mansion, Georgian of 1718; not so elegant is its neighbour in the park, a dark underground hole patronized by the early Italian visitors for worshipping Mithras, their god of light. Inns abound, alluring for solids as well as liquids. Heavy oak beams and Gothic tracery (64) are quite wonderful at the *Red Lion*. A Georgian-fronted *George* screens more beams, the *Marquis of Granby* sparkles in black and white, and behind the *King's Head* I found the Assembly Room in which the surrender happened after the Civil War siege. High up, at the site of a Norman moot hall, the bells in John Belcher's campanile merrily ring out the quarters, chime the hours, very cheerfully by day but oh! in the small hours they woefully dis-turbed my slumbers under the roof of the *Red Lion*. Yet of all the excitements Colchester offers the major one I think is the chase round the walls, a full two miles unique in England. You track past Roman rubble, flints and bonded brick courses (62), postern and bastion, and so to the Balkerne Gate, the largest of

Roman gateways and unmatched in Britain. Above the din of cars mounting the hill as the twentieth century goes by you can fancy, almost hear, brave processions of emperors, centurions and cavalrymen who set out for Aldgate at *Londinium* years after Caractacus went captive in chains to Rome and Boadicea's trails of firing ended.

West of the great Roman road lies Essex at its best, endearing, quiet, rural. There we could spend hours and days in an undulating countryside that leads northward to innumerable "ends," "greens," and chalk hill and valley scenery. Everywhere the district is all the more charming for its heritage of long-settled villages, memorials and homes of ancient families, rambling farmhouses, country towns, the weathered colourings of wrought oak, parge surfaces, mellow brickwork, and tiled roofs. Here are Halstead, Braintree with Bocking, long centres for weaving and full of old appearances. Thaxted and Saffron Walden form two well-known prizes with splendid churches and streets packed with all sorts of attractions (64). Streams and little rivers wind to secluded spots. The Roding from Roman Stane Street runs a course delicately banked with feathery greenery, lines of willows, water meadows; it names the chain of villages from High Roding to Beauchamp and Berners Roding, remote pretty places often half hidden in trees, each generally showing a manor-house, perhaps moated, haunted, or continuing as a farmhouse like Leaden Roding Hall (56). The upper reaches of the Chelmer, Pant, and Colne are lovely too, flowing smoothly between rushy banks, cornfields, wooded hollows. They water the fair lands of north-west Essex in which village scenes have rare picturesqueness made by traditional renderings of light-tinted cottages, grey churches, and an extraordinary number of halls and manor-houses rich in associations of history, myth, and legend. Most of my discoveries in this locality now, alas, must remain unrecorded. I should like to detain my readers at Finchingfield, a queen of villages rightly praised in dozens of books; at its worthy neighbour, Great Bardfield (69), once a weaving centre, where I learned that people who live there never want to leave, and those who have to always return—no wonder! We might visit Little Bardfield across the fields, beloved by Walter Crane, Weathersfield (56), Newport (64), Wendens Ambo, Sible Hedingham (75), Castle Hedingham nestling below de Vere's keep (75), explore onward in a score of places and trace the characteristic white-faced villages over the county border at Bartlow (69), Hildersham, and Fulbourn (70). Steeple Bumpstead, many ancient houses at the three Belchamps, and the Essex borderlands of the Stour all invite—but this river's country more properly belongs to my next chapter.

3. EAST ANGLIA AND FENLAND

SUFFOLK, NORFOLK, CAMBRIDGESHIRE, LINCOLNSHIRE

Pastoral, up-and-down landscapes and heaths in the chalk country, low rural stretches among slow rivers and the Broads, richly cultivated expanses cut by dykes and artificial waterways in the Fens, these are the varieties of scenery offered in the old kingdom of East Anglia and the Fenlands. The coastline, subject to constant change through erosion by the sea, sweeps round from the Stour estuary past decayed Dunwich to The Wash and East Holland. Architectural feats include splendours left by the monks, Cambridge colleges, flint patterning and magnificent woodwork of churches, numerous halls and manor-houses dating from Tudor and Renaissance times. Charming towns and villages retain signs of the age of golden wool that brought centuries of prosperity. At King's Lynn and Boston, two ancient ports, and in various directions the brick gables and details suggest the influence of Flemish and Dutch settlers who came to England. Constable, Gainsborough, Crome, Cotman, their contemporaries and successors gave the district artistic fame, and still much of the scenery they knew remains unspoiled by the wicked deeds of man.

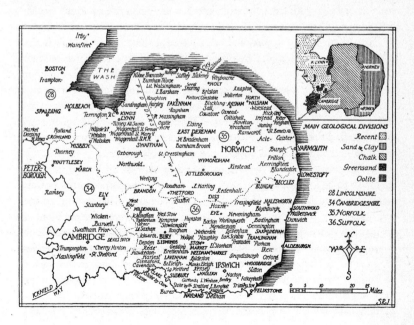

73

THE STOUR VALLEY

The Stour vale, which we reached from Essex in the last chapter, of course means the Constable country to victims of the artistic kink and dabblers who criticize pictures without knowing how to paint them. Not only is this John Constable's land but that of Thomas Gainsborough too, born at Sudbury in the spring of 1727. Great names these for illuminating any few miles of good English earth. Returning a few summers since from sketching in this River Stour country I borrowed a first-edition copy of Constable's "Life" from my friend and neighbour Harry Leslie, himself a descendant of C. R. Leslie, R.A., the author of the classic work on our great landscape artist. At the opening of Chapter I, I re-read Constable's own description of his native land, those happy boyhood scenes that he always said determined his career in

"the fertile valley of the Stour, which river separates the county on the south from Essex. The beauty of the surrounding scenery, its gentle declivities, its luxuriant meadow flats sprinkled with flocks and herds, its well-cultivated uplands, its woods and rivers, with numerous scattered villages and churches, farms and picturesque cottages, all impart to this particular spot an amenity and elegance hardly anywhere else to be found."

The plates added zest to the text. While I studied reproductions of masterpiece after masterpiece, *East Bergholt, Stratford Mill, Flatford Mill*, and on to a glorious finale at *Stoke-by-Nayland* I also recollected more masterpieces from another inspired hand, Gainsborough's *View of Dedham, The Harvest Wagon, The Watering Place, Water Lane, Stratford*, and other scenes in the Stour locality depicted, as Sir Joshua Reynolds said, "by a kind of magic." This grand show of landscape witchery left by these two painters made me realize that my ammunition had been splendidly blown up before launching an attack. Really it seemed nothing further could be done or captured with pen or pencil by an insignificant follower in the footsteps of the great. Therefore I can only recommend my readers to find this delicious countryside, look around, enjoy themselves while seeing so much that is good, lovely, and memorably English.

Though nature's created works, and fine paintings and drawings of them, are things to be looked at rather than written about, this particular tract of our island also owns heaps of additional attractions deposited by man in villages and little towns snugly settled along the river and its borders or mounted on the gentle wooded slopes both of Suffolk and Essex. Since Constable and Gainsborough departed newcomers of course have arrived, spreading the incidence of change over places and prospects. Like the Kingdom of Heaven this portion of England has many mansions; it also shares with the ethereal conglomeration the complications of housing problems due to congestion dictated by an expanding baby industry. Hence the continual multiplication of council dwellings,

Castle
Hedingham
SRJ

Castle
Details

Fireplace Entrance

Hall Window

Sible Hedingham
SRJ

THE HEDINGHAMS. *Top: the famous Norman keep of Castle Hedingham, held for nearly six hundred years by the de Vere family, stands four-square above the village. Below: timbered and Georgian effects in Alderford Street, Sible Hedingham.*

DEDHAM and the Stour valley in the Constable country at the borders of *Essex* and *Suffolk*.

Once a prosperous place of wool merchants, the village is distinguished by a noble church, the varied appearance and good qualities of houses and cottages.

villas and bungalows, various objects of mean shapes and sundry emblems of enlightened progress that afford preludes in the approaches to Dedham, Finchingfield, and Castle Hedingham, to name but three instances from many. Constable's birthplace at East Bergholt, a roomy Georgian house built by Golding Constable in 1774, was pulled down and sold for the cash value of its building materials. To the past also belong the barges, bargees, and river traffic, so picturesque in the paintings of *Flatford Mill* and *River Stour, Suffolk*. Nor in these days of petrol abominations is one likely to find a duplicate of *The Leaping Horse*, one of those powerful animals that towed the barges and were trained to leap the fenced boundaries of the fields at the riverside. Yet villages, old towns, and landscapes still keep innate characteristics to yield joyful sights; they bring the consciousness of treading the actual grounds known to masters of the painting art who learned from nature's infinite book of secrecy, finely accomplished what they set out to do, passed on, and left more than their names behind.

Dedham on the Essex side of the river is a good starting-point for exploring the Stour. One approach can be made along the route A 12 from Colchester to Ipswich and by leaving this highway at the foot of Gun Hill near Stratford St. Mary. Here the vale gives a proper introduction to the quality of the local scenery. It is widely set out. Delicate colourings of water-meadows, willows, high elms and poplars meet the slopes patched with darker woods that frame and complete the pictures. A church tower, high to its battlements and pinnacles built by a Tudor wool merchant, locates Dedham's warm-tinted roofs, white and toned walls. If you clamber into the field at the end of the lane, as I did, gracious views are visible over the village and vale bounded by the uplands of Suffolk (76). Dedham continues lovely. Certainly fame has not spoiled it. Homes of beauty stand as they have stood for centuries. Greenery adds colour and freshness, little streams run this way and that down to the river beyond the fields. Timber and plaster combinations brighten a memorable High Street up to the *Sun* and *Marlborough Head* inns; capital eighteenth-century brickwork makes the dressings of the old Grammar School and another house dignified with a sundial; Thomas Webbe's Perpendicular church tower of flint and stone mounts a centre-piece; a fragrance of the past handicraft hovers in the still air at the master-weaver's gabled house and workshops of 400 years ago. The chief blots that have threatened this adorable spot and its surroundings are the modern housing erections aforementioned and a scheme to erect a pumping station, a proposal vigorously censured by Sir Alfred Munnings. By chance it may be possible to meet this artist and doughty champion of great traditions emerging from Castle House fully armed on his war-horse, zealous to preserve or paint his and John Constable's treasured scenes. But without further dawdling we must wander on, for much awaits to be seen further afield.

Not far down the river brings us to Flatford. The mill, bridge, Willy Lott's house, and the scenery circled within a few hundred yards plant us with remarkable fidelity into the very realm of Constable's many famous pictures. True, the original bridge has gone. It was taken down and reconstructed with Burmese timber; at this particular spot of all others on earth the question might be asked, what is the matter with stout and seasoned English oak? Willy Lott's house stands poised above the mill stream in the simplicity of sixteenth-century timber framing plastered and lime-washed. Saved from decay some years ago by a generous benefactor of Ipswich, it looks very like the subject so often sketched and painted by Constable when Willy Lott had his habitation in the cottage, living for more than eighty years with never four whole days spent away from it. Climbing up the hill we may hear the curious muffled harmony of East Bergholt bells pealing from the bell cage in the churchyard. Sweet tunes resound, as they used to do, over Constable's birthplace, the rectory, the sumptuous medieval church with Cardinal Wolsey's unfinished tower, all of which were intimately associated with the tender love story of constancy, fidelity, and of hope deferred until Maria Bicknell became Mrs. Constable in 1816. The village is a paradise for artists and people able to use their eyes. Over Dedham and the vale the views are superb, actualities jewelled to inspire visions of English landscape fitted for immortality. Further along the ridge at Stoke-by-Nayland, good for timbered and plaster houses (82), the church tower mounts proudly over village roofs, pointing a landmark seen far and wide and frequently captured by Constable. Round about stand home places of old-time squires, merchants and prosperous folk. Going along roads and lanes in the peaceful countrified surroundings, halls and manor-houses are visible, antique retreats, relics of the good old times that flourished and now don't. Beautiful homes, wonderfully mixed in features and meanings, and very numerous in this locality include Stoke Priory, Tendring Hall rebuilt in the eighteenth century by a Lord Mayor of London, Thorington Hall, a near neighbour; Giffords Hall and Hadleigh Deanery, both exuberant in the patterns and diapers of Tudor brickwork; Little Wenham Hall secluded beside a moat, perfect for its date of c. 1260, one of England's earliest examples of house-building in brickwork (87). Departing from these reminders of a squirearchy that owned the gateways, towers, chimneys, and panelling for concealing ghosts during the daytime, our way descends from Stoke church tower on the skyline, soon reaching Nayland lowly by the stream. The little town browses on departed days of wool-thriving by merchants and clothiers, the bridge they built, the church William Abell adorned. It is a quiet place for dreaming of times past, enjoying present delights, or crossing the meadows to the weir (81) for chances of catching perch and certainly for remembering John Constable. The altarpiece he painted is in Nayland Church, and throughout this region the artist's name, life and works ever come uppermost in the mind. Here are the villages, churches, picturesque houses, the streams, weirs, meadows and uplands, all known and loved by our great interpreter of rural landscape. "As long as I am able to hold a brush," he said, "I shall never cease to paint them." To me a score of countrysides are just as fair as this one, but no other is more imbued with the fresh spirit and significance of the English scene. It was Constable's school, the groundwork of his life. Studied and expressed in painting by him, the outlook, feeling, and poetical insight of the man put him in the line of the great traditions traced by the masters of English poetry, Gothic craftsmen inspired by the sweetness in nature.

From Nayland, past Bures prettily reflected in the stream, and on to Sudbury and Clare the Stour vale maintains its loveliness. Elm, ash, willow, and trembling poplar, delicate harmonies of foliage and vegetation, plough lands and sheep grounds, meadows with cattle grazing, all unite in the tranquillity set by the prevailing landscape's shapeliness and colouring. The upland borders, seen gradually mounting higher to wooded skylines, come down to meet the river as it winds to mark the county boundary onward from Wixoe. Old villages, hamlets, and country towns, their light plastered, timbered, or bricked houses and cottages nicely blend with the natural settings.

On a summer day, as I first saw it, Sudbury looks bright, cheerful, inviting, quite a considerable town. Three "wool" churches stand in medieval beauty. Buildings planted in all sorts of shapes and periods (82) line the streets. Bertram Mackennal's statue of Gainsborough faces the Market Hill of the artist's birthplace, and Gainsborough Street—how honourable of you, dear Sudbury folk, to name it—of course contains the master's home. *White Horse, Black Boy, Swans, Rose and Crown*, once Pickwickian "Blue Inns and Buff Inns," were useful to Charles Dickens for the rotten electioneering at *Eatanswill* when the honourable Samuel Slumkey, of Slumkey Hall, paid for a seat in Parliament. Arrived at the town on a bicycle more years ago than I dare mention, a cycle dealer while mending my exploded tyre offered to supply a bed plus breakfast of home-cured bacon and two eggs at half-a-crown a time. He also directed me to Ballingdon Hall a mile or so away.

"The place has been sold by auction," he said. "Gypsies outbid everybody and bought it. They are there now. May be queer customers."

"Not highwaymen or murderers?" I said laughingly.

"You'd better be careful."

"I'll keep one eye wide open."

Though not a George Borrow I advanced and arrived. The sides of an unkempt drive were strewn with gypsies, dozens of them, men, women, youths, girls, babies innumerable, mostly sprawled outside caravans and tents around fires boiling sizzling pots. The hall showed at the end of the drive. A

swarthy Egyptian of whom I asked permission to see the house, directed me to
"'im," evidently the chieftain, a tough short oldish man with a Roman type of
nose betwixt two beady black eyes that seemed to penetrate right through me.
Apparently satisfied with my exterior, in economical language he told me to
go — anywhere, stop as long as I liked. Threading through the massed congregation I reached the front of the hall. It proved to be a good specimen of a
timber-framed and plaster manor-house, overhanging at three gables, lit by
many leaded windows set in four big bays swept upward from the ground to
the eaves (87). But how down-at-heel it appeared! Shabby in the face and joints,
faded, very sentimental, a mere wreck of Elizabethan manorial pride uneasy
among new birds of passage and boiling-pots. Until dusk I sketched and noted,
improved my knowledge of humanity in the primitive state, yet experienced
no "hair-breadth scapes i' the imminent-deadly breach."

"Well?" said the man of wheels and beds on my return to Sudbury.

"Very well, thank you," I replied.

"Quite thought you might never come back."

"Oh."

"And I've got your bicycle here."

"You are something of a humourist."

"Merely a cycle dealer."

"Every man to his trade. I've got Ballingdon Hall in my sketch-book, my
body intact, also retain my bicycle."

"Very true."

"Could I have another lot of bacon and eggs in the morning, please? About
eight o'clock, if convenient. Good-night."

Since that day in the distant past I have not set eyes on Ballingdon Hall, so
cannot say if the gypsies remained in possession or tell of its subsequent fate.

You can take the riverside road from Sudbury for exploring many places full
of attractions in the upper Stour valley. First comes Long Melford, very long
and first-class too for a large green bordered with cosy old homes, Elizabethan
almshouses, a really glorious church both outside and within, three halls each of
them lovely, and an ancient inn to stay at. This last is the *Bull*. Dating from the
fifteenth century and originally inhabited by a rich clothier, its bulky fat timbers
have served in the pub line since 1580. Not always peacefully, however; in 1648
an angry cut-throat in the front hall cried out "Pshaw" (or the Puritan equiva-
lent), murdered Richard Evered, yeoman, and thereby hangs the tale of a funeral
at the church, a trial and a hanging at the gallows. Melford Hall, moated, Tudor
and finely bricked, presides over the main street just as it did when Queen
Elizabeth paid a visit; two more emblems of spacious and picturesque times,
Melford Place and the Elizabethan brickwork of Kentwell Hall within a moat
add further riches to this highly endowed spot, one that it is difficult for me

RIVER STOUR, at Nayland. The pretty town in the vale thrived with the old wool trade. Clothiers built the bridge, adorned the church, and Constable painted the altarpiece.

SALTER'S HALL · MOOT HALL

SUDBURY. *Old patterns in the picturesque streets of Gainsborough's birthplace.*

STOKE-BY-NAYLAND. *Timbered houses on the ridge rising from the valley of the Stour. The high tower of the village church was often depicted by Constable.*

to advise anyone ever to leave. But leave we must and so reach Glemsford, there admiring the great valley view and perhaps making a halt for a Shakespearian interlude enlivened with speeches remembered from *King Henry VIII*. For here came Wolsey's gentleman-usher and faithful friend, George Cavendish. Finding peace at last in this Suffolk village after the turmoil of Courts and the Cardinal's fall in 1529, he wrote his master's biography, died in 1561, passed on to the church where neither flourish nor memorial commemorates him. The biography remained in manuscript until printed nearly a century later. In the meantime Shakespeare undoubtedly saw it, and used the wording for his characterization of Cardinal Wolsey. Nearer the river a living Cavendish stands upright, pleasing to meet for its white houses round the green, thatched cottages nestling below the turreted church tower. While staying at the former manor-house (now a reading-room and institute) I discovered plaster panels of the Cavendish family arms in two of the rooms. These aristocratic symbols reminded me that the village had been a haunt of Sir John Cavendish, a Chief Justice in those sprouting years of the Labour movement when John Ball, Jack Straw, and Wat Tyler rose up and spouted, fired their comrades to pillage and burn all over the country, and the seeds of class warfare were beautifully sown with the popular rhyme,

> When Adam delved and Eve span,
> Who was then a gentleman?

Because Sir John had the misfortune to be a gentleman and belonged to the opposite camp he was unceremoniously trundled to Bury St. Edmunds for the purpose of removing his head, a sad loss for any officer of the Crown, even in 1381. Clare, the near town, matches Sudbury for good looks. If the renowned Earls of Clare, their castle, and the priory they founded now chiefly belong to the realm of romance and memories, the college not far away, re-endowed in 1338 by the Countess of Clare, continues to be one of the present sights at Cambridge. Old beauty unmarred has kept the streets of Clare delightful. Here are seen mixtures of gable and timbering, barge-board and oriel, a priest's house at the churchyard notable for parge ornamentation. Very obvious is the make-up used by local worthies who wished to be modish when wigs and patches were worn. They smartened up their premises, made them fashionable with light plaster fronts, Georgian doorways, sash windows. Yet behind parapets and cornices, peep older roofs and moulded brick chimneys, Tudor or Elizabethan, to tell that the later faces and frills merely rejuvenated ancestral structures (87). This eighteenth-century ensemble gives a charming and dignified character to the town. A few miles away, beyond Stoke-by-Clare and Wixoe, the River Stour parts from the Essex boundary, bends northward, leads us to quiet pastures and fresh lands of promise in

SUFFOLK

These lands of promise, set on part of the Eastern Plain, stretch across West and East Suffolk. The county thus divided into two halves is so delightful and countrified, gentle and pastoral in scene, often so remote and sequestered that it really does fit the title "unspoiled," a popular word now of course meaning that spoliations by man have not been excessively rampant. Here is the placid beauty of warm, wooded and homely prospects. The even surfaces are variegated with little hills, sheltered valleys, slow streams, commons, hedgerows, broad farmlands. Manor halls and farmhouses sit just right for making pictures. Narrow and twisting lanes yield the endless surprises of nature's growth and flowered borders. Fritillaries bloom red and white at Framsden. Dozens of villages delight and capture the eye. The churches are of unusual splendour. Lavenham and more ancient townships show their riches left from years long past. All these particulars imply just the same thing, rural Suffolk, far from the madding crowds and with not many strangers about. It is even possible to see more than one horse, the chestnut and famous Suffolk Punches actually at work in the fields. Flocks of sheep too, lambs, shepherds, send the mind wandering back to the early sources of East Anglian wealth and prosperity. High points on the belt of chalk, far-flung from the Chilterns, top the 400-feet mark around Depden and Rede, offer widespread views right across the county. Further north sandy heaths lead down to the fens below Mildenhall. Travellers of very distant ages left their tracks. The Icknield Way, direct from Newmarket, nears the end of the long course through England; tree-lined and lonely it points from Tuddenham Corner to Norfolk. Only by guessing and speculation may you expect to locate approximate sections of the Suffolk and Peddars Way until the northern county boundary is approached near the woods of Euston Park. Thence beyond the Little Ouse and Thet rivers, the old Way asserts itself, keeps to the heaths and swelling chalk lands right across Norfolk. The overgrown green miles, exhilarating to tread, their very age, the stillness and solitude promote and sustain those suggestions of mystery that always add to the fascination of any primitive trackway. This route apparently started from the River Stour at Stratford St. Mary, ended as it still does at the eastern corner of The Wash four miles from Brancaster where the Romans had their station of *Brancounum*. The Way thus cut a bold vital line right through the heart of East Anglia. It served the ancient territory of the Icenian Britons, survived their revolt and defeat in 61 A.D., gave the Romans a line of communication, then lost military significance, fed no centres of population, dropped out of use. Yet the Way remains, little known and secretive, a limb of early England. It has furnished learned antiquaries with unsolved puzzles for argument; now it offers thrilling miles to antediluvian mortals who still can progress without petrol and walk bravely on through little worlds of imaginative appeal without getting lost in the mires of dusky learning. Along the green stretches little is met to disturb or hinder anyone fancying pictures of the Icenians back on their tracks, rising to join Boadicea's great revolt for massacring the Romans, hurrying south to burn Colchester and London, fighting losing battles, suffering extermination, disappearing from the pages of history. Or conquering Romans can be revitalized marching north to smash pirate raiders on the coast, settling down within hail of the Peddars Way where their villas and relics can be found at Brettenham, Rougham, Stowlangtoft, West Stow, Icklingham; and who, you may wonder, buried the Roman treasure at West Row by Mildenhall, a wonderful hoard of silver dishes, bowls, cups, and spoons, all of superb workmanship, turned up by a farmer's plough on a winter's day in 1942? Anything in fact may be seen or mentally imaged on the old trackways of England; they're captivating, what treasures they lead to!

Prehistoric routes, tribal Icenians, mouldy Roman relics, or the flint mines and knapping at Brandon representing England's oldest industry dating back almost to the time of the Flood are all very well for particular quests, moods, and weighty deliberations. But in thinking of this pleasant Suffolk countryside my liveliest recollections keep a lighter and more delicate complexion. They centre on things more recent, old enough to be interesting and good to look at, and are remembered by churches, villages, houses, and towns that matured before men wore drab clothes below hard black hats and machinery conquered. My thoughts also turn to wool. This commodity I think ought to rank first because it furnished the staple in more ways than one. Sheep far and wide over the East Anglian grasslands, marshes, and fens helped to bring the immense wealth that laid a foundation of the country's prosperity onward from the Middle Ages when England was foremost in the production of wool for Europe. Kings, nobles, and the monks as well as merchants traded in wool; all made handsome profits from the long-woolled Cotswold and Lincolnshire sheep, from the flocks of the midland and eastern counties. The export trade consequently brought fortunes to the ports round the coast including Boston and Lynn on the Wash, Yarmouth, Harwich at the mouth of the Stour. Sheep provided the raw material for the great weaving industry with which England prospered after Edward III encouraged the immigration of skilled weavers from the Low Countries for the improvement of the home manufactures. Kersey, where Flemings settled in 1331, gave the name to the cloth woven from wool of long staple; Worstead in Norfolk similarly named its own products. In towns and villages the weaving workshops and humble homes throbbed with activity. The influx of more foreigners, to Norwich for example in 1508, meant new ideas and new looms for making russets, fustians, and satins. The Springs of

Lavenham, William Abell of Nayland, Cloptons of Long Melford and many master-weavers of Suffolk and Norfolk in the fifteenth and sixteenth centuries rose to fame, filled their coffers with gold. After the seventeenth century had passed the development of mechanical power and the grim factory system of the Industrial Revolution foreshadowed doom for the great days of hand-weaving pleasantly done where flowers bloomed and the greenery of trees and fields added sweetness to the daily labours of handiwork. Daniel Defoe, who lived for a time in Suffolk during the eighteenth century, noted again and again while he toured from place to place, "The trade has much declined." That it did so is evident when you visit the old wool towns and villages. Go to Kersey, an adorable spot, to Lavenham for a breath of Tudor England, to Mendlesham and Debenham both sweet in their decline. Much of the glory made by the golden fleece remains. Perhaps it was a good thing that the trade migrated and the later progress produced its chimney-stacks, smoke, and mean streets elsewhere.

While this material success through wool gathered impetus in the eastern counties during the fourteenth, fifteenth, and sixteenth centuries it was a custom of the times to mix prayer and praise with business. Over towns and villages, the sheep-walks and the fields the Angelus bells tolled notes of salutation and blessing at morning, noon and sunset. Into the churches went wool-staplers and weavers, master men and employed men to observe religious duties, and quiet moments of devotion snatched from hours of work and piling the money shine little soft lights here and there on the pages of contemporary records. And if unrest, class strife, questioning, close bargaining, and devotion to the main chance did ruffle the times in the manner customary to all periods of human society I like to think that men, as they did very well for themselves, remembered their debts to Divine Providence. Certain it is that they directed an abundance of ready cash to build and beautify many churches, now the particular glories on the landscapes of the plains and lowlands in the east. Onward from the middle of the fourteenth century the woolmen became wealthy.

It was a period of high thinking and high doing in the realm of artistic expression. Then England's great system in building, native, home-grown, passed from full flower to its richest fruitage of the Perpendicular style. As the years moved on the profits of commerce, particularly from wool, spread beauty far and wide. Success in work and export marketing allied with the prevailing religious beliefs and innate artistic perception helped sermons in stone to arise, towers in Somerset, loveliness on the Cotswolds, spires pointing over the up-lands of Northamptonshire, and the grand array of churches now visible in the eastern counties. These last, my concern for a moment, developed very notably in the late fourteenth and fifteenth centuries. Elevated schemes, bigly conceived, commonly of large actual size, carried a definite grand manner.

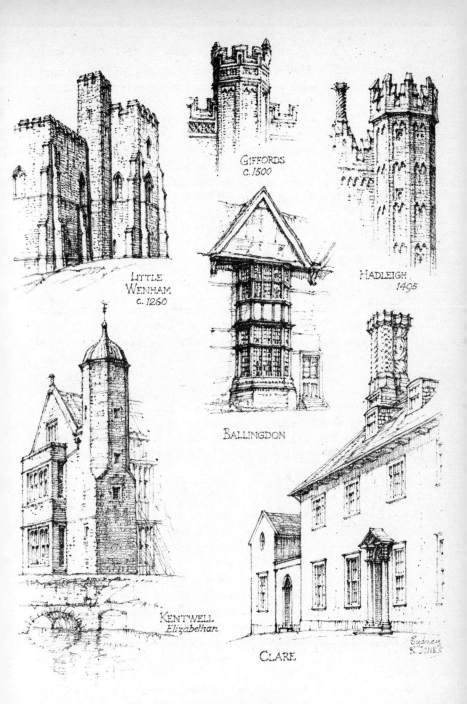

GIFFORDS
c. 1500

LITTLE
WENHAM
c. 1260

HADLEIGH
1495

BALLINGDON

KENTWELL
Elizabethan

CLARE

Sydney
R. Jones

HALLS IN THE STOUR COUNTRY

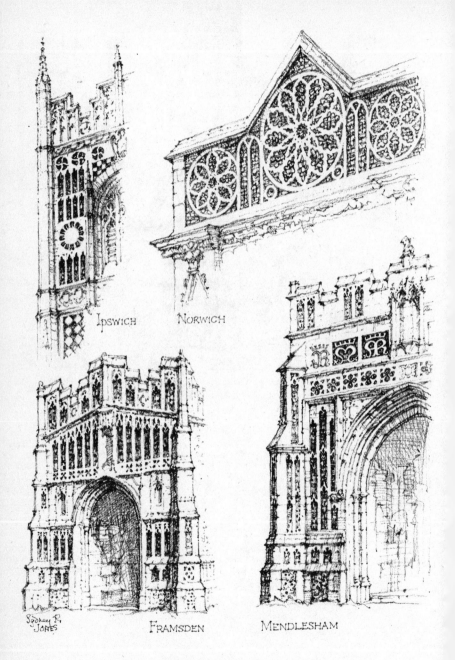

IPSWICH   NORWICH

FRAMSDEN   MENDLESHAM

EAST ANGLIAN CHURCHES. *Flint and stone ornamentation.*

WETHERDEN

St. Mary's
BURY ST. EDMUNDS

NEEDHAM
MARKET

Hammer-beam and angel roofs.

GEDDING HALL. *It stands in a charming tract of the Suffolk countryside. The gatehouse survives from the moated home built by the Chamberlayne family when Tudor kings reigned.*

External flint walling predominated. Structural and fitted woodwork became unusually excellent. Only to see the outside brilliance of dark flint and light stone, the spaciousness and lofty grace of interiors rising to timbered and hammer-beam roofs, the artistry of screens and stalls, is to realize how the fruits of good trade once stimulated a happy union of piety, idealism, skilled design, and perfection in craftsmanship. At Long Melford, Lavenham, St. Mary's in Bury St. Edmunds, Wetherden, Saxmundham, Blythburgh, Southwold, and throughout the area of Suffolk it is clearly obvious that church-building advanced with the upward trend of the times, thus to leave a bequest of architecture beyond worldly price.

Natural products in Suffolk and Norfolk did not offer good building stone; it had to be obtained from distant quarries, notably in Northamptonshire, sometimes from Caen in Normandy. But flints on the local chalk lands and pebbles in the coastal districts were abundant. Saxons, Normans and later generations used them for rough walling. They made the early and frequent round towers, now curious features for inquisitive eyes to see at Little Saxham (west of Bury St. Edmunds), Blundeston, Herringfleet and Fritton (all near Lowestoft), at forty places in Suffolk, with more than a hundred yet standing over the county border in Norfolk. The continuous use of the material brought to East Anglia its pre-eminence for flint churches. Flint however is one of nature's hardest products, small in units, uneven in surface texture, impossible to carve. While East Anglian trade and manufacture expanded in the fourteenth century experiments began for improving walling and decoration. Split and selected in sizes, flints were laid in regular courses. Then followed the use of flints knapped to square shapes, more careful splitting to show even lustrous surfaces, while the introduction of flint patterns, panels and diapers framed in strips of freestone served for general ornamentation and enrichment. This progress, fully in swing after 1450, gave the locality its most distinctive architectural characteristics. Travellers who explore these lands of old fame and light on the churches I have previously mentioned, or who find the exceptionally good tower at Eye, Earl Stonham clerestory, porches at Framsden, Mendlesham, Fressingfield, the sparkling blacks, greys and whites of flint and stone at churches all over Suffolk and away through Norfolk (88), such wanderers perhaps may admire the way the old people made the best job they could with a hard yet humble defier of time and weather—flint. Difficult to work, cruel for the hands in laying, it has endured. Now it recalls pockets full of money, prayer and praise, offerings truly built by men in thanks for their earthly well-being and presented in the custom of their years "To the glory of God" during the great days of medieval trade, wool-dealing, and cloth-making.

If flint was hard and intractable the oak of old England had quite different qualities. It offered free and boundless possibilities to craftsmen. Within its constructive and decorative limits the carpenters of the eastern counties developed one of the great woodworking centres of England. They did splendid jobs, left wonderful sights for us now to see in screens, traceries, stalls, canopies, bench-ends, and all manner of fittings in churches. To their work they also added fresh human touches, expressions of themselves in carved figures, birds, beasts, flowers, and foliage that show better than words can tell their sense of skill, observation, humour sometimes, and always a striving to do well. This display of woodwork, the lively designs and spirited execution add particular zest to the joys of church-hunting at Stowlangtoft, Worlingworth, Dennington, Badingham, in fact in all directions through Suffolk and next door in the county of Norfolk. And the roofs—where can they be equalled? They are a special glory of this eastern region. Set high above earth they close the interiors. Open timbering, rafter, post, beam, brace, and arch glow deep-coloured in the mystery of religious light. Here you plainly trace roof construction with tie-beams developed to the hammer-beam and double hammer-beam roofs, richly effective in the decorative resourcefulness of Gothic design, adorned with symbolic figures and companies of angels carved on the projections to name the celebrated "angel roofs" of the east (89). I need only mention such famous examples as those at Woolpit, Needham Market, Bacton, Mildenhall, and Grundisburgh to send a seeker in search of more magnificence at other points. Clearly the old-time carpenters succeeded in bringing elevated meanings to their lofty work. While I looked upward in church after church and espied the angels with wings outstretched, it seemed to me that they were ready poised to rise and join the angelic hosts in heaven—surely a gracious suggestion for any roof to give.

Around the churches grew the villages and towns of the common life. Guildhalls, quarters for marketing, homes of the well-to-do, houses, cottages, and domestic buildings harmoniously blended with local scenes and decked the calm Suffolk landscapes. Fully matured during the sixteenth and seventeenth centuries the work in timbering, plaster surfaces, narrow bricks, ample chimneys, tiling and thatching carried onward the traditional uses and forms inherited from the golden years of national creative art and handicraft. But the truly democratic style in building had arrived, of and for the people, in tune with the pulse and movements of the times; in this eastern country, as elsewhere, it endowed English towns and villages with their rarity and expression. Here and there steep gables of Flemish bond in brickwork, curved and crow-stepped, reminded foreign weavers of their native lands. In due season the Renaissance breezes of an architectural rebirth blew in, influenced features, dictated designs. The Georgian manner spread, brought dignity and charm to town streets, country mansions, houses round village greens—for builders, like the ladies, generally wished to be in the fashion.

These leaps down the centuries and the stores left by past thought, conduct, and artistic traditions are particularly obvious in Suffolk. Mostly spared from the dreary ugliness imposed by the mechanized industrial era the county has retained much of its home-bred and bright native character to this day. All routes north of the Stour direct through rural scenery, to the quiet and peace of fields, trees, and plentiful oaks, winding lanes between the hedgerows, the luxuriance of wild flowers along the waysides. They lead to villages and towns that took ages to make so comely, now full of delight, holding memories. Castle relics occasionally give antique flavours of feudal times. I name but two—the impressive thirteenth-century masonry at Framlingham, early curtain walls 45 feet high, thirteen towers, once known to the Mowbrays and the Howards, creators of the neighbouring church in which they lie under the blazon of her-aldry, rich carving, colour and alabaster; and the massive keep at Bungay, stronghold of Bigod, the boastful earl who told Henry II to go to the devil,

> Were I in my Castle of Bungaye
> Above the Water of Waveneye,
> I would ne care for the King of Cockneye
> And all his meiny.

Very frequent, the picturesque outlines of halls and manor-houses, often reflected in still moats, impart suspicions of romance first planted, doubtless unconsciously, by Willoughby of Parham, Kytson of Hengrave, and their companion upholders of the settled gentry and wealthy merchants who strode ancestral or newly-acquired acres.

The remaining portion of Hengrave Hall (four miles north of Bury St. Edmunds) is a splendid Tudor sight still flashing the buoyancy of its years of building, 1525 to 1538. Gables, domed turrets, battlements, crocket and finial, bay and carved oriel convey the idea of sumptuous effect in home-making favoured by one of the wealthiest merchants in Henry VIII's reign, Sir Thomas Kytson, who is elaborately commemorated by his tomb in the little church. He traded in the richest of stuffs, velvets, tapestries, furs, cloth of gold, and with such success that he was able to acquire a Countess of Bath for his wife. "Skut-chens with armes" worked in the windows by Robert Wright the glazier gave the impress of ownership and family pride; within the walls were first heard the sweet madrigals composed by John Wilbye, the family's resident musician—for the music of singing at sight from part-books then had a daily place in the art of living. Tudor also is Parham Old Hall (south of Framlingham), matured between 1498 and 1527 on an earlier castle site. Modest in size, tradi-tional in the manner of brickwork and timbering rising sheer from a moat, its air of romance, slightly melancholy, gains from the shades cast by the trees surrounding the water. After the lords of Parham departed the house descended from aristocratic to farming uses and late in the eighteenth century made a home for George Crabbe, satirically called by Horace Smith, "Pope in worsted stockings." Fresh from Hengrave with thoughts of love-making between Kytson and the Countess, or perhaps the scene at Parham appeared to me suitable for the same kind of thing—whatever the reason may have been I happened to dig from oblivion a little verse written by the Suffolk poet and entitled *A Marriage Ring*. The opening lines read,

> The ring, so worn as you behold,
> So thin, so pale, is yet of gold.

Ah! a tender sentiment. Then I learned that Crabbe met and wooed Sarah Elmy, niece of John Tovell the yeoman farmer, they married in 1783, lived happily ever afterwards conveniently sustained by Sarah's inherited fortune, publisher's rewards, plural livings—and it all began because de Parham the knight built the pretty and spookish old house I had seen through the trees above the moat. More tall bays straight up from another moat at Gedding lead brave and lovely touches of the fifteenth century into these years of the twentieth (90). Out from Stowmarket, first finding a Norman castle mound at Haughley and Woolpit's wonderful church, I turned through Drinkstone along the lanes in a rare bit of rural Suffolk, rounded a bend, caught sight of Gedding Hall standing back from a grassy space. The summer sunlight warmed the brickwork tinted in reds and greys. Grouped with trees and green turf here was a picture ready made by the original builders, nature, and a few hundred years of time. I crossed the moat, was welcomed inside the gatehouse, throught to stay for minutes but remained until the next day, rambled downstairs and upstairs— that's the sort of welcome given to a stranger by the natives in kind, friendly, and hospitable Suffolk. Except the gatehouse, the house now used is largely reconstructed. Of romantic arrivals and farewells that of course happened at the great gate I gleaned nothing; like the callers and lovers gone and forgotten, the archways were sealed up long ago. Nor did overgrown foundations at the rear tell me much of the home made by the Chamberlayne family in this calm and sequestered spot when Tudor kings reigned. Up and down the county there are so many more of these halls of families that flourished and those that went to seed, my list could be continued almost indefinitely. From scenes remembered I might have been tempted to tell of Tudors and Elizabethans at Bentley, West Stow, Thurston End near Hawkedon, Columbine Hall outside Stowmarket; to locate knights, squires, and parsons calmly settled in roomy places built in the reigns of the Stuarts, Queen Anne, and the Georges. The small space at my disposal would never do justice to Heveningham's stately classicalism and chaste interiors designed by Sir Robert Taylor and James Wyatt, or Flaxman friezes and the Herveys' long eighteenth-century mansion into which I entered from the wide parklands of Ickworth. But a warning. The time may be short for seeing these historic houses intact. A melancholy note by

BILDESTON. *One of Suffolk's old weaving towns. Here cloth and blankets were made. Oak and plaster frontages line the streets, and inside the Crown inn are long moulded Tudor beams.*

MENDLESHAM. *A quiet and peaceful little place that once flourished with the East Anglian trade. The church remains a monument of past prosperity, splendid with fifteenth-century architecture and flint ornamentation.*

BRENT ELEIGH. *One in the line of effective Suffolk villages leading from Lavenham to Hadleigh. Others are Monks Eleigh, Chelsworth, and Kersey.*

HOXNE. *Light-tinted walls, tiled and thatched roofs prettily surround the green. Here in 870 Edmund, Christian King of East Anglia, was martyred by the Danes, his body being finally interred later at Bury St. Edmunds.*

Lord Euston in the *East Anglian Magazine* sounds the doom of 49 important examples, 37 of which have been demolished recently.

Villages and towns, storied and jolly as old years made them, have managed to keep standing up. They retain appearances invented by the real craftsmen of Suffolk who worked in timber, brick, plaster, tile, and thatch to mould a style of vernacular architecture that seems to have grown out of the very soil. It is sheer joy to wander amongst these places, not as yet unduly mauled by nondescript erections created in the name of modern convenience. Houses, cottages, and inviting inns, domestic groups leading to fine churches, town squares and village greens, guildhalls and almshouses, all demonstrate how local people both planned for everyday needs and constructed the right kind of beauty for matching the richness of their country and environment. Among the towns Lavenham needs no further praise from me. It is a jewel of all England. Nowhere more easily does time push back. Light and dark, oak and colour-wash, the guild and wool halls, medieval shops and Tudor streets foster dreams of the great days when the life of merchants, weavers, and townsfolk busily progressed, while at the church a lordly de Vere with Springs the clothiers created splendour and a joy for ever. The loveliness of Lavenham does not stand alone. More pleasant little towns, Needham Market, Halesworth, Eye, and others scattered across the county, have the characteristic picturesqueness of the East Anglian manner. Gables and overhanging storeys, much oakwork, cream and pink plaster panels, Georgian doorways, and all sorts of details from various periods decorate the active present with signs of the life lived a long time ago. Debenham, Mendlesham, and Bildeston (95) made a delightful trio. If Defoe might have called them "decayed" after doing good business with woollens, nothing could be more successful than their calm and peaceful settling down in age. A guildhall among bulging houses and pretty peeps through archways attracted me in Debenham, and at the *Crown,* Bildeston, a ponderous oak ceiling with moulded beams that I measured 25 feet long made me feel quite Tudor-ish and back in the thriving wool days. It is a bewilderment to choose the good Suffolk villages for mention, they are so numerous. In general appearance and architectural make-up they resemble those we have previously noted in north Essex. Nowhere more endearing than Kersey can be discovered in a day's march or motoring. Brent Eleigh (96), Monks Eleigh, and Chelsworth have neighbours fair as themselves down by the willows and alders along the vale of the River Brett. Hawkedon round a big green with a church in the middle, another broad green at Hartest sheltered by oaks and elms, Hunston much better than a stage setting, the windmill and old houses at Earl Soham, and Hoxne for its shapeliness and colouring (96) are but samples of my findings among these village riches. Whichever way is followed every road and lane yields things to see and remember in pictures toned by age and nature, works made by the sons and daughters of the soil who unconsciously achieved better than they knew.

Routes south, north, west, and east through rich agricultural country meet at the local capital and crown of West Suffolk, Bury St. Edmunds (101). Of ancient fame for the glorious shrine of St. Edmund, King and Martyr, the cradle of law and liberty embodied in Magna Carta, the borough proudly displays its motto *Sacrarium Regis, Cunabula Legis*. This junction of highways and history, now as ever bright with a wholesome air of wellbeing, is full of captivating sights that to me seemed all the better for the presence of jolly Suffolk folk who come in from the villages and farms, throng the streets, noticeably foregather in the Butter Market and Cornhill hard by the elegant old town hall. Monumental buildings, Romanesque and Gothic, sent my feet wandering to ruins of the once powerful abbey, the Norman tower and medieval gateway, two grand Perpendicular churches of St. James and St. Mary, Moyses Hall for eleventh-century domestic rarities, the Guildhall of 1480. Green shades, glades, and flowered gardens deck the grounds and the vineyard trodden by Benedictine monks for more than five hundred years. Proper country-town pictures are everywhere, ready for pencil, paint, or camera. They group in streets busy, quiet, narrow, or opening into squares. Down Eastgate Street I found the River Lark, the bridge over it built by an abbot in 1250, timbering opposite cornered at an elaborately carved angle post, one combination and sample of many good subjects. Numerous biggish and dignified houses even now might fit their younger years when candlelight shone, and ladies fair and tinted stepped through delicate doorways into sedan chairs—one specimen chair without lady being preserved inside Moyses Hall. These same houses, charming in entrances, panelled rooms, and staircases, knew gay days and nights in the town seasons that of course flourished hugely in this little metropolis of the squirearchy. From all around came the gentry for the routs, balls, the gossip and scandal. Then the Bristol family settled down at their manor-house on Honey Hill, the Gages of Hengrave at their handsome establishment you see in Northgate. Youth and pleasure, the sylphs and the dowagers met to chase the dancing hours in the old Assembly Rooms where the Athenæum Hall, still polished in the Adamantic style, echoes the age of elegance. The *Dog and Partridge, Half Moon*, and numerous inns are ancient or Georgian featured. The *Suffolk*, badly mauled outside but comfortable within, claims an ownership by the abbey under the name of *le Greyhounde* until the Dissolution, and the eighteenth-century *Angel* on the top of thirteenth-century cellars looks inviting enough to make anyone wish to stay there for the rest of the twentieth century.

With so much to attract no discerning potterer could fail to like Bury. Earlier sojourners certainly did and said so, Leland in the 1500's, Daniel Defoe in the 1800's when he discovered "the Montpellier of Suffolk, and perhaps of England" while living in the oak-panelled rooms of Cupola House in The Traverse. Dickens fitted Pickwickians into the *Angel*, Louis-Philippe next door may or may not have enjoyed his retreat from France, and Edward Fitzgerald never forgot his schooldays at King Edward's School. Nor shall I ever forget past times of hospitality spent at the Abbey Ruins, the spell of resting for a while at those sacred and historic acres of England. Within sight of my guest-room lay the foundations of Beodricsworth that became the Bury at which men laid the body of Edmund the Christian and last king of East Anglia, defeated by the Danes and murdered at Hoxne in 870. Stonework standing up and fragments strewn on the ground indicated an abbey's magnificence and gigantic life dead and gone. Night brought the shades and the images of fancy—Canute, Cœur-de-Lion, and kings long since dumb; barons at the high altar vowing to extort Magna Carta from King John; meetings of Parliament; miracles at the gorgeous shrine; the ceaseless flow of pilgrims; desecration by Henry VIII; Thomas Carlyle groping round "old St. Edmundsbury walls" brooding on *Past and Present*, Jocelin of Brakelond, Abbot Samson, black ruin, "how silent now." Truly Bury St. Edmunds is a place for visions, memories, a town of perennial beauty, happiness, and new life blending at the Shrine of the King and the Cradle of the Law.

Across country, past the fine churches and through delightful villages, brings us to Ipswich, Suffolk's capital and really big town. This ancient port at the head of the Orwell estuary, thriving in the sweat, smells and smoke of modern industry, and acres of docks, has never failed to accelerate and get on since Edward III and merchants of old sent their ships to fight and trade across the seas. In spite of arrangements made for progress much of oldness among the newness catches the eye. Bits and pieces anatomize past life and times in the present crowded narrow streets, peculiar passages and back quarters. Earlier bones and structure of the place show at timbered houses and plaster fronts particular for their local stamp in oriels and projecting windows, at inns of all sorts, ages, and degrees, at the parish churches, some of them noteworthy and so numerous that it is difficult even to count them—seventeen I managed to find and hope the number is correct. These churches, so closely placed, rewarded my wandering with sights of much good fifteenth-century architecture, the stone, the flint, and pierced parapets paid for by the trading burgesses, a double hammer-beam roof at St. Margaret's, the carved stalls, screens, and a pulpit that still glow for the city lights on their civic occasions at St. Mary-le-Tower. Blest with a fancy for tombs I met old town worthies in aisles and chancels, properly commemorated with death's emblems of furred gown and ruff, hour-glass, skull and crossbones. Merchant Thomas Pounder in St. Mary-at-the-Quay and John Knapp the Tudor at St. Peter's swelled the throng with their portraits engraved on brass—and anybody who pokes around might like to see how a

Flemish artist treated 46 inches of T. Pounder. One illustrious son of the town, Cardinal Wolsey, called me to his gateway by St. Peter's, a remnant of the college he erected on the site of an Augustinian monastery, there founding a tower of learning which rose and then, as Shakespeare tells us, "fell with him."

Of many more subjects offered for inspection at Ipswich I can only mention a few. Christchurch Mansion in its park clearly shows that it came together in a spacious age of luxury, light taxation, and no servant shortage, when people could afford a home with a good frontage, forecourt, projecting wings, gables curved and pedimented, big rich fireplaces, panelled walls, and a minstrel's gallery for their own musicians to perform on viols, lutes, and hautboys. That's how things were done at the mansion before it lost caste and the aristocratic birds fled. Like others of the same class it now democratically caters for all comers who may enjoy this treasure-house of its period, and roam at leisure through stately rooms in which Tudors and Elizabethans once lolled.

> The *Rampant Horse* shall kick the *Bear*
> And make the *Griffin* fly,
> Turn the *Bull* upside down
> And drink the *Three Tuns* dry,

denotes another aspect of Ipswich renown in a doggerel rhyme on a few of the town's many inns during the posting and coaching days. A reconstructed *Rampant Horse* changed its name to the *Crown and Anchor* in the 1800's, but the *Great White Horse* stands where it stood more than four hundred years ago. One of England's very famous establishments, "known far and wide," wrote Charles Dickens in the twenty-second chapter of *Pickwick*, it is still a haven of welcome for travelling gents, and ladies without "yellow curl-papers." The long flat front is conspicuous for a spirited carving of a white animal between two huge lamps elevated above the entrance. Through that doorway passed Mr. Pickwick for his nocturnal adventure, Lord Nelson and King Louis XVIII to sleep, King George II on arrival after a rough wintry passage from Lowestoft and Saxmundham in 1737; in fact, vast assortments of humanity, distinguished and of middle quality, have thanked their lucky stars for the presence of that white animal as they halted in the perpetual careering up and down the East Anglian highway. The plaster-faced houses with their pretty curved oriel windows, seen in Fore Street and elsewhere, I consider the most distinctive features on the town's domestic front. The Ancient or Sparrowe's House, a most lively ornament at the corner of Butter Market, stands as a king amongst them. Built in the sixteenth century with great beams, panelled rooms, and a wide staircase, it made a home for the ardent Royalists who lie in a vault at St. Laurence's church under their motto, *Nidus Passerum* (sparrow's nest). The house went gay at the Restoration, acquired a new face, boldly bore the arms of Charles II to date it. Above, below, and between the delicate oriel windows

BURY ST. EDMUNDS. *Shrine of the King, cradle of Magna Carta. Abbey gateways, churches of St. James (cathedral) and St. Mary, and the old Assembly Rooms from Angel Hill.*

IPSWICH. *External parge decoration at Sparrowe's House. The ornamentation, dated with the arms of Charles II, includes modelled pilasters, figures, flowers, birds, and symbols for Europe, Asia, Africa, and America.*

COASTAL SUFFOLK.

NORFOLK COAST. *Village and church at Salthouse border salt marshes and the sea. The church has a good fifteenth-century interior.*

STIFFKEY HALL, *chiefly built of flint. Here lived Sir Nicholas Bacon, Queen Elizabeth's Lord Keeper and father of Francis.*

NORFOLK HEATH, *near Weybourne.*

HICKLING BROAD, *one of the most beautiful lakes in Broadland.*
It covers more than 200 acres.

Sydney R Jones
Potter Heigham

POTTER HEIGHAM. *The ancient bridge over the River Thurne is*
well known to explorers of the Broads. The village church has a round
tower and thatched roof. Roman pottery was made in the neighbourhood.

E Dereham

Sydney R Jones

EAST DEREHAM. *Cottages known as Bishop Bonner's, dated 1502, show a running frieze of parge ornamentation below the eaves. Names and events of the town include Bonner's rectorship, George Borrow's birth in 1803, Cowper's last years and death in 1800.*

NORWICH. *The restored medieval watergate at Pull's disused ferry. The archway leads to the close, monastic precincts, and Cathedral.*

WYMONDHAM. *Green Dragon inn, Church Street. Twin towers locate remains of a Benedictine monastery and the lofty church with a fine angel roof. The town has a pretty market cross, octagonal and timbered, dating from 1616.*

Sydney
R. Jones
1951

NORWICH. *For more than 700 years trading has thrived in the Market Place, the Great Croft of Norman times. The wide square is dominated by St. Peter Mancroft, commenced in 1530, the most beautiful of the city's many old parish churches.*

107

NORWICH. *A south view of the Cathedral's long Norman nave and lofty east end in the varied architectural setting of the close. The spire, rising from the talles. Norman tower in England and only exceeded in height at Salisbury, nobly dominate.*

the scenes from surrounding points and Mousehold Heath. A Norman keep, medieval
gateways and halls, streets with numerous old houses and very many churches
preserve past interest and beauty in this prosperous capital of East Anglia.

YARMOUTH. *One of the Rows in the curious tight town-planning called by Charles Dickens "The Norfolk gridiron."*

GT. SNORING
c.1500

E. BARSHAM
c.1500-15

BLICKLING 1620

BARNHAM BROOM

Sidney R Jones

KIRSTEAD 1614

Terra-Cotta

NORFOLK HALLS. *Brick and terra-cotta details.*

SANDRINGHAM. *King Edward VII's favourite view.*

The Royal country home, built in the 1860's, was designed by Albert J. Humbert.

TRINITY. *The fountain (1602), great gate, and chapel.*

JESUS. *Bishop Alcock's gateway.*

QUEENS'. *The President's gallery.*

CAMBRIDGE COLLEGES.

PEMBROKE COLLEGE, *the University Press, and Trumpington Street.*

ST. JOHN'S COLLEGE *and Wren's bridge over the River Cam.*

KING'S. *The chapel and Gibbs' building.*

GONVILLE AND CAIUS. *Gate of Honour.*   EMMANUEL. *Wren's chapel and cloister.*

CAMBRIDGE COLLEGES.

appear plaster modellings of swags and pilasters, figures, animals, fruit, flowers, birds, Neptune riding a seahorse, Atlas bearing the world on his shoulders, symbols for Europe, Asia, Africa, and America (101), while the back of the building shows royalty in a chariot drawn by plumed horses and cheered by a spectator perched up a tree. Vivacious, strong, decorative, the scheme was evidently the work of imaginative local craftsmen; not in all England have I met another frontage quite like it or more fantastically devised. The images, set locally on overhanging storeys and pointed gables, seem to burst their bounds, call to far continents, breathe the spirit of old Ipswich, its merchants and mariners, adventure and romance across the oceans.

East of Ipswich lies the coastal plain bounded by the sea, a plain of low altitudes, heaths, scattered woods, wide expanses of flat landscape. Broad tidal estuaries of the Orwell, Deben, and Alde wind down to their endings among lonesome borderlands which smugglers found most convenient in the bad old days. These elements for scenic appeal may not enthrall everybody; I recollect that Crabbe, born at Aldeburgh two hundred years ago, thought the district dismal, weedy, rank, depressing, peopled by "a wild, artful, surly, savage race." Since the poet's time progress and racial equalization of course have brought wonderful changes, yet without entirely obliterating the quiet and out-of-the-way character of this tract of country. Latter-day upheavals and crowds are not very conspicuous in the sparsely placed villages, hamlets, and ancient small towns. Woodbridge, though served by highways, railroads, and motor services, has managed to retain much of its delightful true self. Bits and peeps along the water front make you think of warships built there in the oak days. Rambling streets packed with quaint buildings, a steelyard by the *Bell* inn (102), the Shire Hall that might be sixteenth-century Flemish, and the town's general attractiveness cannot have greatly changed since Tennyson stayed at the *Bull* or Edward Fitzgerald lodged on Market Hill prior to settling down at Little Grange, complete with his Inverness cape, satin waistcoat, and "A Book of Verses underneath the Bough." Among other place-names pleasantly remembered in this neighbourhood I recommend Sutton for its manorial Wood Hall and great barn; Iken on the River Alde; Falkenham with an "angel" roof in the church; Nacton among the trees where Vernon of Orwell Park and Broke of Broke House recall names of fighting seamen; Trimley St. Mary and St. Martin, curious for two adjacent churches and owning Grimston Hall, once a home of the Elizabethan Thomas Cavendish, the intrepid navigator who rivalled Drake by sailing all round the world, pirated on the Spanish Main, and still shines gloriously in the pages of Hakluyt. The coast, never far away, sweeps northward through Felixstowe, Aldeburgh, Southwold, Lowestoft, marking an end of our ways through Suffolk. Here land and seaward aspects are varied with summer holidaymakers, piers, promenades, life and movement in the harbours, fishermen and their quarters. Lighthouses and coastguard stations face epic strands of storm, danger, and heroism when the lifeboats go out. Walberswick is but one of the haunts favoured by artists who find heaps to draw and paint among tidal shallows, boats, wooden piles, little bridges, saltish natives, white-faced and brick-gabled cottages roofed with pantiles. Meanwhile the North Sea continues an ageless battle with the land, swallows it up, changes the coast outlines. Orford therefore retired long ago to be a decayed port; a charming one it is for pretty houses, old streets, and a pictorial lion at Henry II's twelve-sided castle (102) built in 1165 by Alnoth, the royal architect, whose pay for making this unusual design was sevenpence a day! The tides at Alde-burgh have located the town's timbered moot hall (102) on the beach. At Dunwich there is really nothing to see. The place of Bishop Felix, the seventh-century missionary, and a chief city of East Anglia with a fine harbour, palace, monasteries, many churches, hospitals, gates, all fell victims to the waves; when a man told me of churchyard bones sticking out of the cliff I thought of a lost city in its proud days of flesh, blood, life, now a fabled Lyonesse, a phantom below the waters. If the sea did conquer the defences erected by the Romans at Dunwich and Felixstowe the fortress of Burgh stands, defying time and storm a few miles inland at the northern tip of Suffolk. It is a wonderful ruin. Massive bastions, walls ten feet thick, broken flintwork and rubble vivify memories of a far-flung Empire in its little era of conquest, power, and triumph. Mounted on one of the towers I looked out far and wide as the Counts of the Saxon Shore had done when they held in check seaborne raiders and the warlike Iceni.

> The tumult and the shouting dies—
> The captains and the kings depart.

Down below, where trained legions and Stablesian cavalry manœuvred in the dawning time of Christianity, to-day's harvest ripened over the graves of the dead; the Waveney and the Yare flowed on to Yarmouth and the sea; beyond the marshes stretched Norfolk, the county for our next exploration.

NORFOLK

This big shire, England's fourth largest, brings us again to more notable churches with flint walling and splendid woodwork, great houses led by Royal Sandringham, halls contrived in Tudor and later brickwork, to the homelands of more artists and celebrities, and to a fair countryside thickly dotted with villages and towns of long standing within hail of a worthy county capital, the noble cathedral city of Norwich. The chalk formation across England from Dorset, here ending along the sea coast, and the eastern low-lying country of slow rivers and the Broads roughly bisect this old province of the North

Folk who raided in from Germany. Fens, the Little Ouse and Waveney Rivers determine the inland county boundaries. Facing outward to the North Sea a bold arc of coastline sweeps from Yarmouth to The Wash. The sea, "which is full of fish," wrote Camden, "beats upon the shore with a great roaring." Consequently it has perpetually fought and bitten into the land, silted up ancient ports, accounted for pungent smells of herrings and other members of the fishy tribe.

Within this land figure bounded by the sea the landscape forms and scenery are green, pleasant, and satisfying, still "grateful with the variety thereof," as Fuller found three hundred years ago. Here is concentrated a good and typical piece of England. Famous for agriculture and cornfields, it has not been unduly embellished with the smoky effects of massed industrialism. Crossing from south to north, west to east, brings to view the changeful aspects of the county's scenic variety. Landscapes in the chalk country have the characteristics of their kind, smooth and curved surfaces, the dips, hollows, and many small streams, expansive distances, delicate field greens and browns that contrast with deeper colouring of plentiful woodlands. These general appearances, locally diversified, belong to the chalky belt; rarely elevated to more than three hundred feet and containing the East Anglian Heights (311 feet at West Bradenham), it forms the wide and slightly undulating plain from the Little Ouse River to the northern shores at Hunstanton cliffs, Brancaster Bay, Wells, and Weybourne. This same chalk ground yielded flints mined by Stone Age men. You can discover more than three hundred of their pits at Grime's Graves in a wood near Weeting to bring visions of England's earliest and busy industrial centre dating back thousands of years and then worked with picks made from antlers. A few miles from these remarkable acres it was not without a thrill that I found the mysterious Peddars Way, lonely, green, and little trodden, tracing an immemorial course over Roudham Heath and through the uplands to Castle Acre, momentous for its scenes of ruined castle and abbey founded by the Lords de Warrenne. Thence, beginning on the hard road, the Way sends a bold straight line to Holme-next-the-Sea, close to Brancaster, a golfer's paradise at the lost Roman station for repelling raids upon The Wash. The coastline hereabout is fascinating. Corn ripens within sight of white horses breaking upon the shore. Watery channels intersect the salt marshes and sand dunes. A curious arm of land stretches out to Blakeney Point. The haunts of terns and wild birds are famous; the bird-watcher keeps his vigil on Scoult Head. Day and night the North Sea ever beats in, and the beacon tower of Blakeney church, seen far out to sea, served as a lighthouse in times of peril. Great seaward views are visible from the uplands. Churches at Salthouse (102) and Cley stand out. They seem to be fixed anchorages of faith and hope among the eternal changes of watery expanses, marshes, and the moving skies. Cley church, one of the most beautiful in north Norfolk, grew so fine before the shifting sands claimed the harbour. Then the port was influential, wealthy, thronged with Continental wool-buyers. Good business, and thankfulness developed the loveliness of arcades, tracery, fan-vaulting, battlements, now to be seen where the bustling days have gone. Fittingly, near the incessant battling of the waves, Nelson was born at Burnham Thorpe; his birthplace, like "the greatest sailor since the world began," has departed. In these sturdy coastal villages, each facing wind and weather in a sense of community with the elements, I observed remarkable house and cottage walling, patterns and curved gables built in flint. Also did I hear a number of quaint names for fishes, apparently lobsters and crabs:

> Weybourne witches—Salthouse ditches—
> Blakeney bulldogs—Morston dodmen—
> Binham bulls—Stiffkey trolls—
> Wells bitefingers.

Additionally Stiffkey enjoys another fame for "Stewkey blues," commonly called cockles. Landward it is a sweet village in a wooded hollow by the Stiffkey stream, flint gables and a round tower of the hall (103) rising among the trees. Once a manor of the Boleyn family, it came into possession of Sir Nicholas Bacon, Queen Elizabeth's Lord Keeper and father of Francis. He largely built the house. A local seer, who impeded my view for a few moments, told me that Shakespeare's plays were written within these flint walls. Not a Baconian, I thought grains of salt rather larger than flints were needed to swallow this notion.

The heathlands introduce changes of scenery. Here are sandy expanses, wide prospects and loneliness, pines and fir trees, colourings of gorse, bracken and ling, wild birds, huge rabbit warrens, cover for hares. Dwellers in the warrens have made Brandon noted for a trade in rabbit skins for decorating would-be fine ladies, and supplies of hare-fur go to people who make hats. Beyond this town and Thetford stretches Breckland, a district so named from the "brecks" or ancient remains of land broken by the plough in futile attempts to develop cultivation. East Anglia has no wilder tract, nor one more exhilarating for stepping away from time and trouble. It is open, airy, bracing. A number of meres glisten among the heaths. You can cross for miles with rarely a house in sight. I always fancy that from these primitive sanctuaries sprouted the entertaining chronicler *Jocelin of Brakelond*, exposed by Thomas Carlyle as "a certain old St. Edmundsbury Monk and Boswell, now seven centuries old." Swaffham, Massingham, and more heaths and commons, similarly spacious and remote, lead towards the coast, marking the line of the Peddars Way or stretching to the right and left of the prehistoric route. On the verge of Norwich Mousehold Heath remains a breezy tract of gorsy hillocks and dingles. You can look down to the great panorama of the city set round its superb spire, feel the wind

KING'S LYNN. *The house with the twisted columns in Queen Street. Formerly a merchant's home, the frontage and entrance were reconstructed in 1708. Seventeenth-century warehouses remain at the rear facing King's Staithe Lane.*

WICKEN. *White walls and thatched roofs near to Wicken Fen, a preserved fragment of the wide fenlands known to Hereward the Wake. The neighbouring church contains memorials to Oliver Cromwell's sister, son, and grandson.*

MARKET DEEPING. *Once a market town and anciently connected with the powerful Wake family. It lies where the oolite ends and the fens begin. Stone houses continue for two miles into Deeping St. James, notable for its church, bridge, and enriched market cross.*

blowing as George Borrow did, think of Old Crome catching a breath of inpiration for his pictures, *Mousehold Heath* and *The Windmill*. Patches of heath overlook the sea. From Weybourne I crossed Kelling Heath for Holt in unclouded autumn weather. Banks of ling, bracken, and gorse were ablaze in tones of purple, gold, and yellow; sombre greens of fir trees stood out against the blue sky (103). Leaving Holt's heathy and wooded surroundings, past the stately towered front of Blickling Hall, and through Aylsham is a good approach to another distinctive variation in Norfolk scenery. The River Bure, highway to the land of the Broads, lazily courses through calm low country, reaches Coltishall, a most picturesque waterside village. Onward expands the curiously self-contained and flat area of sluggish rivers and streams, weedy pools, small and large meres fringed with reeds, the Broads of Wroxham, Hoveton, Ranworth, Barton, and others of fame and popularity, with Hickling Broad (104) in my opinion the most alluring of all. Much has been written on this strange fenny land since the Broads were recorded as such in 1608, but to go there means gleaning sights, experiences, remembrances. It holds life in many aspects, seclusion undisturbed by the intrusion of the present. Foregrounds and distances yield watery expanses, sedges, flowering rushes, reflected images, foliage vividly coloured, the brilliance of wild flowers, dragon-fly blue. Water-birds, sedge-warblers, herons, and otters make their own sounds and movements. Sunset effects are glorious. Autumn mists steal over the marshes. St. Benet's Abbey ruins by moonlight might be a stage setting ready for the entrance of its ghostly founder, King Canute. Old windmills and dark sails of wherries point up above the levels. Punt-gunners, eel-catchers, anglers, peat-cutters, and the vanishing race of wherrymen hint the mood of traditions and ancient usage. Indicative of the present are the pleasure boats, petrol launches, sailing craft, the gaily clothed or nearly naked bodies on them, the jolly gatherings I found at Potter Heigham (104) and Wroxham bridges, at the inn by Horning Ferry.

If we had lived a long time ago, then it would have been quite easy to account for the close settlement of the Norfolk villages, the many and often large churches, a frequency of attractive halls and manor-houses, the engaging qualities of Wymondham (106), Diss, Aylsham, Fakenham, East Dereham (105), Thetford, and other old country towns. Now pleasant to find and linger amongst, all remind of incentives and fruition in an enlightened and thriving past. Travelling from place to place we can think of much of the land serving for immense sheepwalks through the Middle Ages and until the seventeenth century. Obvious are the results of the later enclosures, fields divided by living hedges, the agricultural progress that changed the face of the landscapes and eventually developed some of the best farmed and most productive acres in England. Before, during, and after the Tudor years sheep reared on the walks were sold and bought in tens of thousands. Lynn fair, for example, regularly penned up to 25,000, and the fairs at East Harling, Briston, Harpley, and other markets recorded similar large figures. Wool, native and foreign weavers, successful merchants, and a prosperous continental trade from the ports made the district centred round Norwich one of the foremost in English commerce and industry. Consequently towns and villages, churches and rich men's homes grew and evolved famously.

The churches share with those of Suffolk the stateliness of the East Anglian architectural tradition. Stone and flint, magnificent interiors, a sureness of design and execution in details, the positive and remarkable renderings in woodwork, all demonstrate the best of craftsmanship at the harvest time of medieval endeavour. How and why much of this loveliness came at the consummation of a type in parish church building I have indicated on earlier pages (85-92). Noble exteriors and internal brilliance, the almost unique display of roofs, screens, stall canopies, bench ends, font covers, and panelling keep beauty alive in scores of places. The following particulars briefly indicate samples of subjects to be looked for amongst the vast store of treasures in Norfolk churches : Woodwork roofs, and the angels at Cawston, Sall, Irstead, Knapton, Blakeney, Swaffham, Northwold, Wymondham, East Harling ; Attleborough's splendid rood-loft (*c.* 1500) spanning right across the church ; flintwork at North Walsham porch, the grand tower of Redenhall (completed in 1518), and at many of Norwich's crowded churches and the Ethelbert Gate (88). And in this county claiming a long artistic heritage extending from the birth of graphic art in the Stone Age to the graces born of the Norwich School, from the spirited prehistoric designs scratched with flint at Grime's Graves to the masterpieces of Crome and Cotman, it is fitting that a middle or medieval period shines with more than a hundred contemporary paintings to be seen in the churches, of which the saints and decorations at Ranworth are particularly noteworthy. Here, too, we are in the land of thatching, of English crafts one of the most ancient, elemental in first providing man with a roof over his head. The beautiful and noted reed thatching swells upward from deep eaves to the ridges of cottages, farmhouses and great barns ; it covers the big spans at Coltishall, Potter Heigham, Irstead, Acle, and more than fifty Norfolk churches, survivors from nearly three hundred recorded in the county about one hundred years ago.

Even in these grim times of nationalized redistribution of wealth and collapse of the aristocracy it is consoling to find in Norfolk quite a lot of the parks and the places that used to accommodate the race of Walpoles, Cokes, Pastons who wrote the *Letters*, Boleyns who gave Henry VIII a transient wife, Astleys, Bacons, Bulwers, and similar families with long pedigrees and high-sounding names. Only a casual glance at the county map shows an abundance of those green spots for turning green thoughts in green shades. They promise echoes of romance and pageantry, reminders of old lineage, and all the sorts of meditation stimulated by the sights of weathered walls, moats, stately façades, or a leaden Pan with his pipes mute amongst the topiary and herbaceous borders. Sandringham (112), Royal and nineteenth-century, of course stands foremost in the list of great places. The preceding century brought the vast Palladian state-liness of the Earl of Leicester's Holkham (1744) and Sir Robert Walpole's Houghton (1738), both with rich and dignified interiors designed by William Kent. They carry an air of their age, pompous, proud, grand, monuments of a bygone time when the upper classes held the upper hand. Then battalions of domestics could be marshalled to do the colossal chores, footsteps of liveried servants scraped the marble floors; fine pictures, treasures, and furniture by the master cabinet-makers adorned saloons and state apartments, and from columnar porticoes great personages emerged to the appropriate showiness of bulky coaches drawn by teams of horses mounted with ornamental postilions and attended by outriders. Everything seemed very splendid while it lasted and no Chancellor of the Exchequer disastrously interfered. Such mansions made centres of government for immense estates. Those at Holkham, which became grounds for the agricultural pioneering by "Coke of Norfolk," grew so extensive that the Earl is reputed to have said, "I am Giant of Giant Castle, and have ate up all my neighbours. My nearest neighbour is the King of Denmark." Defoe on his arrival at Houghton from King's Lynn also remarked, "I found myself out of Her Majesty's dominions and in the capital city of King Walpole." Wolterton (near Aylsham) is another Palladian house of 1736; moderate in size, charmingly built in brick and stone, the excellent design by Thomas Ripley was made for Horatio Walpole, brother of Sir Robert. More notable additions enriched this county of fine country houses during the seventeenth century. Melton Constable, for example, built about 1686 south of Holt, developed into a classic home for the ancient family of Astley, remembered in history by Sir Jacob, the valiant Royalist who fought the last battle in the lost cause of King Charles. Raynham Hall near Fakenham, a combination of classical-ism and curved gables in brick and stone formerly attributed to Inigo Jones, contains the interiors of elegant and refined design used by Viscount Townshend, another celebrated agriculturist nicknamed "Turnip" for his success with the crops. And a glimpse of Blickling from the Aylsham road introduces one of the Jacobean sights of England, beautifully completed in 1628 for Sir John Hobart at the site of Anne Boleyn's earlier birthplace. Time and period trace back to the native and traditional building art of the Elizabethans and Tudors. Picturesquely outlined in gables, brick angle-turrets, and high moulded chimneys, the ramb-ling and commodious homes from old generations vividly suggest the ways of living and doing pursued by the knights, squires, and their ladies who struck roots into the Norfolk soil and are remembered by the memorials and heraldic scutcheons that so often repay the finding in the nearby churches. Figuring conspicuously among many rare pictures are the timbered gables and patterned chimneys of Elsing Hall, an early home of Sir John Hastings (near East Dereham), the Bedingfelds' moated Oxborough guarded by a lofty brick gatehouse of 1482 (south-west of Swaffham), and Sir William Fermor's early sixteenth century gateway and ornamented walls at East Barsham manor-house, a rich and lovely scene for me as I looked from the route followed by pilgrims and Henry VIII on their way to the Shrine of Our Lady of Walsingham. If the big places may not be open to everybody, throughout the county in almost every parish good old houses stand in full view. Halls and manor-houses are charming to see and offer architectural variants ranging from the fifteenth to the eighteenth centuries. Great Cressingham has brick panels of 1513 richly moulded; similar effects at Great Snoring rectory were built for Sir Ralph Shelton in the reign of Henry VII; in Oxnead's pretty Tudor hall the Pastons wrote their letters and entertained royalty. Notable are the renderings of the late fifteenth, sixteenth, and seventeenth-century brickwork, the texture, colouring, and enrichments, clusters of chimneys with elaborate and tall capped shafts. Examples of the patterns appear on page 111. Frequent features and details, gables steep, shaped, and corbie-stepped in the style native to Belgium and Holland, suggest that the merchants, artisans, and refugees who came from the Low Countries to trade, settle, weave, and spin also brought something of their own to the appearance of the East Anglian homes.

Norfolk's two largest towns, Norwich and Yarmouth, bring me to the end of this section. Trippers, sands, piers, shipping, herrings, and smells at Yarmouth· may not be everybody's choice. Yet this ancient port, successor of the Romano-British settlement at Caister-on-Sea, exhibits its picturesque age with the Tolhouse, an Elizabethan merchant's richly built home turned into the *Star* inn, the Georgian fishermen's Hospital, the great wide church of St. Nicholas, founded about 1101 but shattered by war raids when I last saw it. Antique specimens of tight town-planning known as the Rows (110) are remarkably curious. The town's place in literature is ever bright with *David Copperfield,* Peggotty, Ham, Emily, and the tremendous Chapter 55 entitled "Tempest."

Sooner or later Norwich really must be the goal of all explorers in Norfolk. Old in history and new in endeavour, the thriving capital of East Anglia dispenses a joyous mixture of then and now. The city throbs progressively. Streets are noisy. Aloof from the bustle of getting on with the business, sights fine and inspiring breathe the spirit of the Middle Ages and succeeding centuries. Sadly also recent devastations bring tears for things remembered and gone. In these latish years of the city's long standing I looked over wide acres and churches wrecked by German raiders; seeking the *Dolphin* inn, formerly widely admired for Elizabethan flintwork and stone, I found it in a state of collapse. So much

ELY. *Octagon and lantern, the particular glory of the cathedral. This brilliant design, planned to replace the fallen Norman tower, was built between 1322 and 1342. The lantern, sheathed in lead, is one of the supreme achievements of fourteenth-century oak work in England.*

ELY. *It is an inspiring scene from Stuntney across Middle Fen to the gleaming towers, octagonal lantern, pinnacles, and traceried walls of one of England's most striking cathedral compositions. Stuntney Hall (right), now a farmhouse, was the home of Cromwell's mother and inherited by Oliver.*

Sydney R. JONES, Ely

WISBECH. *Georgian setting at North Brink along the River Nene. Bank House (centre), built in 1722, contains elegant interiors, panelling, carving, and plaster decorations.*

SPALDING. *The River Welland and Georgian houses on the Holbeach road.*

for tears, coupled with thankfulness for all that remains upstanding and splendid. Eyes, ears, and excellent guide books will inform onlookers of all they may wish to know of this fair spot enriched with the long cathedral tapering upward to the spire's aerial height, the arcaded Norman keep on its earthwork, medieval churches crowded together, buildings and homes of delight, all contained within lands sloping low to the River Wensum and surrounded by heaths and ridges. Of its moods and graces Norwich needs no new words from me; here I merely indicate a few of my own preferences. England offers nothing more striking in traditional civic pattern than the Market Place (107). It is lively and multicoloured with stalls and people as it was in centuries past. The new City Hall, very fine and certainly large, dwarfs the ancient of days signified by the Gothic flint and stonework of the Guildhall dating from 1407. At the end presides St. Peter Mancroft, most beautiful of all the parish churches. One Sunday morning after sermon-time I watched the civic coach pass through this square, the coachman liveried and powdered, hoofs of dappled greys clattering on the paving, just the picture for a Lord Mayor's coach of fabled story in an appropriate and real setting. Dozens of medieval churches, survivors from more than fifty once standing, lead to interest, beauty, and such fascinating names as St. Peter Parmentergate, St. James-with-Pockthorpe, St. Michael-at-Coslany, and St. Peter Hungate, a fabric restored by the Pastons in the fifteenth century and now a museum of ecclesiastical treasures. Roman Catholic and modern, the church of St. John attracts the eye from many angles; large and impressive, its Gothic form designed by J. Oldrid Scott bigly dominates the chalk ridge. Near this sacred monument, particularly along Chapel Field Road or behind Grapes Hill, it is quite simple to jerk back a few centuries while tracing the city walls, freshly exposed in parts by the recent bombing. Catching the spirits of departed time, of the years and purposes for which these walls were erected, you see within the line of fortifications a wealth of sights for looking at and thinking about. They tell of townsfolk who were alive once, spoke, worked, traded, and enjoyed themselves in the principal and small streets, in the extraordinary alleys and lanes lined with domestic quarters of all ages and shapes around Tombland, the Saxon and Danish town's heart before the Normans centred at Mancroft (Great Croft). Natives heard the preaching Black Friars in the present St. Andrews Hall. Onward from the fifteenth century they saw Strangers' Hall developed to be the rare courtyard building it now is. Other generations passed in and out of the later houses, those with eighteenth-century doorways in Surrey Street, the Georgian Bank of England Court off Queen Street. The Assembly Rooms (Theatre Street) served for gaiety and entertainments; erected in 1754 by Thomas Ivory, master-builder and architect, it is a gem of a spot in which anyone to-day may enjoy a dish of tea—as I did—with the additional savour of past charm and present taste elegantly blended.

The claim has been made that Norwich acquired the habit of fostering remarkable characters. In Haymarket therefore it did not surprise me to meet Sir Thomas Browne (in bronze) and thank him for giving a few words for my Preface (page 6); nor could any artist fail to salute John Sell Cotman, also in bronze by the side of his Georgian doorway facing Palace Street. After much searching a dive through a brick wall and a tunnel from Willow Lane rewarded me with the quaintest little place imaginable, plaster-fronted among bright nasturtiums, the secure hiding-place of the man who so often eluded his pursuers, George Borrow; and the words ,"Maddermarket Theatre," discovered on a former Salvation Army Citadel suggested a new name on the roll of fame, Nugent Monck. Among many pictorial themes to remember, one by the river at Pull's disused ferry composes the ancient watergate, a pretty white home roofed with pantiles (both now restored), and the waterway along which stone passed for building the monastery and great church (106). Following the way the stone went discloses a domain of peace, holiness, and beauty, my last and foremost subject in Norwich. There stands the cathedral, the city's climax, a triumphant expression of art and inspiration developed during 440 years after Herbert de Losinga, Benedictine and first bishop of Norwich, laid the foundation stone in 1096. Elevations vast, masonry gleaming, windows and arcades, remarkably preserve the appearance of a great Anglo-Norman abbey church. The eastern limb mounts exquisitely to flying buttresses and Perpendicular heights above the Romanesque pattern and apsidal chapels. Far-flung towards the heavens the fifteenth-century spire gracefully leads up to its point from one of the richest and certainly the highest of English Norman towers. Prospects seen from Upper and Lower Close are majestic, memorable; perched on a roof above Faith Lane I attempted the drawing illustrated on pages 108–109. Within the church noted sights impress with the long Norman nave ending upward in Bishop Lyhart's magnificent fifteenth-century vault, the choir and arc of the apse brilliantly lit from the lofty clerestory, choir stalls of the fifteenth century's finest, the Prior's doorway richly carved, a spacious traceried cloister (1297–1430). Hundreds of sculptured roof-bosses quaintly depict Bible history and legends, and riches of masoncraft from east to west ennoble this Christian temple's purpose and story spanning over eight and a half centuries. The close, green and tree-shaded, charms with its interest and variety; houses range from the Dean's thirteenth-century hall to Elizabethan and Stuart brickwork, Georgian doorways and windows, behind which life really ought to pass along very smoothly. St. Ethelbert's Gate of *c.* 1320, and the archway of patterned stone and flint erected about 1420 to commemorate Sir Thomas Erpingham, Shakespeare's "good old knight" of Agincourt, both lead to the busy outer world. There I leave my readers to make their own ways, look, and discover among the calm, quiet, and noisy places in the grand old city of Norwich.

THE FENS

Westward across Norfolk from Norwich occurs a transformation in the scenery. Beyond the line of the Peddars Way the land drops from contours of two hundred feet or more, eventually sinking to twenty feet, less, or almost nothing above sea level. Seeming endless miles of flat fenland landscape stretch away to wide horizons. A feeling of being very low down on the earth is relieved by the soaring heights of the churches. Spires, towers, and high-flown masonry rise impressively over the levels. They suggest that natural environment prompted the natives to aspire, aim for elevation, often an inspiration for the architecture of low countries and paralleled not far away by the lofty steeples in the Netherlands. Where stone products did not exist and swampy ground meant difficulties in making secure foundations, only with prodigal expenditures of labour, money, and craftsmanship could these churches be built. Many of them are grand, splendid specimens of the East Anglian style adorned with excellent woodwork. Villages in the marshland around King's Lynn yield rich harvests at the Wiggenhalls, Walsoken, West Walton, the Walpoles, the Tilneys, and the Terringtons.

The drop from high to low, both in altitude and key of scenery, is curiously effective all round the Fens. Leaving the broken hilliness of the Lincolnshire Wolds, when bound for Wainfleet and East Holland, I quickly found roads of the flattest, dykes for field boundaries, vivid meadows, low extended landscapes; over the levels Boston's distant tower of St. Botolph guided me onward through surroundings that one might have thought led to Middelburg, Leiden, or Bruges. Again, from the Midland oolite uplands you can look over the Soke of Peterborough and to flats seeming to go on for ever. Here the stone juts towards the River Welland. It gave character to the low villages, made me think of the Cotswold finish in masonry while sketching in Deeping St. James and Market Deeping (122). Further south outliers of the chalk country command panoramas of the fenland miles. One remarkable viewpoint is Chapel Hill, Haslingfield, formerly a popular place of pilgrimage to the medieval shrine of Our Lady of White Hill. On clear bright days vast prospects visible from this slight eminence include luscious greenery in the near valley, Cambridge sparkling beyond with King's College chapel conspicuous. Northward Ely's towers catch the light, and far away the levels fade to misty distances. Upward points everywhere, towers and spires of Trumpington, Great Shelford, Cherry Hinton, Swaffham, Burwell, and fourscore churches endlessly dot the landscapes with symbols of past ecclesiastical importance and man's aspiring from lowly pitches on the ground.

Though looks over the fenlands can be inviting enough at a distance, not everybody is tempted to explore across country that is popularly thought to be flat as a pancake, watery, misty, dull, featureless, adept in breeding flies, and very good for developing rheumatics. But this is not the whole story. The alluvial land, reclaimed through centuries of labour to be the richest for growing good corn, potatoes, sugar beet, almost everything, presents rich patchworks of colour as seedtime, harvest, and the seasons come and go. Nowhere have I seen wider or more golden spreads of grain in August; like heraldic tinctures the brilliant springtime displays in the bulb fields around Holbeach and Spalding reminded me of the brightness across the North Sea at Haarlem. Willow, poplar, ash, alder, and trees bent by the force of winds break the flat expansiveness with belts of greenery. Dykes, leams, and drains made by Romans, monks, Dutchmen, and recent engineers criss-cross in every direction. The Roman bank facing The Wash, Bishop Morton's Leam constructed about 1480, and the Old and New

THORNEY

Bedford Rivers cut straight as an arrow by Vermuyden the Dutchman more than three hundred years ago are among the peculiar features that tell of an incessant battling to keep the waters in check. Banks raised above the fields enclose river courses. Windmills turn. Little bridges lead to isolated farmhouses. Town streets, often lined with Georgian brick houses, border waterways (130), and Spalding's carillon rings tinkling melodies over the levels. Splendid spires at Whittlesey, March, Frampton, and Boston's glorious "stump" set keynotes for the frequent architectural heights. Overhead the arch of heaven appears all the more ample by contrast with the horizontal lines of the land scenes; great skies move and change, majestic in sunlight and shade, powerful in wind and storm, blue and snow-white, grey or lowering. If these miles of our Holland in England may seem strange or curious their uncommon fascination cannot be

FEN LANDSCAPE *at Postland, near Crowland Abbey.*

FEN RIVER. *The Welland near Spalding.*

FEN WATERWAY *in Boston.*

FEN ROAD *at Irby-in-the-Marsh.*

denied. To suggest general qualities of the scenes I give drawings of a landscape, a river, a road, and a town waterway on pages 135 and 136.

Near the lonely village of Wicken (122) the well-known piece of fen remains primeval and undrained. It preserves an environment that helped to mould the patient and industrious race of fenfolk who fought the waters for ages, lived frugally, toiled on hard-won bits of soil, walked on stilts in winter. And at this plot of primitive England, a survival from the large swampy wastes that in times past were wild, inaccessible, and dotted here and there with reedy islets, it is simple to realize why outlaws, fugitives, Hereward the Wake and his desperate band, or men devoted to religious seclusion sought and found concealment in the Fens. Guthlac's little Saxon chapel foreshadowed Crowland Abbey. The rude huts of Tancred and Tortred founded Thorney. Elsewhere beginnings were made for the wonderful chain of monasteries that rose in fretted masonry to meet the morning sun shining over the sunk and misty hollow land. Memorials of the monks' building, draining, and cultivation now call us across the levels to ruined Crowland, Ramsey gatehouse, the fragment of Thorney Abbey still in its "little paradise"; to Ely crowned with the lantern (127, 128, 129), and Peterborough's west front (154, 155), two marvels of England. The towns have the right kind of individuality for their placing in the wide miles reclaimed after the departure of the monks. Up and down the country the great churches, guildhalls, market-places, streets with old merchants' homes, water ever in view, all mark time-beats in a history of brave continuance through bright times, flood, and tempest. King's Lynn has faced disaster for centuries. Long ago, in 1374, a Grey Friar recorded, "A terrible sea-flood at Lynn, from a gale of dreadful force, which inundated most of the market-place." Yet the town contrived to develop the pictorial prize it now is. The fascinating panorama of architecture gathered through past ages is enriched with fine churches, gates, two market-places, two guildhalls, the Custom House of 1683 and the *Duke's Head* (1685) both designed by the talented local architect, Henry Bell. Winding streets and cobbled lanes lead to endless discoveries at the homes, courtyards (120) and warehouses of merchant princes who thrived with olden trade and far-flung enterprise at the "rich and populous port-town" vividly described by Daniel Defoe. Boston (10) likewise is full of good sights, watery ways (136), and brick-fronted houses centred round the grand church crowned with a sixteenth-century lantern. Southward lies Cambridge, endearing, incomparable, standing where it did when Danes burned it and Hugh de Balsham, Bishop of Ely, founded Peterhouse near Coe Fen and the Granta in 1284. At this jewel, both of our own country and the world, among courts, gateways, chapels, towers, bridges, and storied stonework of Gothic and Renaissance, my pictures (113–116) bring to an end this short note on Fenland.

4. MIDLAND COUNTRY

BUCKINGHAMSHIRE, BEDFORDSHIRE, HUNTINGDONSHIRE, NORTHAMPTONSHIRE, RUTLAND, LEICESTERSHIRE, NOTTINGHAMSHIRE, LINCOLNSHIRE

This section of the old Mercian kingdom is crossed by the ancient Fosse Way. Great northward and other routes engineered by Romans now speed motors on tracks made famous by horses in coaching days. The geological belt of oolite and lias sweeps from north Buckinghamshire and Northamptonshire uplands to the Leicestershire wolds and Lincoln Cliff hills. The Trent, Soar, Welland, and Nene water wide vales, and the Great Ouse winds through borderlands known to Cromwell, Bunyan, and Cowper. Midland forests are

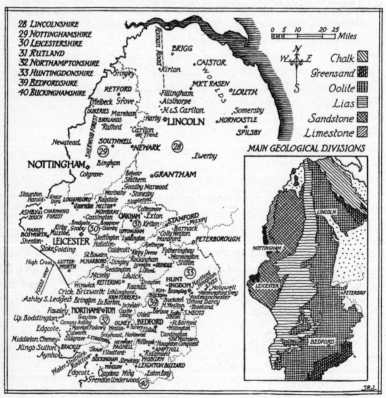

remembered by the names of Rockingham, Charnwood, Sherwood and Robin Hood. Castle remains and war sites mark historic points at Newark, Ashby-de-la-Zouch, Nottingham, Market Bosworth, Naseby, and elsewhere Peterborough, Southwell, and Lincoln shine with the splendours of cathedral building. Medieval churches and high spires grace the face of the land in a brave line from King's Sutton to Grantham and Louth. Stately homes and manor-houses are notable and many, ranging from Burghley and Belvoir to Ashby St. Ledgers and the Washingtons' Sulgrave. The list of lovely country towns includes Stamford, Oundle, Oakham, and Uppingham. Scenery generally is not often spectacular, in places dull, and industrial areas have brought commercial prosperity without improving the landscapes. Yet miles of fair prospects remain to show the good stuff provided by nature and man at England's heart.

DOWN THE GREAT OUSE

The River Ouse, which previously we have traced wandering about Fenland, gives a different account of itself in the middle and upper reaches. Down from grassy Northamptonshire uplands it flows through Buckinghamshire, Bedfordshire, and Huntingdonshire, winding a great deal across the counties. Like cats and human beings it conceals a temperament that can be much affected by changes in the weather. Very pleasant, calm, and slow in movement this river is on fair and bright days; when rain descends and the wind blows it rises up, hits out, and encumbered with too much water viciously floods the borderlands. This circumstance accounts for the unusual number of very long bridges. Many churches, old chapels, and past associations with preachers and men of letters brought to the stream and valley the title of "England's Holy Land." The river further claims to be fancifully lyrical because Cowper lived at Olney, allegoric and evangelical through the Bunyan influences around Bedford, and even delirious at Water Stratford on account of preparations made there for the Day of Judgement. With homes of Gunpowder Plotters in the neighbourhood, and frequent reminders of Puritanic, Cromwellian, and other peculiar folk on the banksides from Buckingham to St. Ives, the Ouse again might be called a nonconforming and rebellious river, which indeed it is in wet seasons when overflowing without respect for persons, settled beliefs, or opinions. Also it is the Great Ouse, superior to little or other Ouses. This fact I gleaned in Buckingham while looking from a bridge to observe a small volume of water coursing between meadows devoted to pigs bred by United Dairies for enlarging the rations of Londoners.

"This little stream I suppose is the River Ouse?" I remarked to a native who stood at my elbow similarly contemplating the liquid.

"Yes," he replied, "this is the Great Ouse. Thirty men have just taken three weeks to clear out the mud."

I meditated on the Walrus, Carpenter, seven maids, seven mops, then further questioned my informer.

"Thirty men did you say?"

"Thirty men for three weeks to clear out the mud," he answered. "United Dairies paid."

"Did they send the mud to London with their bacon?" I asked, thinking of slinging uses for Hyde Park orators and Westminster politicians.

"The mud was carted away," he said, without indicating destination.

"The stream looks rather small, even now," I suggested.

"It's not much certainly," he agreed; but evidently in an effort to sustain local pride in the Great Ouse he added, "You ought to see it in winter when the floods are out. Some river then!"

The Ouse springs from Northamptonshire's green and wooded hillsides where sheep graze and riders in pink follow hounds and perhaps see foxes. Sometimes these sporting cavalcades meet at Hinton-in-the-Hedges, a village prettily named and pretty for its groups of thatched cottages. Within the church a carved Edwardian knight (possibly Sir William Hinton) has his feet placed, rather ungallantly, nearly on the head of his lady; therefore both recline on a tomb of extraordinary length. At Brackley the river settles into its own little valley below the town. On a sunshiny morning, say in early spring when the north wind has spent its last gasp and a mild air comes stealing from the west, Brackley's long, wide, and tree-lined main street is as jolly a place as one could wish to be in. The eighteenth-century town hall stands islanded in the middle, gaily ended with a timepiece and open lantern on the roof-ridge. Magdalen College school of eight centuries' growth, lying well back, makes a memorable group of chapel, old refectory, and dormitories. Stone-built houses of many periods, inns, and almshouses glisten in light and shade, the tower of the big and fine church of St. Peter rises behind, and townsfolk and hunting people meet on the stone pavements, chatter, and very likely discuss last runs of the season or prospects for point-to-point meetings. All in all, whether in springtime or any other season, Brackley certainly is a very jolly country town to visit.

Downstream the river valley begins to open out wider. In no time, after a halt for the attractive village of Westbury, we can be at Water Stratford. Here are charming scenes of cottages, manor-house, chestnut trees, and a church with two splendid Norman doorways all quiet and secluded on the old Roman road passing from Stowe park to Bicester. Not so quiet was it in the reign of William and Mary when Parson Mason went in and out of his church under the tympanum of the south doorway enriched with spirited Norman carvings of Christ in Majesty and angels kneeling. For this deluded man, though one of parts and a considerable hymn-writer, conceived the fantastic idea that on a Whit Monday "the Lord Jesus Christ would appear at Water Stratford and judge the world."

BUCKINGHAM. *Houses, roofs, and the town hall grouped beyond the river bridge.*

RADCLIVE *manor-house in the upper Ouse valley. The distant woods belong to Stowe park.*

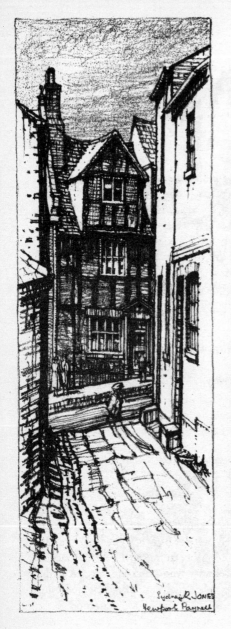

NEWPORT PAGNELL. *Church Passage lead-ing to St. John's Street.*

BEDFORD. *Yard off St. Paul's Square.*

Hosts of people believed him. They invaded the parish, camped on the ground, developed hysteria at religious gatherings, disorganized everything and everybody in the neighbourhood. Even after this prophet died in May 1694, having predicted beforehand that he would rise again in three days, his followers continued to wait in expectation of the appointed time. In vain was Mason's body exhumed and exhibited to prove its *status quo*. Only when the campers had been dispersed by force did the excitement subside and eventually vanish. Thereafter the village settled down to continuance and the peace you now may find there on the old Roman road.

Nearer Buckingham is Radclive, snug in the vale among high trees. A small bridge crosses the stream near a mill-race fringed with willows, a delicate Early English archway leads into the church of Norman origins, and the choice little group has a squirely look from the light gables and clustered brick chimneys of the manor-house showing well on a grassy slope (141). Good oak, carvings, and an original staircase remain inside this old home. Other Elizabethan and seventeenth-century manorial houses are obvious in this district at Shalstone, Chetwode, Foscott, and elsewhere. Hereabout, where the upper waters of the Ouse wind down, the valley gathers in width, woodiness, and landscape attraction. Vivid green water-meadows meet the stream lined with willow foliage bunched on stocky trunks. Tall elms, oaks, and groups of mixed trees richly colour the land surfaces stretching out and up to higher border grounds. The scenes appear all the more homely with thatched cottage roofs, brick and timbered walls, the mills and the bridges, little friendly accents placed in an ample natural setting that reminded me of Constable's Stour valley country.

Higher up in the wide parklands near the Brackley to Buckingham road (A 422) we still may catch a breath of ducal and classic grandeur. Magnificent avenues, archways, obelisks, bridge and ornamental lake, a temple to Bacchus, a temple to Venus, and the vast pile of colonnade and wings extended on a frontage 916 feet long all help to sustain an atmosphere, rarefied and aristocratic, that prompted Alexander Pope and Horace Walpole to set down lively impressions of Stowe. One of England's greatest and most famous houses, this mansion of once upon a time is now a noted public school. Onward from 1760 architects and craftsmen, notably Robert Adam and Lancelot Brown, lavished their talents to make buildings, gardens, and stylish formality fit for the life and spectacular entertainments enjoyed by hosts of celebrities who came and capered in the Buckinghamshire air, These proceedings were rudely terminated by funds running dry and one of the biggest sales of art and literary treasures ever put under the hammer. After the brilliant years, the bankruptcy, and arrival of the schoolboys the air continues fresh, the prospects alluring; the mansion looks much as it did when dukes, grandees, statesmen, the clever notables and witty bucks of fashion walked and talked in the stone and marble halls, promenaded along the groves and avenues, or gathered at the Temple of Friendship to quarrel. Points worth seeking outside the park are the secluded villages of Lillingstone Dayrell and Lillingstone Lovell, the former with an unspoiled medieval church, tombs of the Dayrells, and the family arms carved on the porch of their old home. Roads and lanes go north to leafy domains and high woodlands of Whittlewood Forest, of which the Dukes of Grafton were hereditary rangers. Oaks, genuine antiques, spread hoary branches. At one of them near Potterspury, now hollow, decayed, and called the Queen's Oak, Edward IV is supposed to have met Elizabeth Woodville in a romantic prelude to the later upheavals in the Yorkist queen's life. This past regal event does not much matter to-day, for the surroundings remain delightful, green and shady, still very nice for lovers' meetings or romantic meditations.

You can approach Buckingham in the grand manner by passing under the elms of Stowe Avenue. More humbly the same end can be gained along the road through Tingewick, a village of old standing known for Roman remains and more recently for storing bombs. But whichever route to the town be followed, its location is plainly marked by the church spire, a very graceful termination for the modern church built where a pre-Conquest castle stood on a bold mound almost encircled by the river. Best, perhaps, is the way in from Winslow and Aylesbury. There the town is seen spread over its hill beyond the bridge, winding stream of the Ouse (141), and grouped in a medley of gables, brickwork, chimneys, and tiled roofs, with the town hall weathercock for a top note—this cock being a great swan, the crest of the borough. Below its spreading wings the Market Square opens to Market Hill, the ancient place of the bull-ring. Adjoining stand old houses on an island and the castellated jail of eighteenth-century vintage changed to a peaceful cell for antiques and afternoon teas. Streets diverge curiously, wind up and down hills. Narrow ways obviously keep to medieval boundary lines. A mellow air is fresh with the rural feeling, for the surrounding meadows and green slopes are rarely out of sight. These and other distinctions make Buckingham the really nice spot it is, townish yet countrified, neither too large nor small, often quiet, historic enough to satisfy any old fogey, and offering plenty to-day for pleasing the eye, the mind, and the digestion. A white hart neatly seated on the porch of the white-fronted *White Hart* gave me a hint for excellently satisfying the digestion; a rambling yard at the rear, together with the good old-fashioned wording "Posting House," on the *Swan and Castle* in Castle Street, both convinced me of a long and hospitable road service, dating back perhaps to the years of Shakespeare, when Buckingham stood on the Elizabethan route from Stratford to London. Eighteenth-century houses facing the defunct prison, shop windows divided into little square panes, now used by Mr. French and Mr. Tompkins, numerous doorways to Georgian dwellings, and the square brick town hall, must have united to look just the thing for the poke-bonnet and crinoline years of the town's middle-aged period. The big conflagration in 1725, though it caused half Buckingham to be renewed, did not consume all the older buildings. Peeps under archways reveal black-and-white patterning. Timbered houses and cottages stand round the cattle market. The old manor-house shows gables, timbers, and a twisted chimney at the back built of Tudor brickwork; the churchyard opposite is a forlorn reminder of the original church that decayed, fell, and finally disappeared. Rarest of all, the chapel entered through a late twelfth-century doorway in the narrow street behind Market Square remains the town's oldest architectural prize. This earliest chantry chapel in Buckinghamshire was largely rebuilt about 1474, served for a Latin school, and continued as such long after chantries were dissolved. The age of this building makes one realize the antiquity of Buckingham. When King Alfred reigned he made it a county town. At the Conquest it was a borough. The wool trade, established by Edwardian kings, brought great prosperity. Medieval pilgrims flocked in to the shrine of Saint Rumwold, the precocious infant prince who lived, preached, and died at King's Sutton during his three days on earth. Later the trade and prosperity slumped. Both had so much declined in Henry VIII's time that the local affairs then were reckoned to be in a very sorry state. Subsequently the town settled down quite nicely. It kept clear of the Industrial Revolution, avoided the horrors of the mechanical era, and after all the vicissitudes remains what I have stated it is, a really nice small country town, one that I can fully recommend to my readers, but with this warning—be sure to give plenty of notice beforehand at the *White Hart* if you wish to stay in it, because other knowing people already have discovered that Buckingham hath charms.

A couple of miles below the town the Claydon Brook joins the Ouse after meandering through an ample vale green with pastures and lots of oak trees. A collection of villages well worth finding have the name of the stream. East

East Claydon

Claydon, almost joined to Botolph Claydon, I thought remarkably good, set on rising ground above an expanse of luscious woody landscape spreading to Quainton Hill, Addington manor park, Winslow, and Whaddon Chase. Old cottages and a little thatched *Verney Arms* border lanes continuing to the bigger manorial house topped with Elizabethan chimneys and entered through an arched doorway of stone. Around stand clipped yews. Fine brick walling encloses the forecourt, from which the manorial dogs bounded to bark at me. This otherwise quiet corner ends at the modest church tower, embattled in the style of its period and terminating the neat nave and chancel heavily restored by Gilbert Scott. Across the valley Steeple Claydon on a hillock in command of wide views makes a conspicuous landmark with its spire, erected in the nineteenth century by the Verneys and joined to the old church. Eastward from the fourteenth-century chancel extend noble double avenues of oaks and elms in most impressive order. The village, now with many new houses, numerous old ones, and Sir Thomas Chaloner's seventeenth-century school, once was a possession of Catherine of Aragon, the royal lady to whom is attributed the introduction of lace-making in Buckinghamshire. On the stone Camp Barn I read, "Around this spot the army of the Parliament under the command of Cromwell was encamped, March 1644, and on the 3rd of that month advanced from hence to the attack on Hillesden House." Then occurred the hat episode, one of the flirtings with chivalry credited to the breaker of images. The Parliamentary victor offered his own hat and apologies to the vanquished Royalist, Sir William Smith, whose headgear had been filched by a Roundhead in the fighting. Only earthen mounds mark the place of old Hillesden House, two miles from Steeple Claydon, but near the site the doors of the very beautiful Perpendicular church show bullet-holes made during the attack. Amid the clatter of war Sir William fell in love with Squire Denton's daughter, married her while a prisoner in the Tower, and the romance happily continued in safe and peaceful years.

At Middle Claydon, between the two Claydons noted above, feudal homes and appurtenances are visible. Evidently good-mannered people live there. Natives courteously saluted on meeting me, a mere stranger named Jones—acts which brought reminders of nice old custom surviving in this age of equality. These human peculiarities and buildings point to the presence of aristocracy settled on ancestral acres, to the Verneys in fact, the family that arrived in the fifteenth century, begat sons and daughters for the country's good, and gave King Charles his standard-bearer, Sir Edmund Verney, who fought, died, and still grasped the standard in death at the battle of Edge Hill. Well-placed in the finely timbered park and above the lakes stands the big house, seen on the approach to the village. The stone wing, elegantly fitted inside, remains from a larger Adam design. The near church tower directs to memorials of the Verneys,

OLNEY. *The mill and church by the River Ouse, haunts of the poet Cowper.*

BEDFORD *from the Ouse bank. The view includes the Swan hotel of 1794, St. Paul's spire, and the nineteenth-century bridge. An earlier medieval bridge had a chapel, also a jail, possibly the place of John Bunyan's imprisonment.*

the Giffards, and particularly to the tomb of Margaret Giffard, deceased in 1539, a most gorgeous effect of English and Italian craftsmanship. Stretches of woodland clothe hilly scenes to the south from Knowl Hill to Edgcott and Grendon Underwood. Here, if John Aubrey's words can be trusted, we are on Shakespearian ground. Born ten years after Shakespeare's death, Aubrey originated the supposition that the poet "happened to lye" on Midsummer night "at Grendon, in Bucks, which is on the roade from London to Stratford," picked up tips in the village for *A Midsummer Night's Dream*, and turned "the humour of the constable" into dialogue for Dogberry in *Much Ado About Nothing*. That is the story; whether true or not nobody can say, but the nearness of Aubrey's time to that of Shakespeare suggests probability. The house in which Shakespeare is thought to have lodged more than once stands close to the church. Formerly the *Ship* inn and built of Elizabethan timbering, it consequently acquired the name of Shakespeare Farm. A garrulous man, apparently suitable for the oldest inhabitant and possibly a descendant of Nick Bottom, Francis Flute, or Dogberry, told me of an interior open fireplace at which (of course) the poet sat, and a winding staircase up which (without doubt) he went to bed. "Knock at the door and see for yourself," he said. I could not summon up courage to do as directed.

The small town of this leafy region, Winslow, winds to the brow of a hill. Centuries old at the Conquest, now horribly modern near the railway station, the timbered walls, gables, and thatched roofs in Hurn Street (153) and Sheep Street yet impart a quaint old-fashioned air. Mixed building fashions, predominantly Georgian, and the white front of the *Bell* inn surround the Market Square. Trim and flowered, the churchyard leads from the pavement to the interesting church topped with clerestories and a fourteenth-century tower. Curfew still rings and has done so for nearly a thousand years. Winslow Hall, visible to everybody beyond gate piers and forecourt, is the domestic gem of the town, exquisitely proportioned, a dignified composition in brickwork with stone quoins, cornice and pediment, windows long, doorway classic, and lettered WILLIAM LOWNDES AD MDCC. This rare sight means the Wren tradition, and also the home of Queen Anne's Secretary to the Treasury remembered as "Ways and Means Lowndes," inventor of the saying now obsolete in Whitehall, "Take care of the pence and the pounds will take care of themselves."

The Holyhead Road down from Dunstable, Fenny Stratford, and on to Towcester runs remarkably straight in a length of historic highway that crosses the Ouse at Stony Stratford. This Roman Watling Street, later the road *par excellence* in the coaching days of the horses, spins fresh stories for the motoring age on a surface smooth, fast, quiet neither by day nor night. In some ways this is disturbing if you happen to be thinking of earlier occurrences in far centuries while the new life hurries along. Speed, noise, and petrol have somewhat upset the tricks of old remembrance. Stony Stratford and Fenny Stratford do not show very much to stimulate the imagination on the crowded events in the long past of the great highway. Things seen in the two towns are not very suggestive of such matters, for example, as Queen Eleanor's funeral procession moving slowly towards London, Gunpowder Plotters scurrying from London on a November day, the Holyhead Mail making coaching records, or a Shakespearian line, "At Stony Stratford they will be tonight," indicating that Richard of Gloucester had seized young Edward V for a last journey to the Tower. Among the brick frontages, relics of timbered buildings, numerous inns, and openings to yards of inns departed in the long street of Stony Stratford the *Cock* and the *Bull* yet stand firm, Georgian, exhibiting their signs carried on good ironwork to locate where extravagant gossip during the Napoleonic wars originated the classic expression, "a cock and bull story." Gloomy areas stretch from both towns, one to Wolverton, the other to Bletchley, smoky monuments of the power and iron age that eclipsed the reign of coachmen and horses. The immediate region in fact is not particularly brilliant in spectacular beauty.

Within hail of Watling Street plenty of interesting objects and cheering sights have outlasted the celebrated North-Western coaches of Telford, and were centuries old before they flourished. One is Bow Brickhill church, conspicuously situated high up. Ever since primitive folk dug the entrenchment near it people have been remarking, "Don't you admire the view?"—still very fine, I might add. Leighton Buzzard has the splendours of a medieval town church topped by a central tower and spire. When I admired the curved and foliated ironwork on the door I thought of its maker, Thomas *de Laighton*, the master artificer who furnished the Bedfordshire church doors at Eaton Bray and Turvey (153), and wrought the exquisite grille over Queen Eleanor's tomb at Westminster Abbey in 1293–94. West of the town Norman exteriors and interiors at Stewkley, and a Saxon apse and crypt at Wing, all appearing remarkably fresh for their age, continue to illustrate actual productions of the twelfth and pre-Conquest centuries. Easterly from Watling Street the Bedfordshire grounds mount up beyond Bow Brickhill to Ridgmont uplands and hilly surroundings of Woburn town, abbey, and wide acres of the Bedford Dukes. Beautiful woods clothe the slopes in all directions. Ridges continue towards Ampthill, the place of royal memories and the park where the old oaks stand. High points offer great views opening out to the north, the east, and show that the Ouse valley gains in width. Miles and miles of plain stretch far away, ever so flat but with the appeal of spaciousness and distance. As I watched from above Ridgmont an evening sun lit the Morteyne's sturdy detached tower and fifteenth-century church at Marston Moretaine; light and shade swept across the wide expanses dotted with many churches standing like milestones to locate villages snuggled among trees and broad meadows. The two towns, Woburn and Ampthill, each attract with street frontages of excellent brickwork schemed in a manner that suggests the Georgian and Regency atmosphere or the times of people who wore wigs powdered and shoes red-heeled. Quantities of old inns, now either in service or changed into nice homes for superior occupants, prove how lively the trafficking must have been in the years of coaches with horses; they also demonstrate that the discriminating tastes of local brewers extended to architecture. Not quite so jolly are other aspects of brickwork obvious in the near lower country where brick-makers perform. Huge excavations in the earth, fiery kilns, and scenic effects of much power and ugliness bring shocks to the eyesight. As for high chimney-stacks, they are mounted by the score like forests in uncharted Satanic regions. If poor Christian had met these bricky monstrosities in his passage to the Celestial City they might have been even more frightening than the deserts, pits, hobgoblins, satyrs, and dragons he encountered at Millbrook, the place thought to be the original for the Valley of the Shadow of Death described by Bunyan in *The Pilgrim's Progress.*

Conveniently distant from the production of modern brick shades ancient Newport Pagnell hugs the Ouse where the little Ouzel meets the bigger river. Approached by the old coach road from Woburn the town presents one of its best looks, a tell-tale of its past and present. Beyond the iron bridge and a watery tree-lined foreground irregular buildings are disposed up St. John's Street to Cannon Corner. The church's long length, remarkably well set with chancel, aisle, clerestory, notable porch, and bulky sixteenth-century tower, gives an impressive finish to the brow of the hill on which an early castle probably stood. "God save the King" that I heard played by the church bells seemed to be making amends for Cromwellian episodes. On the lower ground a modernized Tickford Abbey incorporates fragments of a priory founded early in the reign of William Rufus by Fulc Pagnall, one of the family that added Pagnell to the Domesday name of Newport. Outside these once holy precincts bumps on the earth disclose the place of fortifications thrown up during the Civil War. Another good viewpoint can be found by going up the hill, down High Street, and to the far end of the long Ouse bridge. Close collections of housebacks, walls, and roofs warmly coloured in brick and tile group effectively to the embattled church tower, the pretty and broad foreground being made by meadows, the stream, a mill, and seven arches of the bridge. From all angles the town looks just what it is, a characteristic specimen of the country variety containing the distinctive High Street, frontages of mixed sorts, back ways that invite a visitor to explore behind the scenes. Church Passage (142) prompted me to draw it, apparently an unusual procedure, for a man popped along and said,

"Are you waiting for Mr. Smithers?"

"No," I replied. "Admiring the view and sketching it."

He eyed me curiously, seemed to wonder what on earth I could see, then retreated into the *Swan* yard behind me, perhaps to find Mr. Smithers. This long rambling yard, a reminder of the coaches that rattled in and out bound for Holyhead via Chester, belongs to the white-fronted *Swan*, an adornment of High Street with a wide pillared entrance and elegant furniture inside. The inn has been in service long enough to have accommodated Mr. Pepys in 1668 when he inspected Newport Pagnell, "a very fair and like a cathedral-church," then "lay here well; reckoning for supper 19s. 6d.; and rose next day by four o'clock"—a virtue most alarming! In the opposite direction I passed through an archway to enquire for Mr. Bull.

"You will find him inside," said the custodian of the Congregational church as he handed to me the key of the building, one nastily reconstructed since the foundations of the meeting-house were laid in 1660. On entering I met William Bull, or rather a representation of the Puritan's son and minister who smoked pipes in Cowper's summer-house on his fortnightly visits to the poet. For company he had portraits of Wycliffe and John Knox, a piece of John Bunyan's Bedford pulpit, and a memorial to John Gibbs, the town's first Nonconformist minister at the Restoration. The discovery of these worthies and relics was a reminder that dissent, preachers, and preaching strongly whiffled the air of the Ouse valley landscapes onward from the passing of the Act of Uniformity in 1662 when King Charles had come home again. Meeting-houses then built, though they may not have beautified the scenes, flourished plentifully about the river's environment and now offer old-established features for those who care to find them. Civil War earthworks near the confluence of the rivers at Newport Pagnell also make one of many indications to prove how the Ouse valley scenery must have been enjoyed by Puritans and Cromwellians. Whether that breed of mankind be admired or disliked, and whatever opinions may be held on the architecture produced by Nonconformity, without doubt we are hot on the tracks of Parliamentarians and chapels in our onward course through Bedford, St. Neots, Huntingdon, and St. Ives. Newport Pagnell itself became a strong garrison for Parliamentary troops, first held by Sir Samuel Luke, the stern Puritan Commander derided by Samuel Butler in *Hudibras*. Here most likely John Bunyan joined up and certainly Captain Oliver, Cromwell's son, died of the smallpox. An attack by Royalists changed the fortunes of war, won the town for the King, and unwilling Puritan burgesses no doubt could not appreciate the humour of being forced to delve on the meadows in making trenches to stem attentions from their own comrades.

Continuing along the broad vale the quality of the local stone is shown by two fine churches and the houses at Sherington and Emberton. A tall spire, visible above trees by the silent river, guides us into Cowper's town.

The church, a stone bridge, the river, hymns, the house lived in by Cowper, and a pancake race through the streets on Shrove Tuesday each constitute

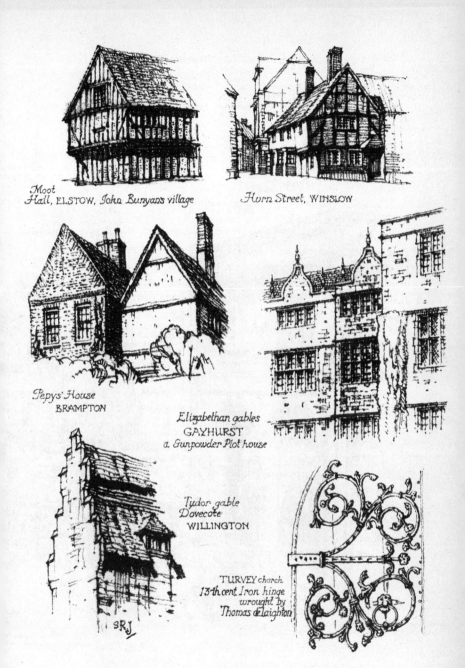

Moot
Hall, ELSTOW, John Bunyan's village

Hurn Street, WINSLOW

Pepys' House
BRAMPTON

Elizabethan gables
GAYHURST
a Gunpowder Plot house

Tudor gable
Dovecote
WILLINGTON

TURVEY church
13th cent. Iron hinge
wrought by
Thomas de Laighton

SRJ

DETAILS NEAR THE GREAT OUSE.

PETERBOROUGH. *The Market Place, remarkably busy nowadays, centres round the arched Market Cross and its upper work, built in 1671. Beyond the gate to the close (adjoined by the*

King's Lodging) rise the immense portals and gables of the Cathedral's western front. This triumph of Early English design screens the long length of the great Norman church.

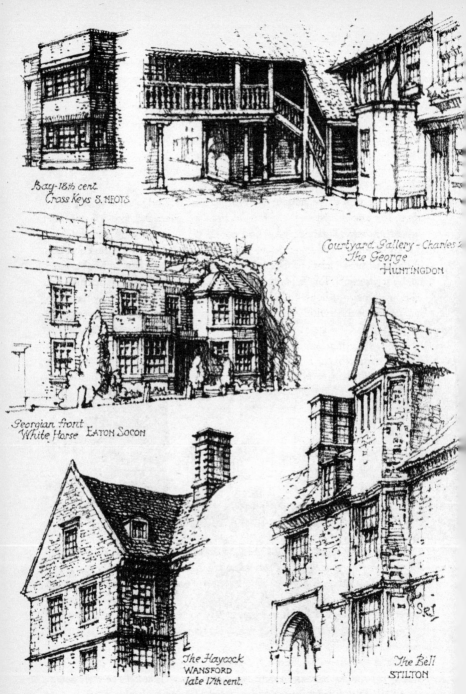

Bay—18th cent.
Cross Keys S. NEOTS

Courtyard, Gallery — Charles 2
The George
HUNTINGDON

Georgian front
White Horse EATON SOCON

The Haycock
WANSFORD
late 17th cent.

The Bell
STILTON

HISTORIC EAST MIDLAND INNS.

particular belongings of Olney. The town centres round a long and partly tree-lined main street. The buildings, mostly constructed of cool grey stone, show various mixtures of appearance and are devoted to the usual purposes of trade, residence, and liquid refreshment. After our visits to such spots as Lavenham, Thaxted, Dedham, or Finchingfield this one might be considered very ordinary or even dull, though not quite in agreement with the words of an earlier writer, "just as doleful a spot as when Cowper took up his abode in it." Natives think otherwise, rate it highly; with proper local pride they told me as much. Towards the church the street widens out in a triangular open space, the market-place, fitted with shops, houses, and the *Bull* inn. Beyond one corner I was intrigued by a double bowed shop-front with square panes and decorations of late eighteenth-century pattern, now used by C. W. Barker for distributing buns more recently baked. Enquiries in various quarters brought a little confusion in the local pronunciation of a poet's name, but the telephone official assisted me by repeating W for William, C for breakfast—with Cooper's (marmalade). Famous among the houses of course is the tall frontage of good early Georgian brickwork pierced with twenty-one sash windows, two stone doorways, and lettered "The Cowper Museum." Adjoining right and left are the premises of Hoddle, family butcher, and Perkins, carpenter, joiner, and undertaker, both jointly catering for the life corporeal and eternal appropriately next door to the sanctuary of a distinguished neighbour who did the same by writing *John Gilpin, The Sofa,* and the *Olney Hymns.* A most intimate literary shrine is this house lived in by Cowper until 1786 while his fame mounted and he penned the delightful letters. There are preserved the rooms, personal possessions, and little things to keep in remembrance the sensitive and lovable man, his devoted Mary Unwin, the fiery parson John Newton, the friendly circle and the three tame hares. Behind lies the garden, smaller than it used to be, with the Summer or Sulking House to which William Bull came from Newport Pagnell and smoked pipes and tobacco kept under a floorboard. The town's most picturesque corner groups round the big fourteenth-century church and conspicuous steeple soaring above roofs, trees, the stone parsonage, a Georgian mill-house, and the bridge with flood arches, partly rebuilt since Cowper trod the "wearisome but needful length" where Prince Rupert defeated Parliamentarians. The mill (147), still thriving, faces a stretch of river winding through a little haven of tranquil and modest beauty. On my autumn day all things seemed fit for the inspired moods of the poet who had known these scenes so well and revealed them with truth, feeling, and simplicity. Here were the banks lined with willows. Smooth meadows spread out widely in low-lying belts of green. Cattle slowly crossed to drink at the waterside, churning the reflections. Field paths by the stream led me to Clifton Reynes and Newton Blossomville, two villages worthy of their tuneful names and poetical associations. In the evening the sun lowered in a rosy sky. Mists began to rise like phantoms over the water. Landscape colours softened, caught the last glow, and nature's harmony at a day's ending reigned in the vale.

Near to the *Bull* a road slopes up, commands views over the river valley, then enters Weston Underwood, the village of Cowper's and Mrs. Unwin's sojourn until they departed in 1795 for the last and tragic chapter of their lives at East Dereham in Norfolk. Cowper thought Weston one of the prettiest villages in England. It remains delightful. Thatched roofs, cottage gardens, the *Cowper's Oak* inn, the poet's pleasant home facing south, and a medieval church containing Throckmorten monuments are secluded among parklike surroundings gloriously decked with elm, beech, chestnut, and lime trees. There is a sense of dignity, too, a suspicion of glory faded in passing between stately gate piers and carved pineapples at the entrance to the village. These, with a length of stabling and chapel remains, constitute obsequies for a hall of an ancient family here gone to seed, long the home of the friendly Throckmortens to whom the poet addressed verses.

Near and far, both in the vale and higher borderlands, scenes have merits of their own without need of garnish from literary associations. Yardley Chase, three miles from Weston or Olney, retains much unspoiled woodland, wonderful for oaks, to say nothing of lowly forget-me-nots in myriads that gave me a permanent remembrance of the Chase in springtime. Gnarled tree trunks look old enough to have bowed to Countess Judith, the Conqueror's niece, who obtained the Chase as a portion of her dowry. One ancient giant, hollow, decayed, yet still able to sprout at the top, acquired the name of Judith because I suppose the Countess must have sat under it; later the tree sat to Cowper for its portrait and doubtful compliments inscribed in *Yardley Oak,*

a cave for owls to roost in.

Down in the valley remarkable windings sweep the river first to the north, then southwards in a series of horseshoe bends to Bedford. Villages in this locality make homely country pictures with churches and towers, generally embattled, nice houses comfortably placed in their gardens, rural buildings and cottages, often of stone and sometimes timbered. Here and there relics from past times and incidents give fillips to inquisitiveness. Saxon masonry at Lavendon proves that the church was there before the Conquest, and a mound and a moat fix the places of an early castle and Norman abbey. Plotters, plotters with Gunpowder, may be thought of at the memorials to the Catesbys on the higher ground at Hardmead, and also at Gayhurst's Elizabethan gables and mullions (153), owned by Sir Everard Digby in 1605, one of the many houses at which the Plot is said to have been hatched. At Turvey the river meets Bedfordshire, an occasion permanently celebrated by a stone figure of Jonah upstanding in the stream and a good picture formed by a long bridge and a mill. Endlessly winding onward through open luscious landscapes the Ouse greets or nears more quiet villages and old-fashioned things that belonged to antiquated years. Harrold bridge is medieval, the church fine and graceful with a spire. Odell has a castle mound overlooking a lovely view. Moated, a castle fragment at Bletsoe marks a site once trodden by Kings, the Beauforts, and the Lords St. John. Circling past Bromham old mill and twenty-six arches of the bridge the river twists and turns yet again, soon to reach the capital town of the county.

Bedford's visible attractions, toned in a minor key, harmonize with the peaceful levels in which the flat town stands. A placid, calm, and prosperous air is imparted by the conspicuous foliage greenery, open spaces, riverside walks, chapels, churches, old inns, a good deal of business, and a suspicion of naïve sophistication due to the presence of innumerable young folk deposited for hatching out at schools of fame and efficiency. Though the town is ancient its shady tree-lined roads, busy streets, and inconspicuous back ways did not greatly help me to make imaginary excursions among the antiquated aspects of the "burh" mentioned in the Anglo-Saxon Chronicle, the place raided by Danes in longships, or even the Norman and Plantagenet castled stronghold. Near the church of St. Cuthbert only a mere fragment of the castle is visible. The great keep vanished as did its ruler, Faukes de Breauté, a veritable bold, formidable, and bad baron who surrendered to Henry III in 1224 and doubtless shuddered when he noticed his own twenty-four and particular knights strung up before the stone walls in the customary manner of good old times. Marks of the early years are best kept at the churches, notably Saxon features and stones fired by Danish raiders at St. Peter de Merton, a Norman tower and transepts at St. Mary's. The town's spacious centre, St. Paul's Square, gains distinction and impressiveness from the overshadowing bigness of the medieval church, restored in transepts, tower, and spire. Outside and inside this church are Bedford's two artistic masterpieces, one a superb figure of John Howard in bronze by Alfred Gilbert, the other a very beautiful fourteenth-century pulpit. Judges had good reason to remember that pulpit. Only by force was Judge Jeffreys restrained from attacking the parson on listening to home truths preached by Thomas Pomfret. Later John Wesley followed with his famous Assize sermon expounded from the text, "But why dost thou judge thy brother? or why dost thou set at nought thy brother? for we shall all stand before the judgment seat of Christ." A trenchant utterance, this, on a high day for wig and gown, yet particularly apt for the locality, long a stronghold of moral fearlessness, religious zeal, Puritanism, dissent, and where the words Bunyan and Bedford can mean much the same thing.

Chancing on a timbered rectory and buildings dating from the thirteenth century at the Hospital of St. John the Baptist, I read these words inscribed on a wall for all to see,

John Bunyan, author of Pilgrim's Progress, used to come here for talks with the rector, John Gifford. In 1653 he joined the St. John's congregation. In 1657 he was ordained in St. John's for preaching in the villages. This place was the interpreter's house of his experience.

A simple statement truly, just one of those little sparks you discern in the open and hidden ways of England to light suddenly a lamp of memory. Here a few sentences illuminate the beginnings of a progress from tinker and man of the commonalty to a universal citizen of the world whose imaginative force in the allegory of humanity's undying struggle with light and darkness, good and evil, touched the hearts of young and old, the rich, the poor, and the learned. A good mile away lovers of the book and the man will find Elstow, the place of Bunyan's birth and early married life, the village and the cottage that call pilgrims of faith and hope to see the things he knew. Here is the green, the original of *Vanity Fair*, bordered with old houses and a timbered moot hall (153). The church tracing from Norman times groups nobly with its detached bell tower. A Renaissance gateway marks the spot of an abbey and its company of nuns governed by the abbess of Elstow, Elizabeth Harvey, all swept into darkness long before the new apostle of light was born. I cannot illustrate the Bedford jail in which was written, "I dreamed a dream," because both claimants for the honour have disappeared and nobody can say with certainty just where the prison stood. More tangible is the Bunyan Meeting in Mill Street, founded in 1650 and where Bunyan ministered from the end of his imprisonment in 1672 until he died in 1688. It houses a unique collection of Bunyan relics. The present building, erected in 1849, might not be considered the acme of æsthetic inspiration; rather did it remind me of a drab architectural period and the singular manner in which a prosperous and grateful nation sometimes commemorated the illustrious dead. Almost next door in the same street stands the Howard Congregational Church, founded in 1772 by John Howard, the country gentleman and immortal reformer of prisons who devoted and lost his life in the cause of the most hapless of mankind. The frontage of 1774, a thin specimen of the classic style, also acquired rear brick quarters that further exemplify the architectural bleakness of the unfortunate year aforementioned, 1849.

If not outstanding for civic and domestic buildings Bedford presents nice fronts of Georgian houses, the old school with a statue of Colley Cibber over the doorway, and in High Street amusing oriels above a fish shop, belongings of a former Court House, the owner of the fish informed me. Keen eyes for quaint peeps will find them along byways and alleys, of the kind that I give from the north side of St. Paul's Square (142). A poor medieval relic maintains a chequered existence in a back yard behind 48 High Street; it may be either a fragment of a house of the Newnham priors or part of an early *George* inn. The *Rose, Saracen's Head, Lion, Cross Keys,* other inn signs, and yards reached through

HUNTINGDON. *The way in from Godmanchester. This bridge, the finest medieval one over the Great Ouse, was rebuilt during the fourteenth century. It directs the Roman road to the North and faces the site of a Saxon castle.*

ST. IVES. *The Ouse bridge with the chapel of St. Leger, consecrated in 1426. Georgian houses line each approach to the bridge, and a near statue on Market Hill commemorates the townsman, Oliver Cromwell.*

archways give indications of long establishment. And as my readers and travellers all need rest and refreshment after sightseeing labours they might fare worse than admire the exterior of the *Swan*, go inside, see the magnificent staircase, then settle down to eat, be merry, and at a timely hour nobly tread the seventeenth-century steps to bed. Built in 1794, the house probably was designed by Henry Holland, architect of Carlton House, London. Its staircase came from the mansion of Houghton Conquest, now in ruins six miles southward, once the home of Philip Sidney's sister, the Countess of Pembroke, and Christiana, Countess of Devonshire. This great place of big names and consequence, long ago fallen, yet keeping beauty in desolation, most likely figured as the House Beautiful in *The Pilgrim's Progress*. The *Swan* contributes to the most impressive view of the town where the nineteenth-century bridge, walks embowered in trees, riverside grouping, and St. Paul's spire peeping up behind (148) compose in the calm and pretty prospect that greeted us on entering and offers a gracious farewell as we now leave Bedford.

Whatever elevation of spirit may have come from thoughts of good John Bunyan, John Howard, and saintly influences associated with Bedford there is no doubt that below the town the Ouse drops us into the flats, miles of wide, flat and woody landscape as the river traces a winding course eastward and north to Huntingdonshire. Heights are only distantly visible, upland country to the north, the southern undulations about Old Warden's abbey fragments, Ickwell maypole, Sandy Warren's pines, oaks, and bracken. Particular sights enliven the valley with their actual good looks and signs of former inhabitants. John Howard, for instance, can be pictured in his house near the new church at Cardington; mercifully he never saw the village's monstrous addition for flying and an aerial tragedy. Willington has a large dovecote (153), truly remarkable and arranged for 1,500 inmates if my informer told the truth. Tudor stables next door accommodated Bunyan, who scratched his name and date of 1650 on the stone fireplace. These two curiosities are all that is left of a mansion erected by Sir John Gostwick, Cardinal Wolsey's Master of the Horse. A bridge of many fifteenth-century arches perceptibly helps to make Great Barford a very picturesque village, and Bunyan's Mr. By-ends, in life a wicked lawyer named William Foster, brought the place a niche of fame by settling down for good in the churchyard. Thatch, white, and green prettily colour Blunham and Roxton. Onward a few miles pointed stone arches below a more recent parapet of the bridge introduce St. Neots and our arrival into Huntingdonshire.

Just at this spot on St. Neots bridge an unfortunate mishap occurred, dated 1254 by Matthew Paris. A gouty gentleman, not good on his legs and out for an airing in his chariot, was summarily jerked into the River Ouse through an unrehearsed act on the part of a careless driver. Consequently William, Earl of

Ferrers, vacated this earth for kingdom come. With better fortune ordained by legs or a car's steering arrangements we quickly see a very large square, a big church remarkably fine, eighteenth-century houses and inns of cool grey brick-work, and other belongings of a town that once upon a time made a strongpoint to keep back the Danes and was named after King Alfred's brother Neotus. More blood shed on the banks of the Ouse is grimly recalled by Civil War trenches down in the fields. One native assured me that many of the townspeople, though far away from north Britain, know how many beans make five—evidently a survival of the Cromwellian and Puritan sagacity—and also are proud of babies to the number of four who make the Miles family very celebrated for quads. Dismissing this trite information on human peculiarities I left the town to spy a little stream joining the big river edged with rushes and willows near Paxton Park, and to penetrate up the Kym valley, a detour I can recommend for rural village peeps, the fresh greenery of meadows and woods. Hail Weston, poetized by Michael Drayton in *Polyolbion*, has its attractions enhanced by a timbered church tower. Great Staughton's old Place House stands charmingly in walled seclusion, a mile from Staughton Green a beautiful park surrounds the seventeenth-century hall of Gaynes, and further up the valley where the Wornditch comes down a graceful spire across the fields pointed me to Kimbolton. This is a bright cheery place of brick and white houses, a Georgian *George* inn creeper-clad, and a Doric gatehouse by Robert Adam gives entrance to the great park and the castle built by the Montagu family at the site of an ancient and royal fortress. All in all a very pleasant spot to find; but not always so, for bullet marks on the church door indicate unpleasant happenings during the Civil War. Tragedies, too, can be remembered. Lord Chief Justice Montagu condemned Raleigh to death; a Shakespearian page titled *Act IV. Scene II.—Kimbolton* tells the pathetic "Farewell" of a dying queen, Catherine of Aragon.

Past St. Neots the Ouse sweeps gracefully round Paxton Hill, then babbles over the weir for the twin villages of Offord Darcy and Offord Cluny. Each amplify the waterside scenery with their modest old-fashioned looks and a manor-house, of 1613 at Darcy, in Georgian brickwork at Cluny. Two miles inland another manor-house attracted me to Toseland, a showing of Elizabethan gables and clustered chimneys in most engaging fashion. Onward again and with more windings the river wanders round Godmanchester and Huntingdon.

This stretch of the Ouse meanders between historic neighbours, the two branches of the great route to the North that meet at Alconbury Hill, as did heroes of fiction, poetry, and gentlemen glib with the words, "Zounds! Stand and deliver!" And as historic highways developed inns to cater for the ceaseless stopping and moving on of travellers down the centuries, apparent slumps in scenic attraction on east Midland stretches of the Great North Road are relieved by houses of entertainment. Among them may be counted a number of England's most noted old hostelries, those mirrors of life and the ways of covering the miles, hereabout evidently pursued by ancient Britons, Romans, King John, Cardinal Wolsey, Cavaliers, Dick Turpin, Georgian big-wigs, and Mr. Jones from Highgate. While the new age speeds along creating the stuff for future reminiscence of the motoring era brightened with electric light in freshened-up bars, coffee-rooms, and snuggeries, these emblems of roadside hospitality still have about them faint glimmerings of their candle and lamp-light years. Solid old walls, cosy rooms, bulging bay windows, and archways leading to the far beyond start shadowy visions of coaches, flying machines and chaises, horns tooting Tally-ho, Tally-ho, mighty sirloins and crackling pork awaiting before crackling wood fires, and the pageantry, the fun, and the miseries of getting about that come to life again as we turn the pages of Harrison, Pepys, Boswell's Johnson, Washington Irving, George Borrow, and Charles Dickens. Time, old Time himself, is never in more illuminating mood than at these hoary contrivances, the English inns.

On page 156 I illustrate features gleaned from some of the east Midland houses of posting associations and fame. Other more modest signs, such as those of the *Anchor* at Tempsford, Roxton's *Pear Tree*, or a *Dragon* at Brampton, locate types of village pubs where local gossip and debates on high matters have been bandied round tap-rooms for generations. But at Eaton Socon, Buckden, and elsewhere in the district we meet the lions of adventurous prime years, the kind of places in which after hot pork and a night-cap you may be startled from slumber by ghosts of royalty, lords and ladies, honest men, bad men, or highwaymen coming out from secret hiding-places behind chimney-corners and massive beams just on the stroke of midnight. Not a fierce carnivorous animal but actually a *White Horse* welcomes us to Eaton Socon. Fat bays stick out from brick walling enlivened with Georgian sash windows, a suitable re-fronting for screening more aged internals and fifteenth-century origins, altogether both outside and inside properly effective for the pencil of a Rowlandson, Randolph Caldecott, or Cecil Aldin. Northward six miles at Buckden the *George's* lines of windows above the archway wink at a real *Lion* squatting on the opposite side of the road. Both inns, much favoured by eaters and drinkers in the coaching days, date from years before those times. Behind the brick front of the *George* built *circa* 1730, anybody so disposed may like to believe the claim that here Queen Elizabeth I reposed in one of her ubiquitous beds, and that Dick Turpin found a convenient hole to bolt through, then disappeared like a streak of lightning on speedy Black Bess. The *Lion's* age dips far back. The house was in being in 1536 when the suppression of monasteries brought to the highway abbots and nobles armed and well horsed, banners bearing sacred emblems followed by the clamour of motley cavalcades, and the Pilgrimage of Grace ran its fiery course up and down the Great North Road, only to lead many an aristocratic and humble head to the block, the stake, countless gibbets, and the gallows at Tyburn. Probably built about 1477, the *Lion's* internal walls, moulded ceiling beams, and timbering correspond with the period of the gatehouse and ruined buildings next door, reminders of a prison for Catherine of Aragon and the palace where bishops of Lincoln lived, died, and left a Tudor picture to charm travellers who halt at the *Lion* and the *George* in Buckden.

North again—and how chilly it can be when an east wind blows damp vapours from the fens and the lodes—the inns at Stilton preside over a width of highway noble and generous. Only to stand under the curly ironwork of the *Bell* sign is quite sufficient for transforming passing saloons and purring engines into coaches and horses, pack trains, lumbering wagons, horseback and pillion, and all the bustling that went on when the *Bell* and the *Angel* had vast ranges of stabling. A worthy stalwart is this *Bell*, true and shapely to record a long past. Its ample front gabled at each end, the inevitable coach archway, a tall bay, original mullions, good chimney shafts, and the general appearances were schemed in the traditional manner dictated by the oolite stone, here projected to this corner of Huntingdonshire from Northamptonshire and the Cotswolds. And the words of old Jno. Pitts, a former landlord, reminded me of something really worth eating. Not only did I read on his billhead, "Neat Post Chaises," but also, "Stilton Cheese as Usual." He obtained these provisions from Leicestershire, regaled travellers with them on the spot, sold cheese at half-a-crown a pound, sent it far and wide by road, spread the name and fame of Stilton to the uttermost ends of the gastronomic world. Such was the ingratitude of John Bull, Pitts did not rise—like another Pitt in the singular—to a peerage. Beyond Stilton and past Norman Cross, a spot commemorated for the captivity of Napoleon's soldiers and sailors, the *Haycock* at Wansford adds a very prince of its generation to the end of the Great North Road in Huntingdonshire. One of the largest seventeenth-century inns, the grouping is so handsome, the projecting wings, central porch, stone chimneys, and lines of dormers are so perfect in detail, the house might be a squire's manorial home run adrift by the arched bridge rebuilt in 1577 over the River Nene. Bridge and inn have been by-passed since a new concrete structure was erected lower downstream. Wise travellers however may keep to the ancient track, admire the view, rest awhile at the *Haycock*, meditate on its painted sign. This artistic effort depicts somebody floating down to the bridge; a man in fact who fell asleep on a haycock, slumbered while drifting on flood water, and only awoke with a start when his curious craft bumped against Wansford bridge.

"Where am I?" he cried to rustic onlookers.

"At Wansford," they said.

"What! in England?" he asked anxiously.

That is the story of Barnabee, one that has been written with frillings and

HEMINGFORD GREY. *The mill near St. Ives.*

FOTHERINGAY. *The eighteenth-century bridge over the River Nene and near the church, splendidly built with an octagonal lantern tower in 1434.*

KING'S SUTTON. *This church is locally famed "for beauty" in the Northamptonshire country of spires and stone villages. It shows the transition to Perpendicular architecture and has a western porch with carved images of the Virgin and Child above the entrance.*

KIRBY HALL. *Ruins of Elizabethan splendour and the Renaissance. John Thorpe laid the first stone of the great house in 1570 and Inigo Jones designed later additions.*

ASHBY ST. LEDGERS. *The manor-house, formerly a home of the Catesby family, dates from Elizabethan times. It was associated with the hatching and consequences of the Gunpowder Plot.*

CALDECOTT. *One of Rutland's pretty and secluded villages with churches and buildings of stonework coursed with ironstone. The bays illustrated are distinctive features.*

LYDDINGTON *near Uppingham. Cottages and the garden tower of the Bede House, a lovely almshouse converted from a home of Lincoln bishops by Thomas Cecil.*

variations for more than three hundred years. It gave a unique name to the inn.
The Haycock, Wansford-in-England certainly became widely known and rose on
a flood of fame and glory at this important stage in the coaching years.

Retracing our ways towards Buckden we diverge from the Great North
Road for Brampton and Huntingdon, soon to see behind the roadside hedge
a white-fronted and gabled house (153). It may be visited. A small payment of
ready cash opens the portals of the Pepys family home. The cash is not likely
to be refunded with interest by searching for hidden treasure, namely the £1,500
buried by Samuel when scared out of his wits on thinking, "The whole kingdom
is undone. So God help us!" For on 10th October 1667, Samuel and his father

with a dark lantern, it being now night, into the garden with my wife, and there went
about our great work to dig up my gold.

From this modest establishment the fine trees lining the highway, park walls,
lodges, and expansive domains show the beauty of unhidden treasures which
denote the nearness of Hinchingbrooke, the great house of the diarist's "My
Lord and My Lady," still the home of the Earl of Sandwich. As some ordinary
mortals even to-day may not be on visiting terms with all members of the
peerage I give the following brief particulars of what lies behind the park walls.
The house began as a nunnery. After the Dissolution wealthy Cromwell knights
added large buildings, a stately gatehouse filched from Ramsey Abbey, and in
1602 developed big windows, bays and walls outlined in the Elizabethan style.
A financial collapse on the part of Sir Oliver Cromwell, largely due to the
attentions of his dutiful nephew, Oliver the Protector, caused the house to be
sold to Sir Sidney Montague. Soon appeared the valiant admiral, Edward
Montague, first Earl of Sandwich. Aware that the Lord Protector had finally
retired from making earthly demolitions and conscious that Charles II had come
back, he began to enlarge the house during 1661, made it "very magnificent,
most excellently furnished," and thereby was "reduced to great straits for
money," Pepys concluded. A later catastrophe, the big fire of 1830, threatened
greater straits and even destruction to this abode of nuns and their successors.
Happily that extremity did not happen. Rebuilt in parts and restored, Hinchingbrooke survived to remain *the* stately mansion of Huntingdonshire.

Forward into George Street, Huntingdon, we find the *George* conveniently
posed to halt us at the corner of the Roman Ermine Street. The inn must have
been there when Tudors reigned. King Charles gave it a date while campaigning
in 1645 and the rare courtyard gallery (156) followed after Charles II had re-
appeared from Holland. The front department, a Victorian rebuilding with a
jolly ballroom, has glittered many a night in the shine of local belles, and when
midnight bells chime over the Pepysian homelands a spectral shade of Tom

Hennesy surely must join youth and pleasure to chase the hours with dancing feet. Alas! poor Tom, incomparable king of coachmen, artist of the ribbons, driver of the speedy Stamford *Regent*. He of the rakish looks, idol of all pretty maids, fell to the slings of his diabolical competitor, the steam engine. Broken in frame and heart, he wound up a brilliant career by driving a two-horsed bus between Cambridge and this same *George*.

Refreshed by comforts bestowed inside the old inn, the outside face of Huntingdon presents a seeker with a number of interesting features, some of them neatly groomed, others wrinkled by age. Distinctive marks of antiquity are visible at two Gothic churches of All Saints and St. Mary. Norman arches at the grammar school for Cromwell and Pepys belonged to an earlier hospital. Castle Hills near the river locate the site of a Saxon fortress erected by King Alfred's son, Edward the Elder. The bridge over the Ouse (161) apparently was largely rebuilt in the late 1300's to replace an older structure mentioned in a survey of 1259, yet partly visible at the town end. Pointed arches, cutwaters, and massive stone piers have defied the kicks of centuries and still finely exhibit the most impressive of the river's medieval bridges. Curious and many were the incidents and services connected with it. One, in 1279, dictated that every Jew or Jewess who crossed over must pay toll of "one penny on horseback, one half-penny on foot"—quite expensive in those days. In more distant times Romans crossed hereabout from *Durolipons,* their station at the junction of *Via Devana* and the route to York. Afterwards the station improved in looks, became Godmanchester, with fertile lands and a charter dated 1212 A.D. Now it is a restful spot of brick, white, and thatched houses, flowered gardens, tall tree greenery, a big and glorious church below the spire, all bounded by the great meadow of Port Holme, the largest in the whole world, a proud native told me!

From Godmanchester and the bridge the Old North Road directs through a long length of Huntingdon's aspects of domesticity, characteristic of a long-settled country town. Mixtures of architectural fashions in building front the pavements, and a number of good original doorways I observed might have opened to R. Cromwell or I. Turpin (the bailiffs of 1609), to Puritans, Royalists, or councillors who sat in the eighteenth-century town hall. Ferrar House, in which Cowper lived with the Unwins from 1765 to 1767, is but one of several dignified Georgian façades in brickwork. Right and left from the great road narrow cobbled alleys give fascinating peeps and further glimpses of how and where the good townspeople previously lived and thrived in varied degrees of comfort, inconvenience, and charm. Where they met for other purposes I have already revealed in our visit to the *George*. The *Falcon*, too, offered conviviality in cosy quarters round its cobbled courtyard, still a sight to invite on looking through the oak doorway in Market Square. Lower down the street the *Bridge* makes another satisfactory picture, nicely perched at the end of the historic bridge. And along this town highway, a bearer of traffic through centuries and on which cars and lorries never cease to speed new years onward, things seen and the intangible unseen join with the realm of memories. It is a street of celebrities. From the hosts of shining lights that have tracked it particular luminaries include Henry of Huntingdon, the archdeacon and twelfth-century historian, the first Queen Elizabeth in progress to Hinchingbrooke, Pepys keeping his early morning hours, young Cowper wandering up and down. Undoubtedly it is the street of Oliver Cromwell. He was born in it (the house behind the priory wall has gone), baptized in it (at All Saints' Church), educated and flogged in the Norman-fronted school. After tracing reminders of Cromwell all down the Ouse borderlands from Hillesden we have arrived at his place of genesis, the nursery of the Man, sometimes acclaimed Great, sometimes judged otherwise. Those who think otherwise can be joyful in believing the story of Huntingdon rejecting an offer of Cromwell's statue to perpetuate his connection with the town. Eventually somebody did something, devised a small inconspicuous tablet. On this solitary memorial affixed to the old school I read,

Oliver Cromwell, Lord Protector of the Commonwealth, attended this school about 1610.

Onward down to St. Ives the Ouse wanders through the low vale of broad green acres stretching to soft distances. The stream winds past Hartford, Houghton, Hemingford Abbots and Hemingford Grey. Here the river scenery is at its best, tempting, alluring, amplifying landscape effects of charming quality. Lush banksides, shapely elms, water reflections, rushes, tall grasses, and bright wildflowers join in the wealth of near detail. Willows clumped together or standing in lines and avenues wave their delicate colours on myriads of narrow pointed leaves hung fanwise from branches and brown wrinkled trunks. Footpaths diverge from quiet narrow lanes to the watermeadows. Houghton and Hemingford Grey mills (167) have the look of old-time toil and use that conspired to make both food and beauty. Brickwork tinted light brown, pinkish, and grey like the Dutchmen used, white plaster and black timbers, thatching swept steeply from ridges of cottages and barns, and ancient weathered churches all help to give the village aspects a harmony with nature's luxuriant handiwork. With so many attractions it is not surprising that this little area became artists' country. Here Dendy Sadler and scores of sketchers and painters perambulated, squatted on stools, sometimes settled for good. Cowper also liked to muse over the lovely view from Hartford churchyard. Perhaps his heart thumped faster when

Two Nymphs adorn'd with every grace

appeared on the scene—the Miss Gunnings in fact out for an airing from their home, the antiquated Norman manor-house in Hemingford Grey. No doubt the limpid village air even enhanced the charms of those two famous beauties who went forth to captivate London town in the 1750's and jointly captured a duke and an earl in the best style of romantic conquest. Alas, too much make-up and consequently too little air through her pores brought an early finale to the celebrated beauty of Maria, Countess of Coventry. Elizabeth, Duchess of Hamilton and Argyll, had better fortune, survived thirty years longer, became the mother of four more dukes.

A long brick barn at the entrance of our next halt, St. Ives, augurs one more dose of Oliver Cromwell. The building looks careworn. Buttresses outside keep it up. Repairs would not be amiss. Nobody does them. The interior, massively timbered up to the roof, would have done very well for a church before the rise and fall of Puritanism. Cromwell's Barn, useful now in the production of food, probably serves better than it did when Oliver, a townsman here from 1631 to 1636, conducted unsuccessful agricultural operations on England. At St. Ives Saxons made another fortress to awe the Danes, and St. Ivo, by tradition a missionary saint from Persia or Celtic Cornwall, fixed the spot on which church and town grew up. The river dictated a bridge, first of wood, in the fourteenth century of stone. A most beautiful bridge it is (162), a fantasy in stonework to rival the one at Huntingdon; the chapel of St. Leger, dating from 1426, served to guard the bodies and souls of all who crossed over the four medieval arches. Situated low in the flats the town does not rise to great spectacular heights except at the Gothic church, impressive at close quarters and when seen from the meadows reflected in the stream. Streets have a number of excellent Georgian brick houses and older gables show here and there. Behind one frontage on Market Hill (in possession of a doctor) Theodore Watts-Dunton made his first squawks to signify he had safely arrived on earth with the kind help of a former physician. The *Lion* inn, quite near, sits cosily round a small courtyard. Outside Oliver Cromwell stands fiercely in bronze on his pedestal, complete with Puritan hat, big Bible, sword handy to prod anybody standing in his way. Groping through darkness, light, falsity, and truth the original may have deduced peculiar notions on uprightness and downrightness, so it is quite appropriate to find his statue on Market Hill—which actually is quite flat!

Two miles distant lies Holywell, most prettily reached by a field way near the river. The small village has a holy well close to the little ancient church. Choice old houses set amongst gardens, flowers, and trees might make covetous people forget the opening decree of the Tenth Commandment. They face the broad green strand, the winding stream, distant horizons. With this last scene for a gracious remembrance we leave the Great Ouse, Cowper's river, where it "glides smoothly and by stealth away" to the Fens.

GEDDINGTON. *Houses and cottages of Northamptonshire stone surround the Eleanor Cross, erected after the Queen's funeral procession halted here in December, 1290. The medieval bridge with big cut-waters crosses the River Ise, and the house beyond has a dormer sundial dated 1767.*

175

Within the illustration:

HERE·LIETH·THE·BODE·OF·LAVRENCE·
WASHINGTON·SONNE·&·HEIRE·OF·
ROBERT·WASHINGTON·OF·SOVLGRAE
IN·TH·COVNTIE·OF·NORTHAMTOM
...LDEST·DAVGHTER·OF·WILLIAM
...DE·TEIS·IN·TH·SO...
...ESOVIER·WHO.

Sydney R
Jones

GREAT BRINGTON. *The Washington stars and stripes on the tomb of Laurence Washington, ancestor of the first President of the United States. Laurence died in 1616 after the family had moved from Sulgrave to Little Brington. Treasures in this church include medieval woodwork and splendid monuments to the Spencers of Althorp.*

NORTHAMPTONSHIRE STONE

Long tracts of Northamptonshire stretching from western boundaries to Peterborough and the fringes of Fenland lie on the stone beds of oolite and lias that sweep south-west and north-east through the Midland Counties. A good satisfying sort of county is this Northamptonshire, though not much in the news or widely known. It has the uplands, called by Horace Walpole "the dumpling hills." The Rivers Nene, Welland, and many smaller streams rise and run down into pretty valleys. Celebrated quarries yielded materials for making countless architectural masterpieces. Consequently the splendours of the parish churches throughout the district are outstanding. Stonework grey and golden sets pictures of delight in villages and towns. Old country houses in extraordinary numbers and varieties present their charms at every turn. Not without cunning and pride did the locals invent the apt conceit for their country, "A land of spires and squires." That adage served very well before the age of mass production and collectivism put churches and squires in the background. Now factories and sprawls of brick housing round Northampton and other manufacturing centres illustrate the idea of man seeing red where Divinity planned grey and green. Within hail of the blast furnaces of Corby devastations almost beyond belief or equal to a Hitler's best machinations are rapidly transforming a once lovely and tranquil area into a rival of Sahara through open-cast mining for ironstone. Recent traversing of threatened ground between Harringworth and Rockingham filled me with gloomy forebodings.

Turning to prospects likely to please, these are many and abundantly exhibit nature's good gifts sympathetically enriched with the works of humanity in times when man was reasonably grateful for products of the fields and stone without developing avaricious hankerings for steel. Over this piece of country the scenery generally keeps true to its geological make-up. You can follow the oolite and lias from Aynho and Evenley, two beautiful villages near the Oxfordshire border, and proceed right across Northamptonshire to Stamford Baron in the north with the certain knowledge of what is likely to be seen. Continuous uplands, not of great height, mould up-and-down curvatures of land surfaces. Panoramas from top points have the fullness of England's patterned miles. Fields and hedgerows, trees and massy depths of woods, steep combes opening to wider valleys, rich borderlands of rivers, the red and brown-tinted earth line and colour great sweeps of landscape. Village roofs, church towers and spires add their features to the vast expanses. Looking from these uplands across near and middle configurations to far horizons brings the exhilaration, the exciting moments experienced in spying over breadth, distance, counties. Here the prospects include Oxfordshire, Warwickshire, outliers of the Cotswolds, Leicestershire to CharnwoodForest, river vales of the Welland, Nene, and

Great Ouse. Moses, I think, certainly Hollar, de Wint, and many artists, had a liking for the big view, a partiality in which I share; from my findings in this locality I record with gratitude and recommendations the viewpoints—and the fresh air—at Honey Hill near Cold Ashby, Cold Higham by Watling Street, the upper grounds of Rockingham Forest, scarps beyond Little Brington, the historic points about Rainsborough Camp, Danesmoor, and Naseby where old battles were fought by Danes, Yorkists and Lancastrians, Roundheads and Cavaliers.

Other sights bring movement and life to the stillness of upland and vale. The best of cattle thrive on rich grazing lands. Foxes steal in and out of coverts and woods. When trees begin to reveal their delicate bark colours and shower carpets of leaves cavalcades of horses, riders and hounds decorate stretches of this famous hunting shire; a meet of the Pytchley at Rockingham Castle makes a picture for enjoyment and remembrance. Sheep still range the slopes. Lambing-time brings new life, new sounds, day and night work for shepherds. I discovered one of these sons of the uplands on a hillside working at his wattle pens roughly thatched with straw, climbed up to him, admired his responsive hands tend long-legged little babies with instinctive care and gentleness. He might have been the actual *Gabriel Oak*, strongly built, features firmly lined, eyes keen, knowing and ready in speech.

"You belong to a dying race," I said.

"Perhaps; maybe not," he answered. "There's quite a lot of us about yet"—news which cheered me.

Where we stood among ewes and lambs, oak trees over yonder, cows at pasture below the hill, set me thinking of wool, hides for leather, bark for tanning, the sources of local village and town industries before machinery and the factory system made these Midlands an emporium for the world.

"Time gone by this was a great centre of the wool trade," the shepherd remarked. "The country families raked in fortunes."

"That was why Laurence Washington settled at Sulgrave in Henry VIII's reign," I added. "He did very well, acquired much land, could afford the luxury of four sons and seven daughters, became mayor of Northampton."

When I further recalled that the same town supplied King John with hand-made boots at ninepence a pair the shepherd looked dubiously at his own boots and my Lotus shoes, said he wished the Northampton machines could do the same sort of economic production nowadays.

Things more lasting than coverings for feet and bodies were piled up to adorn these uplands and valleys. No more than casual observation is needed to prove that much of the regional architecture ranks with England's best. Quarries at Barnack, Weldon, Colly Weston, and others in many places yielded the valued freestone, rougher local stone, ironstone and stone slates, materials handily situated just where they were needed for building anything from a cathedral to a cottage. Masons skilled in the traditional ways of their trade and ready to try out new ideas effectively provided for human requirements and convenience. By using the natural products their constructed works achieved a harmonious union with the scenery and environment. Demand, supply, invention, and craftsmanship thus caused the native stone to become a manifestation of everyday life, of religious aspiration, a medium to localize ordinary people, big personages, and events of history. It is the result of these influences and the consequent effects in stone that now make a special appeal in traversing the Northamptonshire grounds. They lead onward to interest and delight, to monumental Peterborough (154-5), to churches distinctive and graced with spires spread far away eastward from King's Sutton, to mansions and squires' old homes, farms and barns among the fields, the clustered houses and cottages in towns, villages, and hamlets anciently settled on highways and lanes.

Northamptonshire churches add special dignity to the scenes. These emblems of past worship and communal life, their frequent towers and spires pointing upward in the weathered lines of old beauty, stand elevated facing the winds, sheltered below slopes, bordering village greens, or marking centres of populous towns. At Earl's Barton or Brixworth the strong masonry intact after ten centuries of service strikingly illustrates a phase of vernacular Anglo-Saxon culture. Norman works that followed, the massive pillars, rounded arches, the zigzag, chevron, and rich mouldings, are plentifully evident; St. Sepulchre's Round and St. Peter's, both at Northampton, furnish but two examples from many, and the grand manner of the style culminates with the severe simplicity of the interior nave and transepts at Peterborough cathedral. The dawning years of Gothic art heralded new lustre. The masons, ready and dexterous with the native stone and impelled by advancing currents of thought in design, wrought and laid their work. Particularly during the thirteenth, fourteenth, and fifteenth centuries they made their land splendid with arch and column, tracery, clerestory, moulding, carving, and created the wonderful group of medieval parish churches that remain major attractions of the district to this present day. More than that. Designers and craftsmen pre-eminently developed the spire. They built broach spires of octagonal shapes above square tower walls. Stimulated to further possibilities they erected the later spires that rose from embattled parapets, pinnacles, and flying buttresses to mount upward in impressive heights. The sloped surfaces enriched with bands of patterning and little windows opening clear to the skies glistened in the changing lights from dawn to dusk. Crockets emphasized the bold lines of tapering silhouettes. Finials at top points ended with weathervanes to point how the wind blew on summer days or in wintry seasons. Clear of the belfries spires were simply adornments, æsthetic expressions of fancy such as economists of to-day might consider quite useless. Nevertheless they belong to the realm of pure architecture and may be counted among the noblest built works erected by man. As the eye perceives these lovely structures, symbols of faith and high aspiration raised above the workaday world in beautiful rhythm and airy grace, it is easy to realize why they have ever held a warm place in the affections of English people, why Constable and many artists were inspired by them, why poets with Cowper joined in praise of the

> Tall spire, from which the sound of cheerful bells
> Just undulates upon the list'ning ear.

More thickly clustered than elsewhere in England the spires over this east Midland area constitute a most remarkable group. Soaring in graceful lines they stand in all directions over the stone country. Notably they mark point by point at King's Sutton (168), Middleton Cheney (9), Crick, Northampton, Wellingborough, Easton Maudit, Higham Ferrers, Raunds, Kettering, Oundle, Warmington, Nassington, at Uppingham, Empingham, Ketton, and Exton in Rutland, away past Stamford (181) to Lincolnshire's Grantham, Ewerby, and the glorious climax at Louth, a masterpiece triumphantly commanding the levels. If weather, storm, or the downward thrust of sheer weight did cause a number of spires to decay or fall, most of them have survived in original, restored, or rebuilt form largely because they were so greatly valued and admired. Irchester's lofty specimen for example was reconstructed in strict imitation of the original; the beautiful spired proportions above the splendid western porch at Higham Ferrers were much "re-edified" by Richard Atkins, mason, after the stonework collapsed; when lightning in 1826 struck one of the finest early spires at Raunds restorers worked with scrupulous care to preserve the exact appearance of the thirteenth-century structure.

These conspicuous spires and also church towers of the customary Midland type single out many villages of much attraction. Often they occupy very rural situations, see but few travellers, preserve an intimacy that appears related to the surroundings of trees and fields, hill slopes and valleys. People once great in the county lie under splendid memorials in the church chancels and chapels, Spencers at Great Brington, Fermor and Yelverton at Easton Maudit, Knightley at Fawsley, Stafford and Greene at Lowick, Watsons at Rockingham, and others of old lineage. More modestly displayed are the annals of local squires, of merchants and woolmen who amassed fortunes, a slab to Laurence Washington at Great Brington next door to the mighty Spencers (176). Each of them while living landowners, with pedigrees long or pedigrees suspiciously short, settled down on ancestral or acquired acres. They left, like rosemary for remembrance, stately big places half-hidden in wooded parklands, roomy manor-houses built or rebuilt in sight of church spires and towers, the homes now in various stages of upkeep or decay that add special distinction to almost

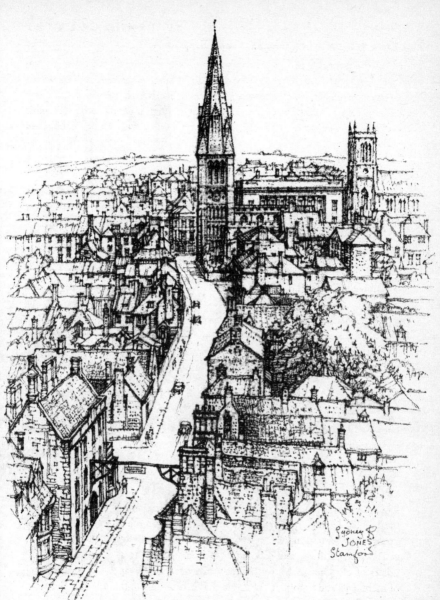

STAMFORD. *A lovely town on the Great North Road tracing history over more than a thousand years. Six churches remaining from sixteen, medieval gateways, hospitals, almshouses, gables and mullions, seventeenth-century and Georgian features contribute rare distinction to the streets. This view towards St. Mary's church includes the George and the Stamford Hotel, two noted coaching inns.*

LINCOLN. *One of England's most magnificent cathedrals soars in fretted masonry from the crown of the hill and is visible over miles of surrounding country. Its west front faces the walls, towers, and battlements of the castle dating from Conquest times.*

Steep streets, ancient houses, buildings and sites, chantries, gates, the Stonebow, and the Roman Newport Arch tell of the city's long standing through more than 2,000 years. The art gallery exhibits fine pictures of local scenes by Peter de Wint.

GREAT BOWDEN. *The classic house faces the medieval church in this village near Market Harborough.*

RAGDALE. *An old hall on the Leicestershire Wolds. It is a beautiful example of Tudor and Elizabethan building, formerly the home of the Shirley family, created Earls of Ferrers.*

every Northamptonshire parish. In shady churchyards betwixt manorial homes and houses of God rest humbler folk, those who were rooted to the soil, toiled on it, ended their days only to be remembered by green mounds, stones overgrown, worn inscriptions bordered by quaint carvings, perhaps amplified with winged cherubs to signify heavenly joy after life's labours. The quarters they occupied have outlived them. Their cottages and small houses continue to charm the eye. Still they make Northamptonshire, and Rutland too, delightful counties for wandering through villages and hamlets with stone, the beautiful stone, ever the great attraction. It gives warm and cool tints to walls, is variegated with bands of ironstone. Stone shapes doorways arched, squared, or hooded, window mullions, dormers snug in thatch, roofs stained with lichen and moss, the distinctive bay windows I found at Stowe Nine Churches, Caldecott (170), and in picturesque villages along each side of the Welland valley. Add the gardens, the tall hollyhocks and white lilies, gilly-flowers, periwinkle, sweet-williams, peonies, all the old-fashioned flowers so often seen in the locality, borders of box, trimmed yews here and there—then the country pictures are complete.

Features I have suggested in the above paragraph are generously disposed right across Northamptonshire from the bracing hilly region about Upper Boddington, Aston-le-Walls, Edgcote and Croughton in the west to Bainton and Maxey church towers where the land drops to the Fen levels. Villages of interest and pleasant with the native stone attract in all directions. One good group to the south-west of Northampton is linked with Litchborough, Moreton Pinkney, Culworth, Sulgrave, Chalcombe, and Marston St. Lawrence where the great yew stands. Other village favourites of mine border the Welland valley through Dingley, Stoke Albany, Gretton, Colly Weston true to its old tradition for fine stone. Rockingham poses a rare centrepiece, a gem set below the ancient stronghold at which early kings arrived for hunting in the forest as foxhounds do to-day. From massive walls and castle mound known long ago to Cœur de Lion and Edwardian sovereigns, you look right into Rutland, of England's counties the smallest, yet large in pictorial appeal and conspicuously free from the blots and drabness deposited by the popular fetish called progress. There among soft landscapes and rural peace the stone theme is continued from village to village, at Caldecott (170), Barrowden, Lyddington (170), Tickencote, Cottesmore, in the delightful streets of Uppingham, at Oakham town full of enchantment and beauty. A trio of towers call us to the Nene valley where the tall lanterns of Irthlingborough, Lowick, and Fotheringhay soar gracefully, adding values of linear height to the placid low landscapes. Irthlingborough has its monks' bridge, market-cross, thatched cottages, but for me the best sight was the detached campanile coloured light and dark, of very unusual design, a fragment of the college founded by a Lord Mayor of London in 1373. Lower down the vale shines the Lowick lantern rich with pinnacles and weathervanes. This striking crown to a church brilliant with Perpendicular windows is also a lasting reminder of the good deeds and sad fate of the man who originated all this finery. For Henry Greene, lord of Drayton House near by, unfortunately backed Richard II instead of Bolingbroke and thus lost his head in 1399. Not for him was the splendour of sculptured monument. His son Ralph gained that; he lies majestically in armour mourned by angel weepers carved by the famous alabasterman Thomas Prentys—but I hope that the angels shed a few tears for father Henry. And so onward to Fotheringhay. To cross the eighteenth-century bridge (167), see the fifteenth-century lantern sparkling above buttress, tracery, fan-vaulting and battlement, and to find a grassy castle mound by the river winding peacefully is more than enough to transport any sentimental soul out of the hard present into a little realm soft in the glow and shades of old romance, beauty, tragedy. The lantern completes the delicate magnificence of a light church, once but part of a stately scheme long since destroyed and royally devised for the Duke of York, killed at Agincourt in 1415. Nave and tower were finished in 1434 by William Horewode, noted master mason. William's contract provided £300 for the job. Times being tough and trade unions not then invented, the contract also dictated that the workmen must work, complete the buildings "within terme reasonable," failing which Horewode "shall yeild his body to prison at my lordys wyll and all his movable goods." Down at the riverside is a dreamland of memories. Where meek sheep graze over the green-faced mounds of vanished Norman and Edwardian strongholds, you can imagine past kings, queens, and princes keeping state, pageantry and colour, the anguish of death, the silence of more than three hundred years ago that settled over this place of lost pomp and circumstance. Richard III was born there. Catherine of Aragon had the castle for a marriage portion. On a grey February morning Queen Mary of the Scots faced the executioner's axe and said to her ladies, "Do not weep." With more to be seen in the village, including the archway to Edward IV's hostel decorated with carved roses, Fotheringhay certainly is an ideal spot for sojourning.

Thoughts of an earlier King Edward and a love story attracted me over wooded uplands to Geddington, passing by way of Oundle, another delightful stone town of streets lined with fine houses, the gabled *Talbot* and other capital old inns. Geddington has a good church with a spire, fat cutwaters of an ancient bridge facing the Ise stream, warm-coloured walls of stone houses and cottages (175). Centrally stands the weathered reminder of royal devotion. This is the Eleanor Cross. Beautifully conceived, the composition shows figures of the Queen, canopies, roses, shields, gablets, pinnacles pointing high. It was erected soon after 1290 by the King's master masons and yet tells of more than beauty in stone. For centuries the delicate work has continued to be a fit memorial for the event it commemorates, the funeral march made by Edward I with the embalmed body of his Queen in the progress of more than 160 miles from Lincoln to Westminster. My first discovery of the cross was in a dull and cloudy late autumn season when bared trees and rustling dead leaves foretold coming winter, a time that seemed to suggest the mood of those days and nights of a distant early December in which the sad pilgrimage happened. Standing by the steps of the graceful tapering monument I recalled the boy and girl alliance of Edward and Eleanor of Castile, their life's happy union broken by the death of the Queen at Harby manor-house, the King's words written to the Abbot of Cluny, "God in his pleasure has called away our most serene consort Eleanor whom, living, we cherished tenderly; whom, dead, we do not cease to love." Pictures at that spot in centuries past came to mind: the King alone behind the bier; rich vestments of ecclesiastics; the procession of mounted nobles, soldiers on foot, attendants clothed in mourning; the wondering villagers who gathered to pay last respects to their beloved Queen, while they saw the sad face of the tall Plantagenet near the purple pall embroidered in gold, and silently watched a dignitary mark the place for a cross to be erected where the bier had rested. Moving indeed must have been the scene in that bleak far-off December dusk. Having thought my thoughts with nobody about to disturb them I left the little plot hallowed by old romance. Low clouds scudded overhead threatening rain. Intent on not getting wet I hastened to Kettering, returned to the big modern world of boots, shoes, mass production, sentimentalities, and a state of welfare in which love matches still may have a place though lovely crosses of beautiful stonework do not commemorate them.

People of other times also left their own monuments, obvious to those who care to seek them by looking around for the big and middle-sized homes that add dignity and charm to these Midland landscapes on nature's foundations of stone. The farmer who gave me a lift from Chalcombe Priory to Culworth manor-house (in which Charles I stayed) said that no English county makes a better showing than Northamptonshire for old country houses—a statement not far short of the truth. They stand in all directions. Few parishes do not possess at least one. They offer wide variations in size and architectural design in masonry. Some of them were rebuilt on Domesday hall sites. Others point to survivals from the spoils of monasteries. Gabled and classic walls swing Time's pendulum through the ages of Tudors and Elizabethans, years of the seventeenth century and Georgian reigns. Tenacious in the British bulldog way these mansions and manor-houses have held tight to their places and continue old ages either upstanding and well tended, socially descended, or falling down. Cecil's vast Elizabethan pile at Burghley House and other great homes of families that climbed high in fame retain a standing in lordly parks. Looking from entrance-gate piers or impertinently trespassing you spy the roomy and gracious strongholds of past squirearchy and lesser gentry. They continue placid in seclusion amongst flower gardens, lawns of old turf, and even rooks cawing in leafy backgrounds of high trees contribute additional notes of long-settled possession. Around farmhouses still lovely to see, the pigs grunting and harsh rattlings of tractors instead of horses neighing and hounds with their tails up plainly tell that the squires, once in residence, departed a long time ago. Here and there, at Kirby Hall for instance or at old Tresham's Elizabethan Lyveden New Building hard by Brigstock, beauty in decay reigns, a tumbling to pieces with lord, squire, and everybody else gone. Whether very large or conveniently big, in good or poor condition, these homes of an out-of-date past now gather an air of museum pieces, for never again will their like be erected. Consequently they afford sentimental excursions into domestic life as it was played in the many parts attributed by Shakespeare to man during the good and bad old times we may like to associate with bold knights in shining armour, landed aristocracy in command of wide acres free from perilous attacks by Super-tax gatherers, when retinues of respectful servants could be acquired very cheaply, and benevolent country gentlemen, secure to rule their little communities from generation to generation, thrived contentedly and kept up the status of a Sir Roger de Coverley or a Squire Hardcastle under such names as Dryden of Canons Ashby or Tanfield of Gayton.

Canons Ashby yet stands in the calm beauty found there by John Dryden the poet; even the leaden shepherd with his pipe really might be tuning an antique melody to steal over the forecourt wall and echo among the yews and mulberry trees. Gayton's gables face the church in which Francis Tanfield lies figured in alabaster. Innumerable reminders of old-time life await to charm admirers of old English homes. They include Apethorpe Hall fancifully gabled, Dingley (classic and Elizabethan), Winwick (sixteenth century), Lilford Hall (Jacobean), Drayton House (fourteenth to seventeenth century), Fawsley's Tudor hall of the Knightleys. Deene appears stately by the Willow Brook, Chalcombe Priory is set between elms and oaks at the place of a priory founded by Hugh Chalcombe in the twelfth century, the fragments at Holdenby remain from one of the largest houses ever built in England, Holmby House of many royal associations and at which in 1646 Cornet Joyce made his dramatic appearance with five hundred troopers to carry away a royal prisoner, Charles I. Of many such scenes visited I only have space to add a few words on three. Castle Ashby, true to its Elizabethan and seventeenth-century origins, is large and magnificent. Wide lawns, terraces, and fine flower gardens add to the lordly look. Avenues I walked along to Yardley Chase on a very hot day seemed miles long, as indeed they are. House within and without, park, everything, have the grand manner. Up aloft at the top of external walls there are curiosities also, texts lettered in stone, rarities occasionally favoured in the old days. The words of one read,

COSSINGTON. *One of Leicestershire's prettiest villages, with cottages and houses of white walls and thatched roofs. It gained fame as the home of Lord Kitchener's father.*

CHARNWOOD FOREST *near Beacon Hill. Tracts of old woodland stretch along the heights northward from Bradgate Park. Wide views are visible from Beacon, Bardon, and other hills.*

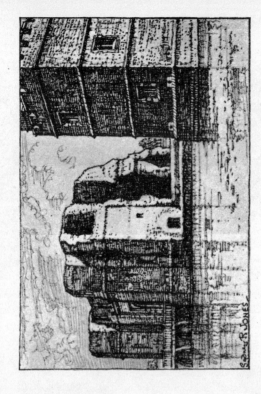

KIRBY MUXLOE CASTLE near Leicester. The gatehouse and west tower, remains of a moated manor-house built in 1474 by Lord Hastings, minister of Edward IV and beheaded by Richard III.

NOTTINGHAM. Castle on the rock and Trip to Jerusalem inn. First erected for William the Conqueror and dismantled after the Civil War, the castle was rebuilt by the Duke of Newcastle. The inn, claiming to be the oldest one in England, is supposed to have gained its name because Crusaders looked in on their way to Palestine.

"Except the Lord build the house, they labour in vain that build it." They were placed in position by the first Lord Compton who, when a bright young man, loved a beautiful girl but failed to be loved by her father, Sir John Spencer, a Lord Mayor of London burdened with fabulous wealth. Nothing daunted and disguised as a baker's boy youth carried off beauty in a bread-basket; they married and of course lived happily ever afterwards. The wealth duly arrived to labour not in vain. It built three sides of this mansion, provided texts, made formal gardens that Capability Brown swept away, and left for us to see a great big memorial of uncommon people who knew how to live in stately times. Ashby St. Ledgers manor-house (169) gives another impression of domesticity: how the Catesby family arranged themselves in a stone residence approached through a timbered gateway. But the old walls, lovely though they be, very likely have spasms of brooding and melancholy. Sir William we all know got a bad mention from Shakespeare in *Richard III*; he departed this life beheaded, and the portrait brass in the church chancel presents his features. Another Catesby, Robert, rode furiously from London on 5th November 1605, pulled up outside the village, sent a messenger to the house with an urgent call for Robert Winter who had just sat down to supper with Lady Catesby. The two men met. Catesby told Winter that Guy Fawkes was arrested, the Gunpowder Plot discovered. Both then rode away to meet death. Doom in other guise overtook Kirby Hall (169). Splendidly roomy and windowed in its prime days, the original hall built for Sir Humphrey Stafford appears to have been designed by that almost mythical Elizabethan figure John Thorpe, for he wrote on the plan, "Kerby whereof I layd the first stone 1570." During the next century Inigo Jones made the classical additions. Long deserted, forlorn among green fields, the extensive ruin is one of the most romantic places of the Midlands. In the silence I roamed through empty courtyards and banqueting hall, admired high-flung windows, pilasters, exquisite carvings in relief. Two tall bays at the south faced out like poops of galleons that sailed to fight the Armada. This empty shell from the high noon of a vanished time, a phantom of its true self yet mysterious in the afterglow of Elizabethan animation and the stately Renaissance, survives as an ancient monument. Saved from extinction it offers curious people wonderful things to look at while Corby's furnaces, smoking beyond the tree-tops, indicate how beautifully we have advanced since John Thorpe and Inigo Jones departed.

LEICESTERSHIRE TO THE LINCOLNSHIRE HILLS

Typical Midland scenery of the middling sort attracts us to Leicestershire and Nottinghamshire whither we now go forward to seek and enjoy medium heights commanding expansive distances, wide river vales, level landscapes in the flats, good grazing fields patterned with hedgerows, fertile farms, hunting country of the best, the wooded survivals of the old central forests with hoary trees in them to make anybody think of Robin Hood, merry men, and ever so long ago. The ancient Fosse Way, route of all ages, cuts a bold immemorial line. It leaves Watling Street at High Cross, enters the Roman corner of Leicester, bisects the county, crosses Nottinghamshire to the Roman station near Bingham and grim ruins of Newark Castle, leads on to the glory mounted on Lincoln's hill. A straight passage over the roots of antiquity is this one, brave and direct, with lots for the finding to the right and the left. Another line from south to north, from Lutterworth to Nottingham, offers further signs of various times, some of them grey and antique, others newer and obviously concerned with humanity's under-garments that are produced by the highly concentrated manufacturing in this long-established centre of the hosiery industry. Lough-borough, for instance, gave me the sight of a fine church with lofty arches and a grand tower containing John Taylor's bells; also in view were acres of modern red bricks and a high sign to locate the whereabouts of I. and R. Morley. Lutterworth from certain aspects to-day may not appear very thrilling, and the bulky church tower, a notable mark, had to be partly rebuilt after a collapse in the eighteenth century. Nevertheless church and town still might be called John Wycliffe's. Here from the pulpit thought to have been his own the first English Protestant raised storm clouds that thundered in the Reformation, then died in December 1384, rested for a while in the grave. Condemned as a heretic after death, his bones were dug up, burned, and finally the River Swift carried away the mortal ashes of Lutterworth's most illustrious townsman.

Foremost among these industrial towns stand Leicester and Nottingham. Both models in the pattern of up-to-date wellbeing and representing bigness and commercial prosperity developed on a fabric of historic antiquity, each city presents offerings to satisfy seekers who like to dwell on signs of progress backward rather than forward. Up from Watling Street the Fosse Way led me straight into the castled and Roman corner of Leicester, a most remarkable and compact area for descending through centuries of time. Tesselated pave-ments can be inspected below ground. Excavated remains of the forum and basilica are in full view near the place curiously called Holy Bones. St. Nicholas and St. Mary de Castro churches mount conspicuously from Saxon founda-tions on Roman sites. The Newarke gateway, originally an entrance to the enclosure of the Church of Annunciation and collegiate buildings, is well preserved from the fourteenth century. Pretty gardens by the riverside extend below scanty relics of the great stronghold once ruled by de Montfort and Dukes of Lancaster. This assortment left from bygone years made me think that Leicester, the progressive city of commerce, keeps in a small full space a wonderful record concerning its origins and story. Of course much else is visible for looking at and starting meditations. Only to enter the courtyard of the guildhall, first in possession of the Corpus Christi Guild, induces a quick change from a throbbing working day into fourteenth-century peace. Scevington House, now the county museum, contains a fascinating collection of objects used by local ancestors; as for Daniel Lambert's breeches and waistcoat of dreadful dimensions, these really do indicate the enormous size of Leicestershire's heavyweight at fifty-two stones. Pleasant grounds mark the place of the great abbey, now gone, to which Cardinal Wolsey went to die—and also to leave a name and a trademark for posterity's good underwear. At the castle, latterly in range of missiles from the "Pex" socks and stockings factory, Simon de Montfort forestalled modern politicians by thinking out a few ideas for a welfare state. And so on, and so on; there is ever so much more for which we ought to present votes of thanks to Leicester as we travel out of its past, feel grateful for it, and sit down to a good twentieth-century meal such as I discovered inside the *Grand Hotel*. Nottingham, progressive and forging ahead like Leicester, presents a good account of itself when seen from the precipitous rocky height where Peverel erected the first Norman Castle. The panoramic view directs over factories, chimney-pots, tall stacks, recent red and white buildings closely packed, the dome of a dignified new Council House, a sprinkling of roofs and grey towers in the low tones of age. Principally it is a prospect of a city very much alive, one eagerly reaching out to the brilliant future promised by guided missiles, chemical sprays, compact medical doses, and quick revolving wheels in place of old-fashioned blunderbusses, brimstone and treacle, and travel at four miles an hour. Looking over this scene it may be considered quite moody to think, as I did, of Norman and Plantagenet kings at this same spot, a city with a Royal Charter five hundred years ago, Charles I unfurling the Royal Standard on Standard Hill in 1642, early inhabitants who existed in holes hacked out of the sandstone rock, miles of lace manufactured when bustles and aspidistras were fashionable. I have to confess that relics of the old strain attracted me most at this thriving centre of action. Drury Hill, St. Peter's Churchside, Trinity Walk, and Castle Street are some of the names of ways still with bits of picturesqueness left from a good many years ago. Three or four houses, quite little masterpieces of the 1780 period, can be spotted among good Georgian effects. Abel Collins in 1709 bequeathed the jolly group of almshouses with an elaborate arms panel over the arched entrance. Ancient inns include the *Flying Horse* on the top of huge rock cellars in the Poultry, a house of call four hundred years ago; and the *Trip to Jerusalem* (190), also with caverns in the rock below the Castle, claiming to have gained its name because Crusaders, bound for Palestine, called in for drinks. The wooden stalls, buying, selling, and the fun of the Goose Fair I remember in the huge market-place, all were swept away to make the civic square clean, tidy, flowered, and respectable. Castles number one, two, and three departed, leaving not many traces visible. Number four, erected in robust classic style for the Duke of Newcastle onward from 1679, was burned by the mob of rioters in 1831. Now it lives again, doing good deeds. It makes the registered trade mark No. 13,645 for John Player's Castle tobacco. It serves for a picture gallery and museum to show people of a machine age the lovely things produced by earlier generations who cunningly used their hands. Once more I mention the view from this rock because it is so wide and comprehensive. You look over the city's brightness and dullness towards open country, fields, trees, Trent valley, Charnwood and Sherwood Forests, the immense and grandiose Elizabethan pile of Wollaton Hall near at hand, Belvoir Castle visible far away on clear days. Into these fresh lands and away from man's industrialism we next continue our travels.

East of the Fosse Way in Leicestershire takes us to hill and stone country, a continuation of the Northamptonshire uplands similar in heights and sights to those indicated on my previous pages. Village houses and cottages of stone add light colourings to green hillslopes and valleys, as may be seen at Great Bowden (184), Hallaton, and elsewhere above the basins of the Welland and Soar rivers. The local town, Market Harborough of foxhunting fame, also bids for hunting to find the church with a high tower and beautiful broach spire, the timbered grammar school standing below, and a show of superb ironwork, so wonderful that it urged me inside the *Three Swans*, an inn known to sixteenth-century callers and used for headquarters both by Cavaliers and Roundheads during the Civil War. Hereabout good old families built good old homes in the good old styles. Their works and names remembered, evident in many places, led me to Nevil Holt erected by the Nevils, Skeffington Hall and Skeffington memorials in the church high on the hill, Stapleford Hall curiously shaped and carved. Three halls lie close together near Hungerton. Ingarsby, of the fifteenth century, occupies a Roman site; Baggrave, with a Queen Anne front and older back, developed from the spoils of dissolved monasteries and Wolsey signed the title deed, still preserved; Quenby stands for an early seventeenth-century prize, a fine achievement in brickwork and stone, but alas, the elaborate wrought-iron gates used by departed owners now only serve for a showpiece at the county museum in Leicester.

Down in the River Wreak valley the splendid Perpendicular finish of a glorious church, a cathedral in miniature, calls us to Melton Mowbray, the seat of powerful Mowbray barons ages before it became the Utopia of huntingmen and eaters of pork pies and Stilton cheese. Beyond the wide vale, the willows, aspen trees and open greenery, the Leicestershire Wolds trace curved wooded outlines from Six Hills on the Fosse Way to Belvoir. High up the near and distant scenes rejoice the heart. You look to irregular heights in

NEWARK. *Ruined and grim on the river bank stands the castle in which King John died. Attractions in this pleasant town include St. Mary's church with a lofty interior, the big market square, ancient inns, and the Georgian publishing house for Lord Byron's first poems.*

GROVE PARK *and view to Sherwood Forest. The hillside park with fine old trees recently has been spoiled and denuded of timber.*

SOUTHWELL, *a small town with a large church, now the cathedral of Nottinghamshire. Much of the minster remains as rebuilt in the Norman style during the twelfth century. Reconstruction from 1234 to 1300 brought the choir and chapter house, masterly achievements in Gothic design elaborated with wonderful naturalistic stone carving.*

Charnwood Forest, over miles of Nottinghamshire, down into the rich Vale of Belvoir; on a bright day I caught the gleam of towers shining far away at Lincoln. Quiet lanes, grassy slopes, and woodland solitudes all invite. It is not surprising that a poetically rural George Crabbe confessed to "spinning flimsy verses" in the calm and green shades yet to be enjoyed around Stathern and Goadby Marwood. Place-names frequently ending in "by"—Wartnaby, Ab-Kettleby, Stonesby, and Saltby for example—indicate where Danes settled. Stone and timbered cottages lived in by their successors are not so conspicuous as the more recent buildings in red bricks, tiles and slates; the quality of the latter prove that in this particular district and generally over Leicestershire and Nottinghamshire the art of village building did not flourish at its best. On the northern tip of the Wolds the towers, battlements, and pinnacles of Belvoir Castle rear proudly in the ducal manner. At the opposite end of the hills I found Ragdale Hall (184) sitting rather forlorn. Hens and chickens greeted me on the front grounds once trodden by the valiant Shirleys, created Earls of Ferrers and allied by marriage to Queen Elizabeth's Earl of Essex. Well and truly did they build their Tudor and Elizabethan home, its wall textures, gables, clustered chimneys, the tall bay windows and the porch brave with armorial shields. Neglected as I last saw the house it was lovely still, settled down in old age above the squat and ancient church—an ideal place to lure anybody with a fancy for brooding over memories, great names, faded beauty, ghosts, and the real meaning of words displayed on a signboard, "This property for sale."

My hours at Ragdale being ended like those of the Shirleys, I walked down to see Hoby village and spired church, then tramped onward under the hot sun of a July day. Presently the driver of a car stopped and offered me a lift.

"Which way are you going?" I asked.

"Anywhere you like," he answered.

The good Samaritan added that he was a doctor bound for nowhere in particular, and when I explained my likings and cranks for places and things he said,

"You really must see Cossington. It's the prettiest village in Leicestershire."

We went on, passed through Thrussington pleasant by the River Wreak, mounted the hill commanding a big view over the Soar valley and Charnwood, crossed the Fosse Way, arrived in Cossington, visited the house in which Lord Kitchener's father died, found the good old church, thatched cottages, white walls—and all this happened through one of those many acts of kindness that make the whole world kin. The impression on page 189 illustrates how attractive the village appeared to me.

The half of Leicestershire in which Cossington lies, namely to the west of the Fosse Way, particularly directs our wanderings to the rugged and high forest grounds of Charnwood. Away from Mountsorrel and Hugo Meynell's foxhunting headquarters at Quorndon Hall, and stretching north to south from Grace Dieu priory ruins to Bradgate, the district stands out like an island peculiar in its geology and visible effects. Bold ridges, sharp heights, exposed rocks, thick woodlands, and bracken (189) combine in lines, shapes, and colours of picturesque and romantic landscape. Top points at Beacon, Bardon, and other hills lead the eye over miles and miles to distant horizons. One choice little region within easy reach of Leicester contains Bradgate Park and the ruins of Lady Jane Grey's home, Newtown Linford village lying so snug and peaceful that I could not resist sketching it, Groby old hall lived in by Elizabeth Woodville, and Groby pool, a dreamy spot for watching bird life and sunsets reflected on the water. The near grass and hedge country presents Kirby Muxloe castle (190), a very special example of a moated and fortified manor-house built in brickwork about 1460 and now admirably cared for after years of neglect. It was erected for the powerful minister of Edward IV, Lord Hastings, to whom Richard of Gloucester spitefully said, "I will not dine until they have brought me your head"; consequently My Lord quickly departed this life at the Tower of London. Near Market Bosworth in the same Leicestershire direction Richard himself completed his mission on earth; the name of the town immediately suggests a place and a date for one king going down and another king rising up, the end of the Plantagenets and the beginning of the Tudors. The quiet streets did not offer me particular excitements nor yet the dullness experienced by young Samuel Johnson when he taught at the old grammar school. An oak bench in the church porch provided me with a subject for my sketch-book until most of the woodwork was obscured by an ancient fat man who sat down upon it. He entertained me with a vivid account of his rheumatics, talked about the battle as if he had been there on 23rd August 1485, and eventually told me how to find Bosworth Field on which Richard III lost his crown in a hawthorn bush. A walk of two miles led me to the historic ground between Sutton Cheney and Shenton, the actual place of the shouting,

A horse! a horse! my kingdom for a horse!

and where Richmond's five thousand men quickly completed their job against the King's ten thousand. In sight was the slope used for crowning Henry VII near Stoke Golding. Remembering my own soldiering on the Somme and in Flanders this battlefield did not seem to me very impressive—just one of those little scenes of warfare for settling differences in the old-time style when people who wanted to fight buckled on their armour, killed each other if they could, managed to change courses of history in a speedy, compact and respectable way. And I thought how nice it might be just now, how much more comfortable for most human beings, if only the quarrellers all the world over scrapped among themselves, followed the example set by Richmond and Stanley the victors, Richard, Norfolk, Ferrers, and Brackenbury the casualties, and the small companies of men that fought and fell on Bosworth Field because they did not happen to agree on explosive matters.

Travelling northward our eyes really must be on the alert for the Staunton Harold group of park, empty Georgian mansion, and a unique Cromwellian church founded in 1653 by Sir Robert Shirley. Entering the next county we reach the pleasant Nottinghamshire landscapes, the broad Trent vale, a long belt green with trees directing to Sherwood Forest and the Dukeries, the central line of hills, the flat expanses spreading for miles to the Isle of Axholme and Lincoln Cliff range. Many admirers of England's natural grandeur know the fascination of Sherwood Forest scenery, hardly to be matched elsewhere in the land. Antique oak monarchs, glades, avenues, and the wild beauty of Birklands and Bilhagh may at any moment start gallant thoughts on Robin Hood's semi-mythical adventures or revive a few pages in *Ivanhoe*. The ducal magnificence of mansions and splendid domains adds to the riot of spectacular effect at Welbeck, Osberton, Clumber, Thoresby, Rufford, the Byrons' Newstead Abbey, but thinkers given to facing the facts well may wonder if Ministries Super-tax, and coalmining will leave any future aristocratic meanings to these names.

The central hilly plateau, running southward from Gringley to Nottingham, specializes in many viewpoints for tremendous panoramas. Standing on the encampment at Gringley Beacon I surveyed vast prospects to the Dukeries, Yorkshire, Lincolnshire and its cathedral visible beyond the Trent winding through limitless miles of flat land richly variegated with meadows, cornfields, village church towers and spires. From Retford, where the cruciform church broods near the noise of the Great North Road, a short walk took me to Grove, a small place finely situated for more of these distant views; the condition of the hall in a bad way, gardens overgrown, trees prostrate in the park formerly noted for beauty (195), the Harcourt Vernons gone, told a now familiar story of people who do not fare very well in a welfare state. Other villages, usually true to the average style of make-up and scattered far and wide over the Trent borders and flat country, might lead us to Cotgrave's needle spire, white gables at Carlton, to Marnham near the river crossed by Edward I to reach his dying Eleanor at Harby manor-house. Two towns in the vale impart the spell of history's meaning and beauty. Newark Castle (195), ruined and grim since King John died there, frowns near bright old inns and houses, St. Mary's lofty church, the animated market-place in which loyal inhabitants fought Parliament men during the Civil War. At the *Saracen's Head*, Southwell, an oaken establishment royally patronized by Edward I, Edward III, James I, and Charles I, the comforts enjoyed inside the inn prepared me for admiring the cathedral's naturalistic stone carving (196), some of the most wonderful ever done in medieval England.

Trent vale at the east meets the Lincoln Edge, with the Roman road on the top running imperially direct to the Humber. Village after village below the Ermine Street, the Carltons (201), Aisthorpe, and Fillingham with a castle (201) to Kirton church tower, border the edge of flat expanses stretching far away. Beyond Brigg and again to the east the Lincolnshire Wolds break the skylines. Soft curves of chalk hills mount to elevations for more views, views over to Louth spire, down to the Fens, away to Lincoln. Round about are cheerful market towns, Caistor, Market Rasen (202), Roman Horncastle for remembering chapters on the horse fair in *Romany Rye*. Out at Somersby (202), Tennyson's birthplace, the Lymn stream still sings as the poet thought,

> For men may come and men may go,
> But I go on for ever.

At last, with this chapter's pages already full, we reach the point so often seen in the distance, Lincoln, the city of my own happy days, a meeting-place of centuries tracing far back to the mists of unrecorded time; a wonderful city of dreams crowned with beauty made by man to the glory of God (182-3), set high above the noise, factories, and smoky activities of to-day—and really one most dreadful sign of the present is the red light by night that must shine at the tip of the Cathedral's masonry to warn aeroplanes not to knock it down! Seen either from the low town or more distantly from the surrounding levels, the Cathedral presents a grand spectacle, one of our country's finest, majestic both in situation and architectural splendour. Near inspection reveals phases of magnificence hardly to be matched at any other English cathedral. Below three towers on the hilltop sights memorable and famous lead to the west front raised above tall Norman arches, the sculptured south-eastern porch, the chapter-house of 1220-1235, thirteenth-century cloisters on the north side completed with the arcade and library of Sir Christopher Wren's design. Interior vistas of column, arch, tracery, and vault are superb; they open out across the north and south transepts to the Dean's Eye and Bishop's Eye, in the long perspective from west to east terminated by the Angel Choir, of human works none more lovely. With no further descriptive words I must leave my readers to their own observations and enjoyment as they find the great scenes around the holy hill; castle gatehouse and walled enclosure; the Stonebow and Roman Newport Arch; Norman Jews' houses on Steep Hill and the Strait; High Bridge mounted with timbered buildings over Glory Hole; Georgian and other homes of many periods; local views pictured by Girtin, de Wint, and Callow in the art gallery; upward prospects from the River Witham; the *White Hart* for sitting down, eating, and sleeping gloriously; and all the magnificence and interest of a storied past that make Lincoln fascinating, a jewel of high rank among England's ancient cities.

FILLINGHAM. *A Georgian "castle" approached by fine avenues in a park enclosed by an eighteenth-century squire. The village church has greater fame for associations with John Wycliffe, rector from 1361 to 1368.*

LOWER TRENT VALE *from the Cliff above South Carlton. Viewpoints on Lincoln Cliff Hills, and Nottinghamshire uplands command wide panoramas over flat country and the river dividing the two counties.*

MARKET RASEN. *One of the cheerful market towns in the region of the Lincolnshire Wolds. Others are Brigg, Caistor, Horncastle, and Spilsby.*

LINCOLNSHIRE WOLDS *near Somersby, Tennyson's birthplace.*

5. NORTH TO THE BORDER

CENTRAL AND EAST YORKSHIRE, DURHAM, NORTHUMBERLAND

The Plain of York, generally level, is bounded southward by the smooth chalk uplands of the East Riding Wolds. Lias and oolite in the North Riding border the Plain with fine elevations of the Hambleton and Cleveland Hills. High moors extend to the north-east, divided by Bilsdale, Rosedale, and a succession of remote valleys. These lead to the stretch of bold headlands and rocky bays along the north Yorkshire coastline. Pennines to the west of Durham county give the wildness of limestone mountain scenery. Moorlands and fells, austere and lonely, continue to the Cheviot range. Down from the heights and the dales famous Yorkshire streams feed the Ouse bound for the Humber. Valleys of the Tees, North and South Tyne, the Coquet, and other rivers charm with their loveliness of steep banks, wooded borders, currents hastening over rocky beds. Northern history in the ways of peace,

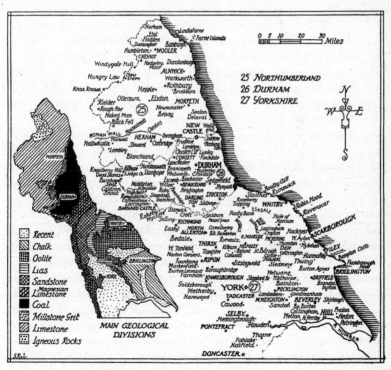

25 NORTHUMBERLAND
26 DURHAM
27 YORKSHIRE

Recent
Chalk
Oolite
Lias
Sandstone
Magnesian Limestone
Coal
Millstone Grit
Limestone
Igneous Rocks

MAIN GEOLOGICAL DIVISIONS

religion, war, robbery and industrialism are plainly illustrated by the buildings and appendages on the face of this area. Signs of many times include Hadrian's Wall, Roman roads and relics, the chain of monastic ruins, castles by the score, Northumbrian peel towers, lone mountain farmsteads, pretty riverside villages, and country towns. Mining, large concentrations of manufacture, grimy towns, and dull suburbs show how wonderfully the wheels of progress have spoiled the heritage of natural beauty.

PLAIN OF YORK TO THE COAST

The River Ouse, widened by many tributaries from the Pennine foothills, runs through the Plain of York, finally to meet the end of the Trent and swell the Humber. About 25 miles from this watery meeting-place thrives the grand old city of York, settled at the river's banks and centrally placed on the rich lands of the Plain.

The metropolis of northern England for centuries, now a rich source of antiquities, history, mellow beauty, and fascination, needs far more than the scanty pages at my disposal to tell its story and reveal its charms. For in York you can feel that here is a city in possession of everything, that is all the things that generally are thought worth having or thinking about. The background, old and weathered, is livened with the new look of a thriving present. Public buildings, places and open spaces, first-class shops and others of all sorts, factories, acres of railway station and lines below medieval walls, suburbs reaching out, a famous racecourse for the celebrated Gimcrack Stakes, and a horrid electric affair belching smoke in sight of the cathedral's central glory all make known that life, action, and progress throb in the ancient city.

If excursions from the present into the past happen to appeal, the visible reminders of bygone ages promise exciting travels down the avenues of Time. Roman foundations and the base of the Multangular Tower dig down to *Eboracum*, the city's beginning. Clifford's Tower of *circa* 1310 gleams white on the castle mound thrown up by William the Conqueror. No city has a more warlike appearance, here made by medieval walls, battlements, bars, gateways, and barbican, the most impressive in all the land. The Minster, very splendid and unmatched for early window glass, offers wonder piled on wonder at England's largest medieval cathedral (208-9). Thirteenth-century ruins of St. Mary's Abbey, still lovely, survive from the rich monastery first begun with the foundation stone laid by William Rufus. A score of parish churches lead from treasure to treasure. Their stone features, towers, spires, and the lantern of All Saints, Pavement, rise serenely over busy streets. Others need finding, are tucked away like Holy Trinity, a most captivating conglomeration of quaintness and periods hidden in quiet behind Goodramgate. In this shrine, at All Saints, at St. Michael,

Spurriergate, and at other churches the old glass supplements that in the cathedral for presenting the most complete and brilliant spectacles of medieval colouring in the British Isles.

Streets, byways, and alleys of the antique stamp, narrow, winding, closely packed together, are not better represented anywhere. Standing on lines planned by Romans, Danes, and townsfolk of the Middle Ages, Petergate, Stonegate, Whip-Ma-Whop-Ma-Gate, and many more thoroughfares keep the Danish name of "gate" meaning road. Twists and turnings, gabled façades and picturesque frontages substantially help in bringing to the mind's eye pictures of the city's doings and the people in times long gone. Particularly after nice dinners at the good hotels—I have just enjoyed one cooked by a former college chef—all sorts of shadowy forms can be imagined stealing along these arteries of the centuries. Look here, watch there! Fancy re-creates the traders and money-lenders of the Jewry (hundreds died in the great massacre of 1190), the soldiers off to fight the Scots and to battle at Towton on Palm Sunday, 1461. Stirring again are the Merchant Adventurers, Taylors, and members of the many guilds bound for their halls; the glass painters and glaziers who lived in Stonegate. Scenes and actual places revive memories of the York Mysteries acted on wagons at a dozen stations in the streets; rebels brought to be hanged or beheaded, Archbishop Scrope, Robert Aske, the Earl of Northumberland; young Guy Fawkes, probably yelling for gunpowder, piloted to baptism at St. Michael-le-Belfrey; Parliamentarians clattering in to complete the surrender after the battle of Marston Moor; My Lord Burlington viewing My Lord Mayor's new Mansion House (207), the Assembly Rooms, and proudly claiming the designs of both. Marks and graces, visible on every hand, respond to the mood of the old days and enhance the present. But alas, Hitler's men in 1942 blew up the fifteenth-century Guildhall, its oak pillars and fine roof.

Warring by another foreign power made the city instead of destroying it. A long time ago advancing Romans had trouble with the northern natives, the British tribe of Brigantes, who threatened their flank from the earthen ramparts now existing at Stanwick and Forcett between Richmond and the River Tees. The tribesmen skirmished and revolted. Eventually they settled down, but not before Caractacus, their refugee from Wales, had been betrayed into the hands of the Romans by the queen of the Brigantes. Though the tribe ceased fighting and kept their place the words of Tacitus suggest that the Romans thought prevention better than cure for further trouble. Consequently, in 71 A.D., they laid out the first fortress of York strengthened with earthen mounds and defences. Walls and buildings of stone followed. The *prætorium* of the military head-quarters occupied the site of the present cathedral, the *castrum* was augmented by quarters for a large civilian population, and *Eboracum* grew fine on the Roman pattern. To the splendid capital of their British province the Emperors came.

There the great Septimus Severus and Constantius, "the pale," both died. Early in the fifth century the symbols of imperial conquest and power, "that other Rome," began to crumble and also passed away. Now foundations of the *præ- torium* columns lie buried under the cathedral crypt; pavings marked by chariot wheels are hidden underneath Stonegate; collections in the Museum vividly illustrate the stirring years of rule departed. Saxons settled on the ruins, thrived, established an illustrious school of learning, erected a wooden church that was followed by two stone ones, prototypes of the Minster. Danes came in, stormed, pillaged, traded, left names for the streets. William the Conqueror arrived, destroyed with fire and sword, piled up castle mounds and fortifica- tions, refounded the city, gave Thomas of Bayeux the job to begin a new metropolitan cathedral on the Saxon church foundations at the spot where Paulinus had won King Edwin of Northumbria to Christianity in 627 A.D. Demolitions and reconstructions brought a fourth stone church, finally a fifth, the present Minster, completed during about 300 years from the early 1200's.

Phœnix-like the medieval city rose from the ashes of war and destruction. Its large population, then exceeded only by London among English cities, prospered with weaving and commerce, and the merchants' ships sailed down the Ouse to trade with the Baltic towns. Two monasteries, friaries, many hospitals, half a hundred churches, elevated workaday life with an air of piety, benevolence, and beauty; in part these works remain to tell their tales. Century by century the streets gained their looks, civic, domestic, picturesque. Early buildings, others in the fashions of Tudor, Elizabethan, and Stuart times yet stand, keep their flavour, mark the passage of years. Their frontages, backs, interiors, features, and details are visible at scores of points, from street pavements, down lanes and alleys, at the guild halls of St. Anthony, the Merchant Advent- urers, the Merchant Taylors. Timbers and gables overhang the narrow roadway (six feet wide) in the Shambles, a street noted in Domesday Book. Later devel- opments on medieval beginnings are shown at the King's Manor (with a carved doorway (207) used by James I and Charles I), at the Treasurer's House, and St. William's College, lovely round a courtyard. When Yorkists, Lan- castrians, Royalists and Roundheads had ceased to fight and wars and rebellions were ended, red heels tip-tapped on the pavements. Wigs and brocades appeared at classic doorways and tall sash windows of fine stately houses erected for the loyal subjects of William and Mary, Anne, and the Georges. Dignified buildings amply tell of the life, work, amusement, sporting (and crime) in those times, enlivened with the presence of Lords Burlington and Rockingham, Dick Turpin, John Carr, Tobias Smollett, David Garrick, and a host of celebrities. Thoughts of that age and its people spontaneously come to mind with sights seen at the Mansion House (1725) and Assembly Rooms (1730), both doubt- fully attributed to Lord Burlington's invention, at the remains of the first race-

Bootham Bar

Monk Bar

Walmgate Bar & Barbican

Micklegate Bar

17th. cent. doorhead King's Manor

Regency shop-front, Stonegate

Mansion House 1725–6

YORK. *Medieval and later details.*

YORK. *England's largest medieval cathedral built within the walled city for the northern archiepiscopal see. This south-west elevation includes the elaborate fourteenth-century west front, the high nave (1291–1338), the great central tower (early fifteenth-century), the thirteenth-century transept with famous rose window, the Perpendicular eastern limb, and many windows which contain unique early painted glass. Stonegate, the Roman line of Petergate, and buildings closely packed in ancient streets, gates, and alleys occupy the foreground.*

Sydney R. Jones
York

KNARESBOROUGH. *A hilly town in the West Riding and a place for views. Here the River Nidd, down from the Dales, winds to the Plain. On a rock above the stream are the ruins of the historic castle, begun by the Normans and knocked down by Cromwellians.*

course stand (in the paddock) designed by Carr in 1754, Carr's Assize Courts of 1777, and the good elevations at the old prison, Dick Turpin's last lodging. Eighteenth-century and early nineteenth-century years are further suggested by distinctive houses in Lendal and Duncombe Place, white facings and iron balconies in St. Leonard's Place, Georgian and Regency shop fronts (207), and numerous variations of the period's charming architecture.

Through all the changes in York's long development the defensive earthworks and the city walls continued influential and marked boundaries. First put up by Emperor Severus, later knocked down, mended, and rebuilt with stone in the Middle Ages, the walls stand much as they did when the Wars of the Roses were fought. To walk more than two miles along the battlemented parapets from bar to bar (207) past gateways, posterns, barbican, and portcullis is a wonderful experience, a progress unique in England; so enthralling I found it when evening shades were descending, only my rescue by a policeman saved me from being locked in for the night near Bootham Bar. Standing on foundations laid more than 1,700 years ago you look over the pack of streets, crowded buildings, towers and spires, superb vistas of the cathedral, the highways and byways of centuries, a square mile of petrified history. Not only along the walls from Monk Bar to Bootham Bar, but sooner or later all the city's ways lead to the crowning glory of York affectionately called by the inhabitants The Minster.

Nothing new can be pictured or told of the cathedral and metropolitan church of St. Peter in York, of size immense, vast in scale, progressively developed during the great reconstruction carried on from 1227 until the fifteenth century. Now shining and serving gloriously the lofty towers, crocketed skylines, rich façades, arcades, and traceries preserve the heritage from the prime times of spiritual faith when devotion, function, and art united to make beautiful rhyme with stone and handiwork while the English genius ripened to golden harvest. Here are the memorable sights, the famous scenes—England's largest central tower schemed in the grand simplicity of Perpendicular design; the exuberant but finely balanced composition of the fourteenth-century west front topped with fifteenth-century towers; soaring heights inside the broad nave and the transepts; the long length ended with magnificent single windows at the west and the east; rare impressions under the tower at the crossing; transepts terminated by tall lancets of the Five Sisters and lovely lights of the rose; and most precious of all, 120 painted windows, the wonderful glass of six centuries with John Thornton's masterpiece of 1408 at the east, the greatest area of medieval painted glass in the world.

The cathedral's wonders, their visible stateliness, and the purposes for which they were created pre-eminently belong to the services at this sacred place where the daily offices have been sung for more than a thousand years. The bells mark the quarters, chime the hours, burst into melodies played on twelve bells, call for Matins, Eucharist, and Evensong; considerate for near night sleepers they kindly retire at a respectable evening hour to wake up again at 7 o'clock in the morning. Thus called at my room in the *Dean Court* hotel opposite, first to rise for breakfast, later to consume luncheon, I crossed the forecourt of the west front as the bells rang for Evensong on an August afternoon. There, most unexpectedly, I met my old master, my early mentor in architecture, likewise going to the service. We entered the nave, threaded through crowds of sight-seers, passed the cords stretched to exclude them from the choir, and occupied seats in the stalls immediately behind the singers. Prayer and praise proceeded, "Dearly beloved brethren," Psalms, *Magnificat, Nunc dimittis*. The organ pealed. A full-voiced choir sang the anthem, "The Lord is King," and the blind tenor in front of us, reading Braille notation, sent heavenward his sweet offering of song. Words and music blended with the harmony of clustered columns, soaring arches,

> And storied Windows richly dight,
> Casting a dimm religious light.

Rays of the western sun shone from the central lantern above William Hynd-ley's splendid stone screen, a myriad colours glittered from John Thornton's exquisite glass in the great east window. Organ notes mounted in final cadences —then stopped. Sounds of one more service echoed and faded away to the ancient shades.

Leaving the choir we found the transepts and nave still crowded with sight-seers wandering round and looking about. Among them were numerous ladies clothed in little more than shorts and brassieres.

"They seem a bit queer," I remarked to my mentor. "Not quite *comme il faut* in a holy of holies?"

"New times, new manners, society classless and naked," he answered, "*Si monumentum et cetera*. Look around at the poems in stone and glass. Couldn't have happened when they were made. Archbishop de Gray or fighting William Zouche would have made the girls put on their skirts."

We departed from the cathedral, admired lovely old buildings in the streets, noticed plateglass shopfronts, cinemas, blow-ups by Germans, the smoking electric affair. But on wishing each other good-bye we sincerely hoped that for a few more years at least the old city would continue beautiful and capti-vating as we had found it.

From York city we next expand over the Plain of York to find it resembling a huge basin with long sides but no ends. Northward it sweeps to the valley of the Tees, southward to the mouth of the Ouse and drained marshlands in the region of Thorne Waste and Hatfield Moors. The eastern sides of its length are contained by the Wolds, Hambleton and Cleveland Hills, in the west by heights rising towards the dales. Proper English vale scenery belongs to this Plain. It is expansive, generally level, but the hills, never far away and often in view, excite the exhilarating thought that if you may not be particularly exalted on the levels you soon can accelerate, mount up, look down over wide panoramas. On the flat the Plain can be seen in total by road or rail. Jump into a train at Doncaster, travel to Northallerton along the straightest runs of railway lines imaginable, and the carriage windows frame pictures to tell just what the Plain scenery is like. Two big roads will serve just as well. One, the Great North Road, now proudly designated A.1, leads straight on the bold Roman traverse from Doncaster to Scotch Corner. The other is the lower road travelled by Dick Turpin (according to Ainsworth) through Thorne, Selby, York, and if the highwayman had not swung on the York gallows in 1739 he might have continued onward for Easingwold, Thirsk, and Northallerton to inspect the amenities of the Plain and prospects for robbery.

Of the Plain scenery I have no exciting or new disclosures to tell. The landscapes belong to the flat sort, extended over broad hedgerow country developed for prosperous agriculture in big fields of pasture and arable land. Trees, woods, and parks, nicely interspersed, add richness, diversity, and colour. The original surface character of dense forest is suggested here and there by sprinklings of greenery and copse, and names survive to recall the Forest of Galtrees, a horrible place to get lost in a long time ago; for that reason the York church of All Saints, Pavement, kept a beacon night-light burning on the lantern tower to guide forlorn wayfarers and wandering medieval lovers. Bumps, not very conspicuous, rise to minor altitudes, and round the lowly Howardian Hills the Plain stretches to the Vale of Pickering. More flat country, separated from the Plain by the Wolds, comprises the coastal district of Holderness; here the famous group of churches, rather than the heights of trees, make the soaring landscape lines of most distinction. Waterways are many. Varied, placid, and winding stream scenes consequently abound, for the rivers include lower reaches of the Wharfe, Nidd, Ure, and Swale, long even courses of the Derwent, the Ouse meandering to the Humber. Interesting and historic villages, Stamford Bridge where King Harold fought his last victory before meeting William of Normandy, Topcliffe on the Swale (234), West Tanfield on the Ure, and many others gain in pleasantness from charming riverside situations. Certain districts need not detain us for the kind of sightseeing we seek. Pontefract for instance—the deathly Pomfret for Richard II with its mighty castle blown to bits by Cromwellians—is perilously marooned at the south of the Plain amidst the scenic features of concentrated industrialism.

Country villages of the Plain and the lowlands, pretty enough in their contents and placings, clearly inform us that we have reached the North. If you like to ponder on such matters they demonstrate that not only mileage but an indefinable distance separates us from the climatic, physical, and mental influences which brought to the villages of the Midlands and South their strongly marked characteristics in traditional building. The prevalent brickwork of subdued colours, the whitewashed walls, pantile roofs, the manner of usage in local materials, each indicate that practical demand and function rather than niceties in detail, surface pattern, and style determined the appearance of these old Yorkshire village homes. Where the narrow fringe of magnesian limestone extends from the River Aire through Tadcaster, Knaresborough (210), Farnham, Burton Leonard, Ripon, and Bedale to the Tees, and the local stone served for building, I found it handled in this same northern way, the chief aims having been for use, strength, and long service. Among the generally pleasant and often lovely environments of the Plain and the lowlands we therefore may not expect to discover regional village architecture exceptionally abundant in the quality nowadays popularly called charm. Outstanding villages however disprove the rule. One, Bishop Burton near Beverley, whitewashed, pantiled, snug round two ponds and two greens, justly has its ardent admirers. My adventurous readers will not be disappointed in finding other choice quarters to attract them. Coxwold would serve very well. I particularly recall reaching it from Byland Abbey, ruined, solitary, quiet. The sun began to set behind the fine octagonal tower of Coxwold church, lighting up cottages and houses on the grass-lined street, telling the time for natives to go up the hill to the Fauconberg Arms facing the living relic of a great old elm. Here was a charming picture, ample in delight. As the evening glow brightened the gables and massive chimneys (222) of Shandy Hall—well, it must have shone a literary light for Laurence Sterne, who finished the last volumes of *Tristram Shandy* inside! Villages naturally introduce the villagers, the sturdy types that we all respect, downright, sometimes short in speech, but with trusty and warm hearts. One of them asked me what I could find to waste my time in drawing at Great Barugh (234); when I said pantile roofs he seemed amazed, responded with peculiar expressions that sounded like " fer thissel," "nivver want nowt," and other enigmas beyond the scope of my limited intelligence. But that happened in 1926, since which date no doubt instruction in the English language by the B.B.C. has penetrated to remote places.

So large and important a county as Yorkshire clearly needed lots of quarters to accommodate ancestral squires, big folk, and prosperous arrivers. While the face of the land developed in the customary English way, was cleared, tidied, and the manorial open fields, common pastures, and wastes were followed by enclosures, parks, stately domains, and landscapes of chequered fields, the Bigods of Settrington, Nortons of Norton Conyers, the Colvilles, Marken-

Sydney R. Jones
Ripon Nov 1950

RIPON. *Seat of a bishopric in 678 A.D., the cathedral is notable for a Saxon crypt, mixed architectural styles, and the choir's fifteenth-century woodwork. In the adjacent large market-place the Wakeman keeps the immemorial custom of blowing the horn every evening, and the town hall displays the motto, "Except ye Lord keep ye Cittie ye Wakeman waketh in vain."*

TWO FAMOUS YORKSHIRE ABBEYS.

RIEVAULX (above). *Cistercians settled in 1131 below the moors in Ryedale. During the thirteenth century they enhanced their perfect natural surroundings with Early English architecture.*

FOUNTAINS. *Extensive and celebrated, the monastic ruins grace a lovely glen of the River Skell near Ripon. Architectural feats include the Norman buildings, a vaulted cellarium, the Early English Chapel of the Nine Altars, the great tower erected in Tudor years.*

216

fields, Ellerkers, Fairfaxes, Belasyses, and scores of families settled down. They built their homes, enlarged old inheritances, from time to time refurbished exteriors and interiors to be in the fashion, planted gardens and avenues as well, and the ladies I quite expect admired males, the peacocks, strutting across smooth lawns. As sundial shadows marked fleeting hours of days, years, and centuries the country homes accumulated. Made with the proper look of northern stone and brick in the domestic building styles bred through medieval, Tudor, and Elizabethan times down to the late Georgian periods, they displayed low gables and heavy mullions of traditional type, mixed Jacobean and Stuart effects, trim outsides with sash windows and chaste doorways of the polite classic manner. Large or medium sized, all in their several patterns denoted the presence of lordly and squirely personages, and the aristocratic and benevolent air about these high places whiffled to neighbouring dependent villages. The above particulars, which everybody knows, are only mentioned now because past people of fame and consequence gave to Yorkshire a generous supply of satisfying sights at castles, great houses, halls, and manor-houses. If my space permitted they might detain us at Markenfield (fortified and moated), Cawood gatehouse (relic of the palace where Wolsey was arrested for high treason), Burton Agnes (1601–3), Goldsborough (1620), Newburgh (with Cromwell's body possibly inside), Gilling (shorn of its magnificent Elizabethan great chamber), Hovingham (George III), Forcett (near towering ramparts constructed by British Brigantes for their stand against the Romans), and at houses in dozens of more pretty places. Vanbrugh's lordly frontage of Castle Howard, and Harewood designed by Carr of York and decorated by Robert Adam, present two good leaders in the group of splendid mansions. Imposing or comfortably homely, many of these reminders of past times await their doom from the twentieth-century revolution, just as the earlier strongholds of feudalism awaited doom from decay or the gunpowder of Cromwell's revolution that shot destruction to the castles of Richmond, Knaresborough, Helmsley, Pickering, Scarborough. At present Yorkshire's survivors from systems now gone remain in plenty for us to discover and look at, visible either as well-kept homes full of treasures, farmhouses, schools, quarters for strange inmates that the original owners would not recognize, or deserted and ruined. They offer material for makers of pictures, students of architecture and craftwork, and their appeal is enormous for sentimental souls given to ruminating on the pomposity, bloodshed, roguery, pedigrees, fellowship, or the quiet of the good old days when the Gascoignes and the Huttons, the Smiths and the Browns went up and down in the world.

And of the good old days the Plain of York keeps good old towns to tell their stories. They stand in a western line from Richmond to Pontefract, more to the east from Northallerton to Selby. Among them I call Richmond the plum. Grey and rugged on the crag where the Swale leaves the wooded dale and leaps to meet the Plain below Easby abbey ruins, the very look of the place speaks of romance and beauty. The lofty Norman tower-keep and castle masonry of old fame (221), downward views from the cliff walks to the bridge, the river, and woods luxuriantly grouped compose in most telling pictures. High and low there are quaint corners and cobbled alleys, streets so steep that I am sure the inhabitants must develop marvellous hearts and lungs. The market-place, big and cobbled, is bordered with stone and whitened houses and shops, the nice Georgian front of the *King's Head* offers comfort behind it, and the castle walls stand high for a background of mellowness and history. Artists, skilled and otherwise, have sought the town since they first began to draw and daub, its beauties have been sung for a long time, and though Surrey tries to grab one of them *The Lass of Richmond Hill* continues firm, defiant and lovely in Yorkshire with the bright memory of Frances I' Anson of Hill House. Evidently Henry VII knew what he was about when he changed the name of Sheen on the Thames to Richmond, in honour of his earldom derived from the old strong-point on the Swale.

Southward, past Bedale's pictorial wide street and old cross, we gain the Ure vale, soon to find Ripon cathedral piled up from the bridges and Skell stream or standing well in near views (215). Small for a cathedral, it exhibits many architectural styles developed since the first foundation in 670 A.D. and the great reconstruction initiated by Archbishop Roger during 1154–81. Where Danes burned, kings devastated, suppressors ruined, and rain descended through leaky roofs, treasures remaining for joyful contemplation include the Saxon crypt, unique renderings of transitional Norman-Gothic design, the eastern limb of the choir (1286–96), a fifteenth-century screen or pulpitum (shorn of its images), exquisite choir stalls of finest fifteenth-century workmanship. From the Early English west front (1216–55), standing as Gilbert Scott left it, a few yards lead to the Market Square, an airy wide space befitting a town incorporated in 886 A.D. by King Alfred the Great. The market-cross, a high obelisk erected in 1781, is surmounted with the golden horn, and the town hall of 1781, elegant, cream-fronted, and pilastered, displays the motto, "Except ye Lord keep ye Cittie ye Wakeman waketh in vain." Hard by stands the gabled Wakeman's House with black beams inside. If my readers cannot join me behind the animal rampant at the *Unicorn* hotel it is worth while making a date to be in the square at 9 p.m. for seeing and hearing the Wakeman perform on the horn, a blowing that (perhaps!) may have been blown ever since the great King aforesaid reigned. On market day also (Thursday) this square is a great place for all the fun of the marketing. I found the local farmers congregated at the corner near the lavatories, heard news of the land, sheep, weather, and while the rain came down one farmer remarked to another, "Nar a very good day," got the reply, "Eh, it's mucky." Away from the workaday world monastic ruins most perfect call us to the lovely glen of the Skell stream. Old beauty shines at the sublime wreck of Fountains Abbey (216), a sight of worldwide repute. I can think of no past centre of piety and learning more stimulating for the eye and imagination. Masonry weathered by centuries and the stately green environment make an instant and lasting appeal that is amplified by memories of an illustrious past and original purpose—for of course the abbey and its uses fell in the doom of 1539. In 1132 came Richard, sub-prior from St. Mary's Abbey, York, and a small company of brethren to follow the strict discipline of Cistercian life in this wild valley, "remote from all the world, uninhabited, set with thorns," as the contemporary record tells. They met privation, cleared the wilderness, with faith and courage began to make a home and shrine beside the stream. From these beginnings the abbey grew in size, influence, and fame. The buildings gained impressive yet severe late Norman architecture, cloisters, chapter house, domestic quarters; the glorious Chapel of the Nine Altars (matched elsewhere only at Durham) was created during the great building period between 1203 and 1247, and early in the 1500's Abbot Huby's tall Perpendicular tower nobly completed the scheme, all fine and ready to be knocked to pieces when the Dissolution soon followed. For the sum of six hundred marks this monument of holiness, enlightenment, and art was surrendered, its treasures ransacked, the site sold. Left for us to see are the relics, the extent and quality of inspired accomplishment at one of the largest and most beautiful monastic ruins in England. About the year 1611 the owner, by name Sir Stephen Procter, used abbey stonework to build Fountains Hall. He changed fallen Gothic into good Jacobean and out of the wreck made a new sight to please us with towers, battlements, curly gables, many windows, a central oriel (222), and pretty gardens that face green acres where Cistercians once prayed and toiled to transform a wilderness into a heaven on earth.

More interesting old Yorkshire towns really ought to be carefully explored. Among them the following regretfully are crowded out of my limited pages— Boroughbridge round a cobbled market-place; Knaresborough with castle ruins high on a rock (210); Wetherby on the Great North Road; Tadcaster marking Roman *Calcaria*; Northallerton and Thirsk each with a big church bordering the wide highway; the colour-washed walls and pantile roofs of Pocklington (222) and Market Weighton nestling below the Wolds. And being very observant people in our travels along the roads and great highways of the Ridings we shall notice in the old towns many capital establishments that catered for man or beast in times past and now offer good cheer to humans behind petrol engines; fine historic inns, some very ancient, others Georgian-fronted, and all surviving from adventurous years, when horses were ridden and driven to transport crowned, coroneted, well-born, and lowly heads.

Thirsk has the *Golden Fleece* (222), Northallerton the *Golden Lion* and gabled *Fleece*, Market Weighton the Georgian *Londesborough Arms*, Pocklington the *Feathers* that gave me a cosy tea. So we can continue our ways brightened with thoughts of welcomes at a whole collection of *Lions, Unicorns and Dragons, Greyhounds* (Boroughbridge), *Swans* (Bedale, Pickering, Helmsley), and a galaxy of birds, beasts, crowns, kings, and angels of heaven.

The *George* suggests Selby, a very ancient place with big modern mills standing in a prosperous agricultural district of wide and flat landscapes due south of York. Though neither a Bruges nor a Boston the town's oldish brick houses, tiled roofs, and towers look quite attractive from the River Ouse crossed by a wooden bridge, a good spot for sketchers and photographers. Early pattern and actual beauty are concentrated at the abbey church. First built with Norman stonework by its wealthy abbot, de Lacy, later fired, damaged, and restored, this church alone survives from the rich and famous Benedictine monastery founded in the eleventh century and suppressed in the 1530's. Ancient and modern, signs of the life spiritual and ephemeral, mix very well here on market days (227). Many people, motors, fish, and dry goods all arrive to settle down in sight of the abbey's west front and three towers with added tops. Lively crowds, stalls served by wideawake Yorkshire natives (of whom it is said they never sleep), bargaining, gossip, quantities of babies pushed about in prams by proud producers, all have the benedictions of hymn tunes sent by the carillon to the market-place. If the lure of the stalls or the hubbub chance to pall a quick change can be made by retreating from the noise and babies into the haunts of de Lacy, there to find quiet and a soft religious light shining as it gleamed long ago on nave arcades, bold rounded arches, the fourteenth-century choir terminated with a great window rich in flowing cusp traceries and painted glass. This serene work of old time, the eastern limb of the church, is the glory of Selby and has been since it was completed in *circa* 1360.

Selby choir, both inside and out, introduces to our travels the quality of façade and bay design that made south-east Yorkshire conspicuous for notable achievements in ecclesiastical architecture. The first pointed or Early English style advanced to new richness and dignity while invention and construction progressed under the geometrical and curvilinear impulses of the Decorated period, particularly in the scheming of east fronts, transept ends, and window-tracery. Later came the soaring rectilinear compositions in Perpendicular building, often due to designers and craft workers, usually laymen, and wealthy folk who prospered in the local cloth and other industries. Together they created melodies in stone and tuned songs of active life through art. Thus Hedon tower, a perfect and grand feat designed by Robert Playser, the mason, began to rise in 1427 above the sumptuous church of the thirteenth and fourteenth centuries; it was

RICHMOND. *The strong point of old fame and memories stands on a crag in the wooded gorge where the River Swale leaves the Dales for the Yorkshire Plain. Massive walls, towers, gateways, and a keep developed from early Conquest years.*

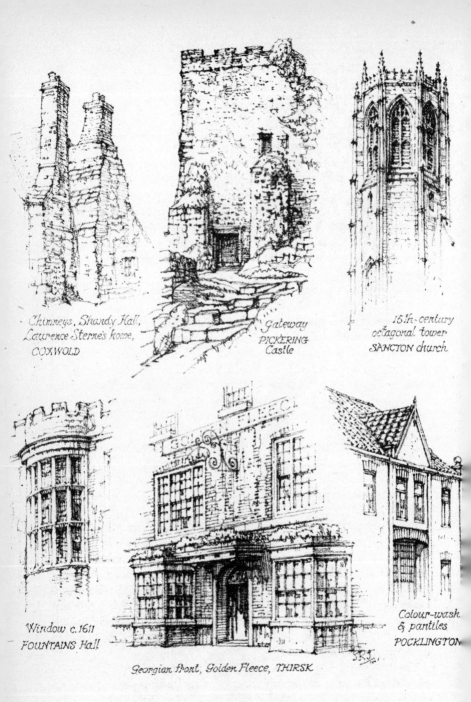

Chimneys, Shandy Hall,
Laurence Sterne's home,
COXWOLD

Gateway
PICKERING
Castle

15th-century
octagonal tower
SANCTON church

Window c.1611
FOUNTAINS Hall

Georgian front, Golden Fleece, THIRSK

Colour-wash
& pantiles
POCKLINGTON

IN THE YORKSHIRE RIDINGS.

made possible and paid for by the united cash contributions of all the substantial inhabitants at this once thriving port. Gothic work of medieval stylists through three centuries is richly scattered over the Plain and through the levels o Holderness. Searchers in quest of it certainly should see Howden's frontages and tower; Hatfield and Fishlake churches among the dykes; Holy Trinity, Hull, large and lofty, and its neighbour at Cottingham; Hemingbrough spire, and another one beautifully proportioned at Patrington. Other Perpendicular towers of Holderness soar over fourteenth-century and earlier designs in rural villages from Preston, Skirlaugh, and Brandesburton to the old-fashioned town of Driffield. Beverley, if not exciting as a town, of course mounts the climax. St. Mary's church is handsome enough to attract any pilgrim; the Minster, Early English to the east (227), fourteenth-century in the nave, magnificently towered at the west in Perpendicular majesty of the early 1400's, and with arcades and screenwork of the first order inside, is the pearl of the lowlands, a sublime harmony for one of the most splendid parish churches in England.

Between the Plain and Holderness the Yorkshire Wolds turn a crescent line from the Humber to the coast. Heights mount up from North Ferriby and Welton villages, near to-day's shipping and Hull, to Hunmanby in sight of Filey Bay, an early anchorage for Roman galleys. Graceful contours, smooth hillsides, the coombs and sheltered hollows (228) clearly indicate chalk country and the northern limit of the long formation through England which ends at the white walls of Bempton Cliffs and Flamborough Head. All the characteristics of downland scenery are here—near expanses and scattered villages; Bainton Heights, Tibthorpe Wolds, and lonely tracts; points for seeing long views and distances over York and beyond Beverley; sheep grounds of ancient fame; fields of arable and pasture, rich and productive since the Sykes family of Sledmere led the way in skilled agriculture. The kindlier slopes show wooded parks, the layout at Londesborough made by the celebrated Earl of Burlington. An air of remote antiquity hangs over the numerous entrenchments and tumuli left by the flint-age men and their successors. Goodmanham is a landmark of Christian faith; the wooden cross in the churchyard commemorates the conversion of King Edwin of Northumbria through the preaching of Bishop Paulinus in 627 A.D. The "thorpes," Wetwang, Thwing, and other place-names survive from Scandinavian raids and settlement. Withal it is fine airy country, good for the legs and comfortable hill-climbing, a homely English region of old standing, one that has been improved and not very much spoiled by recent generations of humanity.

The chalk wolds drop to the Vale of Pickering. Beyond the levels the Yorkshire Moors rise up in unmistakable forms of stone landscapes at this northern termination of the oolite and lias in England. Winding dales and undulations lead from Pickering vale to the heights. Escarpments of the Hambleton (233) and Cleveland Hills bound the York Plain. Rocks thrust out to the sea at the impressive stretch of coastline from Scarborough Castle to Boulby Cliff. Within this North Riding area the hills have the shapelinesss common to limestone scenery. Slopes direct to enclosed or wide valleys. High open spaces extend above lower wooded places. Banks of purple show in heather time. The warm tints and greys of stone-built villages, farmsteads, and boundary walls remind us of Northamptonshire and the Cotswolds. Here again, as on the Wolds, many tumuli, funeral stones, dikes and camps record forgotten pasts. It is a capital district for exploration on foot or wheels along quiet ways where smiling nature spreads beauty far and wide over moor, common, and valley to those distant hills of promise that every mile brings nearer. Two main roads cross from south to north, one through Bilsdale to Hasty Bank, the other along remarkable stretches of moorland magnificence past the Hole of Horcum to Goathland Moor and the River Esk. Between these two routes innumerable little rough lanes turn up valleys, continue in footpaths, lead to joys in high yonderlands. Here are the loveliest dales imaginable, each watered with its stream—Baysdale leading to Eskdale, Riccaldale, Bransdale, Farndale. Rosedale, charming as its name, descends to Cropton (235) and to Lastingham, famed for the Norman church and crypt at the monastery site visited by Bede. Days of pleasure can end with watching sunsets, nowhere better seen than from the western eminences at Kilburn White Horse (shaped in 1857), Sutton Bank on Whitestone Cliff (Wordsworth's choice), Osmotherley Moor (above Ingleby woods and Carthusian ruins of Mount Grace Priory), Roseberry Topping in Cleveland. From these and other vantage points the expansive verdant plain stretches far away to the Pennines defined in silhouette against the glory of the evening sky as the sun goes down. Standing on Black Hambleton I saw churches and tree-tops catch the last gleams of light, long shadows fade, colours deepen in the afterglow. While one more day passed to illimitable yesterdays twinkling motor lights picked out the courses of the great north roads and night began to steal across the broad historic grounds travelled through centuries by saints, scamps, nobles and workaday folk, Romans, Danes and Normans, soldiers who fought at Towton and Marston Moor.

Up from Helmsley you can approach Rievaulx Abbey. Or the ruins may be reached by coming down from the Cleveland Hills through Bilsdale, passing Bilsdale old hall (now a farmhouse), Chop Gate opening to Raisdale, and a Temple Moore church on the roadside by the Fangdale Beck. The stream called Seph babbles along for company all the way, fed right and left by sparkling becks fresh from the moors. Heights slope, climb, and wind in all directions, enclose the valleys, keep secrets in lofty places at prehistoric graves and the Bride Stones. Vistas of hill and dale stretching to the far away, watered pastoral hollows, a few stone cottages and farmhouses here and there, the meeting of the Seph and the Rye, all unite to give the idea of being in a fairyland of delight, particularly in heather time, as I saw it, when curved purple expanses heightened the richness of autumn colour and beauty (236). From the dale road a steep way descends, then turns sharply. Surprise, wonder, even rapture come next—at least these words seemed right for my emotions on finding Rievaulx Abbey set like a jewel in the sylvan scene (216). Turner, Cowper, and Dorothy Wordsworth evidently were similarly moved, for each in their own way recorded the enchantment of Rievaulx. Doubtless thousands of famous and ordinary mortals who have visited this spot ever remembered the first excitement of lighting on the very lovely ruin in the vale, a memorial of piety, devotion, and art framed by monks in their Eden on earth. These monks were Cistercians. Here they made their home in 1131 to be governed by the strict interpretation of St. Benedict's rule. First they built in the austere style followed by their order. The abbey prospered. Time brought the great church, cloister, refectory, vaulted undercroft, an infirmary, extensive domestic buildings, a warming house for comfort in the cold Yorkshire winters. How and where monastic life progressed in this lonely valley can be traced by many fragments and ground plans of the eleventh and twelfth centuries. With the thirteenth century the breath of Gothic time stirred in Ryedale. Reconstruction changed the earlier simplicity to the refinements of the Early English style. Choir, transepts, and tower of the church blossomed anew, delicate with pointed arches and lancets, deeply-cut mouldings, foliated enrichments. Chaste and comely, these features in part remain to adorn the ruins and give to this hallowed spot a most exquisite rendering of the Cistercians' work.

Castle remains at Helmsley, Kirby Moorside, Pickering, and West Ayton, marking the southern boundaries of the Moors, stand in a line dotted with a chain of stone-built villages from Nawton to Sinnington, Thornton Dale, Ebberston, and Wykeham. Edged with hills, dales, and woods each rural place and hamlet is attractive. The tumbled castles of Normans and Plantagenets impart to the present a mouldy flavour of old romance. Worn stonework and mounds still can suggest kingly visitations, pageantry, bloodshed, Richard II a doomed prisoner at Pickering (222), the second Duke of Buckingham uncomfortably settled within the Helmsley ruins battered by Cromwellians (235). The scene for the Duke's finale was Kirby Moorside. At the gabled house near the Tolbooth the far too brilliant, much too witty, and lastly broken-down George Villiers quitted his earthly stage with appropriate lines, "The world and I shake hands, and I dare affirm we are heartily weary of each other." These three little towns of winding streets, grey houses, and *Swan* inns invite halts for an hour, a day, or a week. In Pickering church a long time can be spent at the remarkable medieval wall-paintings, formerly hidden by whitewash because the parson noticed that congregations were more intent on the pictures than listening to his sermons. West Ayton castle, overlooking the river bridge, guarded the opening to the Derwent gorge centuries ago. Garrisoned for religious insurgents, it had dramatic moments in 1536 when holy emblems on banners led the Pilgrimage of Grace in fiery courses through Yorkshire, and nobles and prelates, armed and well horsed, fought and died in the hopeless attempt to save the monasteries and their old faith. Overgrown, defunct, the ruins now point pilgrims of peace to beauty in the Forge Valley. The stream runs fast over a stony bed, winds past rocks, steep banks, and tree-clad hills in passages of extreme lovelinesss. Fresh from the moorlands and Langdaleside the waters meet Hackness village, charming and squirely with the Georgian hall and ancient church wonderfully set among beeches, chestnuts, and noble trees at a meeting of narrow wooded dales. Through the park and up at the top of the hill we glimpse the sea and Scarborough.

Popular seaside resorts are not my choice because they attract quantities of holidaymakers who do not always shine as divine creations for beautifying seascapes and landscapes. But in spite of crowds and complete accoutrements of a modern pleasure town, nature's job at the rocks and bays of Scarborough still remains intact to give this resort one of the most magnificent coastal settings in all the land. From its castled promontory to Boulby Cliff beyond Staithes the headlands, rock forms, and bays, grand, majestic, and alluring, shape a section of England's finest coast scenery, in my opinion only matched elsewhere in north Devon and Cornwall. Towns and villages poised high and low are true to the Yorkshire type. Long ascents of steps, unsuitable for short-winded parties, lead to jumbles of houses and cottages that seem to hang at giddy elevations for the special purpose of looking queer, quaint, and catching breezes to dry washing on clothes lines. Queer people called artists have long known of these particulars, hence the presence of easels, sketching stools, and quaint figures under big hats in old Scarborough town, Robin Hood's Town, Whitby, Runswick Bay, and Staithes (11, 241). Ancient harbours, boats, fish, nets and anchors, fishermen, fishermen's wives and fish markets, stormy seas, heroism in the lifeboats, belong to the more permanent values on this holiday coastline. For those who like to think back there are the places of antiquated picturesqueness and historic meaning. Remains of Henry II's keep stand on Scarborough's almost impregnable rock from which Romans watched, centuries before Smollett arrived below to discover amusing adventures at the "chalybeate spaw" for *Humphry Clinker*. Early English ruins of Whitby Abbey crown the Streoneshalh slope traditionally linked with Cædmon's vision and song in the seventh-century dawn of English poetry. Robin Hood's name at the town and bay suggests a Yorkshire claim for the legendary hero and Little John; and much more than

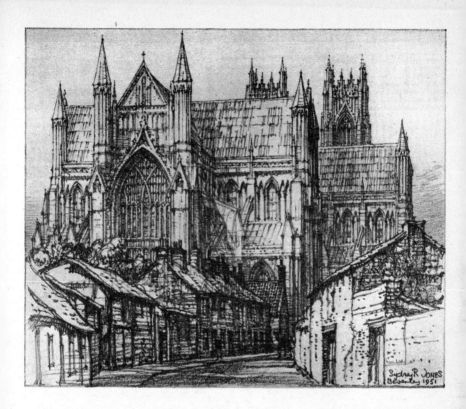

TWO OF YORKSHIRE'S FAMOUS CHURCHES

BEVERLEY (above). *The east end and Early English transepts of the minster, one of the most splendid parish churches in England.*

SELBY. *The abbey church borders the market-place.*

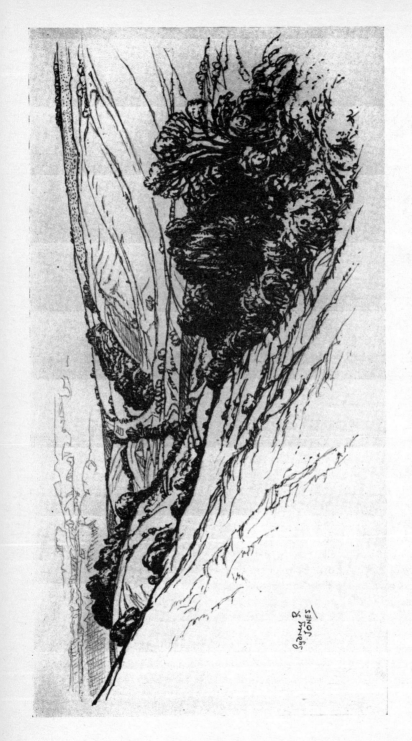

THE YORKSHIRE WOLDS. *Chalk hills near* GOODMANHAM *in the East Riding.*

I now can tell abounds for delight and contemplation on this rugged seaboard where summer suns shine, wintry storms beat, and old smuggling tales are remembered.

DURHAM COUNTY

It must be few observant daytime travellers going north by train from London or southern England who do not look forward to the great moment promised after York, the Tees, and Darlington have been passed. The train runs through a cutting, shoots out of it. Suddenly and quite near Durham is revealed. Cathedral towers, castle masonry, and old town group in stately grandeur. They form one of Durham's several prospects of great dignity (247), scenes deservedly famous and with not many rivals in English cities.

Set on a bold cliff of shale, coal seams, and hard rock almost encircled by the River Wear, Durham occupies a commanding position of natural strength. Obviously it was marked out for early settlement. The site offered ideal situations for building to the glory of God or erecting works to frighten man. Not surprisingly it gathered both signs of power, spiritual and temporal. Mighty prelates, skilled in the professions of worship, strategy, and force of arms, piled up their church and castled home while onward from the eleventh century they reigned supreme in their northern palatinate. Later, many years later, after centuries of prayer, praise, war, and strife, the artists came along to storm and capture on canvas and paper the original of Walter Scott's

Half church of God, half castle 'gainst the Scot.

Though built on a hill surrounding uplands enclose Durham. Consequently it is a place for discovery at close quarters rather than one known for memorable distant visions of gleaming stone and towers, sights such as call us from miles away to Lincoln or Ely, Salisbury or Wells. Yet this city on a rock yields place to none for spectacular grouping of unusual splendour and romantic appeal. To follow the river's course from bridge to bridge brings more than enough to captivate the eye and fire the imagination. At the weir below Framwelgate the castle's massive walls, turrets, and battlements, once emblems of force and now of learning, frown down on the arched bridge, reconstructed two hundred years after Bishop Flambard first erected it in the twelfth century; the three cathedral towers rise beyond, crowning a wealth of greenery that clothes the gorge to the river's edge (242). This noble composition remains little altered since Turner and Girtin found it and painted their pictures. Shady walks known as the Banks lead on to Prebend's Bridge, a graceful construction fitting the date of 1777. Near are the points for two of Cotman's subjects finely painted about 1805, *The New Bridge, Durham*, and the *Durham Cathedral* now in the

British Museum. Hereabout the scenes assemble peculiar magnificence. The silvery stream meanders between luscious green avenues. Steep wooded slopes reach to the galilee and monastic buildings of the cathedral, to the castle crouched like a powerful and weathered guardian. Above clerestories and roofs the three towers predominate. Strong in Norman proportions and the vertical lines of Perpendicular pattern and fenestration they give impressions of immense height raised over St. Cuthbert's shrine. More awaits on following the Banks round the bend to Elvet Bridge. This is a centrepiece for another series of great views both up and down the stream where the up-built town is always overshadowed by the grand massiveness of the cathedral, Chapel of the Nine Altars, and the castle (247). The bridge makes an effective and ancient showing with stone cutwaters and pointed arches. Originally Bishop Puiset's work in the twelfth century and once furnished with two chapels, it was partly rebuilt after flood damage in 1771 and subsequently widened. Scrambling down the bank is repaid by finding a ready-made picture of houses standing on the first low arch at the Elvet end, a rare survival from the medieval custom of building dwellings over the water, as seen in Hollar's print of old London Bridge.

Leaving these memorable spectacles, the very steep ascents, most suitable for spiders or steeplejacks, lead from either of the two medieval bridges to the old town contained within the circuit of the stream. Market Place at the top locates the core of the city's body civic, the heart ecclesiastical and castled being tucked away from this busy square of worldly commotion. A live policeman on a perch attempts to control traffic ever on the move and a large Lord London-derry in bronze perpetually prances on a horse that never advances. Ways open out in various directions, Silver Street precipitously downward, North Bailey pointing to the holy grounds, Saddler Street leading to Elvet Bridge and the *Royal County* hotel over the water, a comfortable anchorage in which a way-farer may rest, refresh, and ascend an old staircase to bed.

Packed lively streets, shops of long standing, newer invaders offering the multiple up-to-date lines, the continuous movement of people and petrol engines turning all clearly indicate an ancient cathedral city and county capital keeping abreast of the times. Up, down, and everywhere the northern character-istics of building are obvious in the sombre dull-coloured brick walling and local stonework. There are tall houses, old-fashioned square and gabled front-ages. Many of them occupy curious elevations that afford opportunities for spying on the domestic deeds performed at more lowly habitations. Best architecturally are the seventeenth-century and Georgian façades in North and South Bailey. Classic doorways with delicate fanlights open to elegant interiors and fine staircases. Close to the cathedral precincts they suggest how nicely life still may be lived and how good it must have been in the times of candlelight dining and bottles galore. Three Gothic churches of St. Margaret, St. Oswald, and St. Giles preserve medieval features; a carved wooden effigy of an Elizabethan in St. Giles's cheered me with his Latin motto, one of those morbid witticisms favoured by the old stock and meaning, to my unravelling, "To-day is my turn, to-morrow yours." A fourth small church, St. Mary-le-Bow, now has come into the fashion for its delightful late Stuart interior of the 1680's enriched with a chancel screen and other notable woodwork.

Very intriguing are Durham's byways and back quarters. Screened from the bustle in the streets, pleasantly drab, sometimes mouldy, yet relatively peaceful, the narrow openings and up-and-down quarters can offer endless surprises. In passing or coming out of the *Castle* hotel by Framwelgate Bridge, for example, probably not many strangers in a hundred notice the adjacent cavernous hole named Moatside Lane. A most promising hole is this one. Burrowed between house walls below first floors it rises step by step, winds steeply upward, might even promise Everest or Heaven in a last final climb. It looks spooky, the sort of mysterious haunt for quite naturally meeting a Norman ghost, a Middle Aged cat, a knight in shining armour, a Prince Bishop's retainer left over from feudal years. Actually I particularly observed a modern democratic Hebe got up to her idea of a film star and piloting her brats who joyfully yelled while leaping down the inclines and steps. But throughout this city mounting to the rocky plateau the progressive and vivid present is variegated by many a feature of old stamp. Looks and streaks of age make it easy to picture the past town life when pilgrims crowded in, religious street processions passed to the churches at Christmas and Whitsuntide, when mounted soldiers clattered away to curb marauding Scots, and Richard Neville murdered the bishop's officer on the bridge in the proper manner fit for a contemporary thriller of 1318.

Peace usually reigns over one secluded area when the sightseers and Mothers' Unions have departed. This is Palace Green, reached from Market Place via North Bailey and Owen Gate. Around it are centred the glories of Durham, the genesis of the city's being. In stately calm, aloof from noise, trafficking, and shops, the cathedral stands neighboured by the castle. Here beauty and romance unite, beauty with strength, the romance of saintliness and origin.

The story of Durham's beginning has often been told and the scene at Palace Green hilltop amplifies it. Towered masonry, column and arch swing thoughts back to the old tale remembered. Here, particularly, the events of St. Cuthbert's life and death hold their immortal place and the saint's pilgrimage on earth can be created anew. Time recedes to the seventh century, to the humble shepherd boy of the Lowlands who joined the monks at the mission station of Melrose in 651 A.D. Grown in stature, fired with religious devotion and poetic insight, the peasant preacher and persuasive orator spread the Christian message to the strongholds of heathenism as he wandered far and wide over the hills and solitudes of Ettick and Teviotdale, Yarrow and Lammermoor. While year followed year Cuthbert became prior of Melrose, Ripon, of Lindisfarne on St. Aidan's Holy Island. Then the anchorite settled at the lonely rock cell on one of the Farne Islands. Though unwilling to leave seclusion, the earnest bidding of Egfrith, King of Northumbria, called him away to become bishop of Hexham, later of Lindisfarne. Soon he returned to the island hermitage. There his last day dawned. After the sun had set a faint gleam of light flashed from the island over the dark waters. Seen by a monk who watched on Lindisfarne tower, the light signalled Cuthbert's death as his brethren in the priory church chanted the Sixtieth Psalm, *Deus, repulisti nos*. The saintly life spent in Christianizing Northumbria had ended.

Cuthbert's works, in common with those of men truly great, lived after his earthly existence. Two circumstances of his life and death however developed very peculiar results. The holy man enjoyed that curious and rare gift known as an aversion for women. This notion, whether indicative of strength or weakness, affected architecture; how it did so will be explained later. Cuthbert also left definite instructions for the disposal of his corpse and thus unwittingly founded his romantic posthumous story. He willed to be buried at Lindisfarne priory. Further, he expressed a dying wish that if heretics or minions of unrighteousness ever attempted to profane the sanctity of the grave, then the monks must unearth his incorruptible remains and carry them away to wheresoever the Almighty directed. The burial duly took place at Lindisfarne in 687 A.D. For nearly two centuries the grave remained undisturbed. Then the forces of heathenism, which Cuthbert once subdued, threatened again and attacked vigorously. Conquering Danes from the strongholds of Woden and Thor appeared in hosts to ravage and desecrate Northumbria. The time had come for the monks to flee and obey the last command of their master. They lifted the body from the grave. Contained in a wooden and richly carved coffin Cuthbert's second pilgrimage began. It progressed through strange intermittent wanderings of more than a hundred years, for rarely could a secure resting-place be found. At each point where the body lay a church was dedicated to St. Cuthbert and so, as a matter of course, the bishop's see of Lindisfarne continued in survival. The mournful journey proceeded from place to place, reached Yorkshire, then Carlisle, and later

> Chester-le-Street, and Rippon saw,
> His holy corpse, ere Wardilaw
> Hailed him with joy and fear.

But at Wardilaw the guardians of the coffin found themselves in a quandary. Their charge held fast, refused to be moved. Soon, as so often occurred in the old days of faith and divine inspiration, the unexpected happened. The name of Dunholme as the Saint's own choice for burial was mysteriously revealed to one of the monks. None of them knew its situation. A woman opportunely

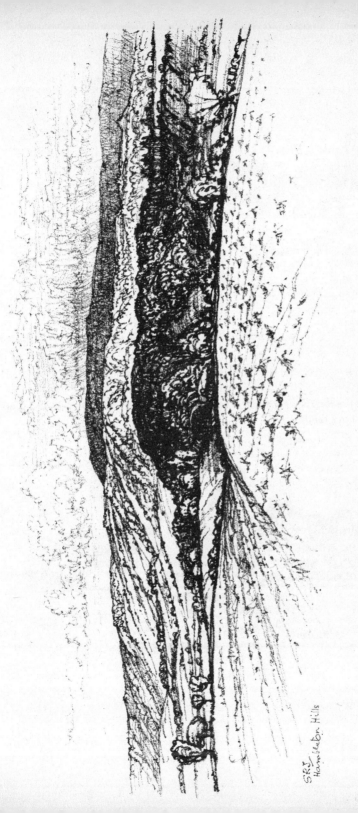

THE HAMBLETON HILLS *and Black Hambleton* (1,257 *feet*), *Yorkshire North Riding.*

GREAT BARUGH. *Pantile roofs and white walls in the Vale of Pickering.*

TOPCLIFFE, *on the York Plain, the River Swale, and near Maiden Bower, the first English home of the Percy family.*

CROPTON, *at the end of Rosedale.*

HELMSLEY. *Norman keep at a pleasant market town on the edge of the Yorkshire Moors. The great castle, badly smashed in the Civil War, was the home for the last years of George Villiers, second Duke of Buckingham.*

BILSDALE *in heather time.*

Sydney R. Jones

appeared in search of a lost cow, gave the location, directed the way for the final stage of the journeying. The coffin responded, could be moved easily again. In the year 997 the monks "with great joy arrived with his Body at Dunholme," a wild and elevated fastness on a rock above the river, a secure retreat fit for the burial of the saintly missionary and hermit. There they made the last grave, erected over it a "little church of Wands and Branches," and by so doing located the site on which we now see Durham cathedral.

On this foundation the little church soon was replaced by a stone one and the seat of Durham's first bishop, sanctified by the mortal remains of St. Cuthbert, advanced to great spiritual fame. Not many years hence the signs and trappings of power, both ecclesiastical and worldly, began to accumulate. William de St. Carileph, second Norman bishop after the Conquest, ejected the secular canons and envisaged a great new church for the Benedictines on the height above the river. There he laid its first stone in 1093. Forty years later, under the episcopacy of the third bishop, Ralph Flambard, the structure was complete with choir, transepts, and nave. The mighty work crowned the rock with twin western towers, immense nave columns diapered in chiselled patterns, lofty arcades, clustered shafting, billet and chevron carved on mouldings; the ribbed stone vault soared over all in a boldness of scale never before attempted in monumental building. Erected to last and weather the centuries this church of the Norman bishops remains to this day, captivating with sights and impressions of grandeur, dignity, and massive strength almost bewildering, of their style and period surely unsurpassed on the English island. Southwards spread and developed the monastic buildings. Still they preserve the plan and arrangements made for the cloister, priors' quarters, the long dormitory over an undercroft, the refectory with cellars below, the octagonal kitchen vaulted to a central louvre for dispersing the smoke, the two prisons that did not lack use. In the monks' garden you may think of the brethren who tended herbs and flowers, who counted serene hours on a sundial's face and during fleeting times of leisure played in the bowling alley. Hard by stood the castle on its eminence. From earthen motte and bailey it grew to be the stronghold of grim stone walls, towers, and gateways now seen frowning riverwards above the steep declivity. Within the enclosure were built the present great hall entered through a splendid Norman doorway, the Norman chapel, and later enlargements suitable for the home and fortress of mighty prelates. For these bishops also had the title and sway of earls. They ruled with the sword and a rod of iron while serving under the Cross of Christ. Predominant in their own palatinate, princes of a state within a kingdom, they wielded authority and judicial rule with no less power than that of the King and claimed, as they still do, a premier place in the House of Lords. They guarded the border country against incursions by the Scots. Their own troops sallied forth to war. The famous banner of St. Cuthbert led the Scottish campaigns of Richard II and Henry IV; it waved over the Bishop's men on Flodden Field. When King David of Scotland advanced in 1346 while Edward III tarried in France after his victorious Crécy, it was the army commanded by the prelates of Durham, York, and Lincoln that stemmed the tide of invasion at the battle of Neville's Cross, captured the Scottish king, and monks anxiously watched the fighting from Durham's cathedral towers. Bishops, monks, their supporters the Percys and the Nevilles, all entered the great church to offer solemn thanksgiving to the King of Kings for victory.

Meanwhile what of St. Cuthbert? Through those times of continuous prayer, praise and strife, aristocratic churchmanship, building to the glory of God and sometimes for the glorification of man, the saint exercised his beneficent influence from the tomb now marked by a block of squared stones behind the high altar. His exemplification of the holy life and the miraculous powers sought and found at his resting-place brought kings, princes, great nobles, and pilgrims in vast numbers to worship in pious adoration. The shrine became famed above all others in northern England, rivalled that of St. Thomas of Canterbury in popularity and potency for healing the ills of body and mind. On solemn occasions the relics were exhibited to the wondering devotees. Written records preserved vividly picture the scenes. The tomb glittered with "fine and costly green marble all limned and gilt with gold." The cover on it, raised by ropes worked on pulleys, concealed the feretory, or casket, containing the chief relics of the saint. Attached to the ropes were six silver and "very fine-sounding bells." Panelled aumbries to the north and south, "varnished and finely painted and gilt over with fine little images," held other relics of St. Cuthbert. Round about gleamed costly gifts and jewels, "being accounted the most sumptuous and richest jewels in all this land." In these gorgeous surroundings the saint's day and other festivals were celebrated. A blaze of candlelight shone on colour, decoration, the beauty of wrought stone, hanging banners of benefactors, the treasures accumulated through long years of religious ardour. As the cover slowly rose the bells pealed, "stirred all men's hearts within the church," and the feretory, brilliant and sparkling, was exposed to view. The concourse of pilgrims, like those in Chaucer's *Canterbury Tales*,

> Kneeléd down to-fore the shrine,
> And sith the holy relikes each man with his mouth
> Kisséd, as a holy monk the namés told and taught.

The air was hushed in the impressive moments of visionary faith. Bright rays from the shrine softly glowed to mysterious shades in the Chapel of the Nine Altars, one of the loveliest thirteenth-century creations made by the Church's high-thinking aristocracy and paid for by pilgrims in a golden age of art.

If truth and legend agree Durham's saint continued active after death in the province of architecture. Previously I have mentioned his extreme dislike for the female sex. This trait in character is reputed to have caused no end of trouble in building operations and also dictated one outstanding performance. Late in the twelfth century it was proposed to erect a Lady Chapel in the customary position at the eastern end of the fabric and thus adjacent to St. Cuthbert's shrine and grave. This idea evidently agitated the saint. The prospect of a chapel dedicated to the Virgin on his immediate frontage surely invited complications that no self-respecting woman-hater could tolerate. To combat such a possibility defensive measures and drastic quick actions were needed. When workmen began to execute the threat by commencing to build the saint counterplotted with rumblings in the earth and opened cracks on the ground to start a series of structural collapses. The project therefore ended with nothing accomplished and had to be abandoned. For this reason the Lady Chapel eventually took shape in a most unusual position, at the western termination of the cathedral. There we now find it, an exquisite feat of its period, five aisles in width and divided by clustered pillars from which spring arches richly carved with chevron mouldings. Possibly the circumstances that determined the almost unique situation of this rare Lady Chapel accounted for it being misnamed a galilee, the term applied to a spacious western porch or antechapel, generally considered less sacred than the main building and sometimes reserved for the use of women. At Durham the monks guarded St. Cuthbert's grave from feminine disturbance or intrusion by decreeing that no female foot should advance from the galilee beyond the second pillar of the nave, the point yet being marked by a marble cross in the paving.

High days and festivals at the shrine, the worship, and the healing came to an end. The candles flickered out. The last sounds of pilgrims faded away. Empty and cold stood the Chapel of the Nine Altars. Visitors other than devout worshippers had arrived in the dying month of the year 1540. These were the emissaries of Henry VIII. They dismantled the gorgeous settings, grabbed the costly gifts and jewels, opened the grave, looked at St. Cuthbert, saw his vestments and the golden metwand at his side, then sealed him up again. Later the Dean's French wife burned the sacred banner in her fire, the famous banner of St. Cuthbert that had hung over his resting-place and led soldiers to victory in Scottish campaigns. Lastly prying nineteenth-centurions opened the grave again in 1826. On sundry occasions very learned gentlemen gifted with logical reasoning and bleak common sense doubted the authenticity of the body and thus tried to reduce the whole fabric of veneration for centuries to a hoax for pilgrimage and profit. Certainly there is not much to be seen after the glitter of past years. With the monks long gone ladies can wander fearlessly over the saint's private pavement. But the plain unadorned stonework, the original base of the shrine, and the word *Cuthbertus* cut on it to mark the grave continue to radiate the light of memory, record, and example of a holy life.

Another famous and saintly name calls us to the galilee. Below the beautiful Romanesque arches is a plain tomb of post-Reformation date bearing the nineteenth-century lettering, *Bædæ venerabilis*. It locates the place of the grave and destroyed shrine of Bede whose years began when those of St. Cuthbert were ending; the Venerable Bede who became "a servant of God, and priest of the monastery of the blessed apostles Peter and Paul, which is at Wearmouth and Jarrow," and whose wisdom and liberal opinions were surpassed only by the noble personal character of this father of English learning. The life consecrated to the service of the Church and quest for knowledge, to writing and teaching, ended at the age of sixty-two in the year 735. Bede was buried at Jarrow where most of his tranquil years had been spent. Nearly three centuries later his grave strongly appealed to the sacrist of Durham. This wily monk, an expert in the medieval art of body-snatching, stole the body to provide an additional shrine when re-interred at his own cathedral. Jarrow preserves stonework within which Bede worshipped, worked, and taught. It is situated between South Shields and Gateshead, a gloomy district more celebrated for ugliness than natural beauty and now conspicuous for drab additions of industrialism such as the modest monk never dreamed of during his quiet years of learning and prayer spent in rural peace. Therefore it seems to me much nicer, vastly pleasanter, to think of the first great English historian at rest in the galilee of Durham, and to pay homage to the beloved and venerable scholar at the grave shaded by lovely stone arches. At that spot it is fitting to recall the master's last day remembered by the words written in Green's *History*:

The dawn broke on another sleepless night, and again the old man called his scholars round him and bade them write. . . . Amid tears and farewells the day wore away to eventide. "There is yet one sentence unwritten, dear master," said the boy. "Write it quickly," bade the dying man. "It is finished now," said the little scribe at last. "You speak truth," said the master; "all is finished now." Placed upon the pavement, his head supported in his scholars' arms, his face turned to the spot where he was wont to pray, Bæda chanted the solemn "Glory to God." As his voice reached the close of his song he passed quietly away.

Of the various approaches to Durham cathedral and castle the quiet and picturesque way from the river Banks, across Prebend's Bridge, and along South Bailey undoubtedly is the most attractive. From this direction are seen the best near views of the cathedral and precincts. First the close is entered. Around its greensward stand grave and dignified homes of cool-coloured stone. Towards the river spread the monastic buildings. After the stress of centuries they remain unusually complete for showing how and where good and bad monks lived before King Henry wished them an unhappy New Year by sending them away on 31st December 1540. The priory house now accommodates the Dean. A refectory renewed after 1662 is conveniently near the fourteenth-

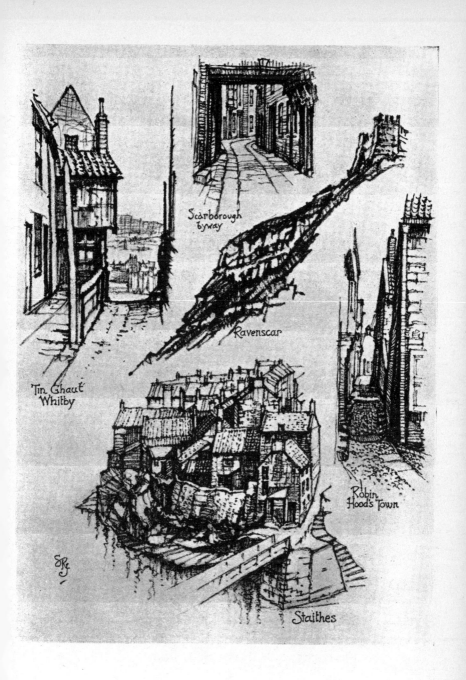

Scarborough byway

Ravenscar

Tin Ghaut Whitby

Robin Hood's Town

Staithes

NORTH YORKSHIRE COAST.

DURHAM from the weir below Framwelgate Bridge. Massive castle stonework and towers of the Cathedral crown steep banks of the river gorge. Here Turner sketched and Girtin painted the picture now in the Whitworth Art Gallery, Manchester.

century kitchen, octagonally planned, one of the finest extant. The long dormitory and undercroft—the length is nearly 200 feet—was built during 1398–1404 and retains the original weighty roof constructed with trunks of oak trees. Since the sleeping inmates departed their quarters have served for the library, rich in early illuminated manuscripts and books, remarkable Anglo-Saxon crosses, and many treasures for which Durham is celebrated. Here, too, after the strange eventful wandering, pieces of St. Cuthbert's carved wooden coffin are preserved, offering exciting evidences of fact such as are met with here and there to flash the light of truth into old stories and legends. Within the quadrangle formed by these buildings and a reconstructed Norman chapter house lies the cloister, somewhat changed from the original stonework, yet perfect and secluded in the four walks and court.

Facing the close and monks' quarters the great elevation of the cathedral soars upward. It reaches final points at the thirteenth-century additions to the western Norman towers; the central Perpendicular masonry of 1474 rises majestically to rule over all. The main grouping composes powerfully in the strong Norman lines of south aisles, clerestories, and transept. Eastward the length terminates in the lighter stone rendering at the Chapel of the Nine Altars; erected over an earlier Norman apse, it constitutes a thirteenth-century transeptal ending of a kind unknown elsewhere except at Fountains Abbey. The south-west door, elaborately ornamented with hammered ironwork, leads inside the nave. The galilee is screened at the west. Spellbound any sensitive observer may feel on looking to the east. There Durham's most famed sight of sights opens out, an achievement in twelfth-century building little altered since the Anglo-Normans accomplished it. The display of strength and dignity in Romanesque architecture has few rivals in England or Europe. Seen from the west end this vista fascinates by its immensity in scale and proportion, bold surface forms, contrasting effects of light, shadow, and stone colouring. Columns, arches, billet and chevron mouldings repeat in sequence to the far distance closed by the Neville Screen at the line of the high altar. Mighty arcades of pillars, clustered shafting, and semicircular arches support triforiums and clerestories; arch responding to arch, pillar to pier, mount upward to the vault of the roof. Massive indeed are the cylindrical nave columns, of girth almost equal to the width of the openings between them. Even the diapers chiselled on their surfaces exemplify early ideas in mass production, for whichever way the stones were laid the carved patterns on them automatically fitted. Crowning this great interior from west to east is the vaulting of ribbed stonework supporting tons and tons of weight, a most daring and original feat in architectural adventuring. Widely celebrated as the earliest specimen of this form of construction applied in the big manner, the sweeps of the rib lines also plainly show that they heralded the use of the pointed arch. Though the contents of later date within this Norman framework are striking and beautiful—they include the splendid altar screen of 1372–80 given by Lord Neville of Raby Castle, the pinnacled throne due to Bishop Hatfield, seventeenth-century woodwork in choir stalls and the elaborate font-cover contributed by good Bishop Cosin—these lesser works incline to rank as minor features amongst the stupendous effects created by the first builders. Remembering the early history of the cathedral and its neighbour castle, built to serve the line of prince-bishops, this wonderful interior always gives me the impression of being not only a church for the worship of God, for saintly shrines and pilgrims' devotions, but a warriors' church, massive enough to withstand a siege, a symbol of worldly power.

In spite of apparent strength both cathedral and castle gave ominous warnings of structural weakness. Though Richard and William, the Durham designers of the galilee, achieved most beautiful effects, only the heavy buttresses later erected by Bishop Langley to support the western wall kept the chapel from falling down the incline to the river. In recent years a similar danger threatened the riverside masonry of the castle. Steel and concrete, the modern weapons, prevented disaster. Now castle and galilee firmly stand maintaining their traditional watch over the gorge of the Wear. The western sun lights them, shines on battlements, buttresses, the towers high over the place of St. Cuthbert's lost shrine. With a last look from the bridge at this wonderful scene, symbolic of ideals and functions now passed and gone, we leave Durham, city of old time and present delight.

The eastern half of Durham county would yield a bumper harvest if our present quest happened to be for the depressing ugliness of mining villages and straggling towns. Northward from Ferryhill to Sunderland, South Shields, Gateshead, and Consett these dreary blobs exist in strong supplies for observers who admire the scenic effects developed from scientific civilization. Bishop Auckland with its park, domain of the palace where the bishops live and use their splendid medieval hall for a chapel, surrendered charm in the interests of coal. So, too, did historic Chester-le-Street, once the seat of a bishopric in St. Cuthbert's years of body-wandering. Now hilly and horrid, the town retains semblances of ancient glory in the collegiate church with a spire and the section of highway along which Romans padded and charioted to the Tyneside end of the Wall. For touches of brightness the Consett works regularly display illuminations. Very impressive I have thought them when lighting the night sky; but they also suggested the Devil at work stoking fires to warm up destructive and sinful man. Worshippers of the American George may hie to Washington, as I did, full of hope and expectation, only to find the ancestral hall of the de Wessingtons amidst a squalid, coaly, and chemical environment. True it is that trees shield the seventeenth-century gables of the stone house, that Stars and Stripes hang in the village school, and a few miles distant Durham cathedral library preserves Washington family deeds dating onward from the thirteenth century; yet for an American pilgrimage I would rather discover the Washington homes prettily embowered in Northampton-shire. The near coastline also might not be called exciting for natural or con-structed beauty, being punctuated with Sunderland, the Hartlepools, sundry collieries, and the lovely glen of Castle Eden Dene, now commanded by King Coal. Elsewhere the catalogue of effects, variegated or gloomy, might be continued indefinitely.

Other directions offer changes of scene with different characteristics for possible relief. Lovely is the Wear in the neighbourhood of old Sunderland Bridge. Deeply wooded and greenly coloured its vale frames pretty places, Whitworth Hall and park, Croxdale Hall avenues, choice bits for a setting to the gatehouse, dry moat, and mansion remains of Butterby Hall. Brancepeth Castle, warlike and spectacular, looms over the valley, a medieval counterfeit touched up by Anthony Salvin, the early-Victorian architect. Existing bits and pieces of the original fortress belonged to the mighty Nevilles until they fell from grace in the northern rising of 1569. Members of the family still keep their names bright in the near church. The structure, one of the county's best parish churches, is rich inside with much notable woodwork, resplendent Nevilles on monuments, and the prominent fighting Robert, very lanky, but fortunately in a recumbent posture. Downstream below Durham the Benedictine remains of Finchdale Priory, ruined arcades, circular pillars, and a thirteenth-century west doorway make a telling picture amidst the seclusion of woods and meadows. Past more bends of the winding river and just clear of the coalmining two inhabited castles, Lumley and Lambton, command the valley. Lambton, above a luscious glen and old stone bridge, gained the dramatic aspect of imitative castellation from Bonomi, the Italian architect, during the vogue for neo-Gothic in the reign of George III. But at Lumley, picturesque on the hillside, we light on the genuine Plantagenet article. Grey and weathered, it broods over past baronial times in the fourteenth-century dwelling of gateways, angle towers, and a proud heraldic display of the Lumley family emblazoning. Away up the river a greater and slightly later brother of Lumley still serves its purpose of habitation for the Chaytors, a race settled for centuries on a bank of the stream at Witton-le-Wear, near to Bishop Auckland and the rare little Saxon church of Escomb. Though partly restored after a fire and enlarged, the castle carries itself with the stately air of romanticism (261), seeming quite aloof from the near quest for coal along the Beechburn Beck. Outlines broken with towers, turrets and crenellated walls, the keep, the courtyard, machicolations, and the gateways bear the Froissart look, flaunt of chivalrous years and old time's gallantry amidst to-day's fragrance of flowered gardens. Developed round an earlier manor-house in 1410, too late in date to be a real feudal frightener, this most arresting group is of the same strain as Raglan, in Monmouthshire, and tunes a peaceful swansong for the military building epoch of the Middle Ages. Clear of the coal measures a countrified district, pastoral and undulating, stretches towards the River Tees and the magnesian limestone district north of Darlington. Here rural ways led me to Sadberge, a tiny place once of great importance to prince-bishops, to the Vanes' Wynyard park magnificently wooded, and to the little town of Sedgefield, old-fashioned with nice houses and a fine big church notable for more good woodwork. Other interesting churches may be discovered at Aycliffe, now sprouting into a satellite town, and in the little village of Heighington prettily set on a hill. The older cottages and farmhouses hereabout, built with the native limestone, have a pleasant regional character that harmonizes with the landscapes.

Westward ho! it is in Durham for meeting the best of the natural scenery in a fresh unspoiled showing, to be spied along the rivers, on the moors and the mountains. So first to the Tees we go, the watery line that defines the boundary between Durham and Yorkshire. Rising on the Pennines' highest altitude of Cross Fell in Cumberland, and descending from Caldron Snout and High Force waterfalls, it delights with stream scenery in England's most alluring patterning. If the Tees inclines to be short undoubtedly it is sweet, and lovely too, in most of its 75 miles length. Sprightly currents hurry, swirl, and leap over the rocky bed. Wooded margins and tree forms mount in graceful shapeliness along the curving miles—for these luxuriant banksides, reflected in the brown peat-tinted water (257), constitute special charms of this truly beautiful river. A chain of pretty rural places with stone houses and colour-washed cottages hug the stream below Middleton-in-Teesdale and Barnard Castle. In quiet churchyards there—Gainford has one—the forefathers of village and hamlet sleep on and on while everlasting melodies chant in eddies rippling over the rocks. Another singer, Walter Scott, made Teesdale ring with his song of *Rokeby*. The descriptive verses, lighting history's scenes and watered loveliness, swing the river along.

> Tees in tumult leaves his source,
> Thundering o'er Caldron and High-Force;
> Condemned to mine a channelled way,
> O'er solid sheets of marble gray.
>
> By Barnard's bridge of stately stone,
> Old Barnard's towers are purple still,
> To those that gaze from Toller-hill.
>
> And from the grassy slope he sees
> The Greta flow to meet the Tees.

DURHAM, *the city of the Prince Bishops. Impressions of the famous west view (top) and from the River Wear near Elvet Bridge (bottom).*

Sydney
R. JONES. Piercebridge

PIERCEBRIDGE. Remains of the Roman station on the road which led from York to Binchester (Vinovia), Lanchester (Longovicium), and Hadrian's Wall.

He views sweet Winston's woodland scene,
And shares the dance on Gainford-green.

Here rise no cliffs the vale to shade;
But, skirting every sunny glade,
In fair variety of green
The woodland lends its sylvan screen.

Unlike its neighbour the Wear, the Tees steers clear of the ominous coalfield. Forgetting the existence of Middlesbrough, Stockton, their chemicals and smokiness, we find the river quickly begins to show its own true self by performing a series of remarkable windings from Middleton St. George, Low Dinsdale, past Sockburn Hall and ruined church (interesting for Saxon Crosses), back to Neasham, and so to Croft. Curving one way, then another, the stream doubles and courses between wooded banks. Each change of direction reveals fresh delights, unexpected vistas of watercourses, leafy borderlands, radiant colour qualities. Away to the south and west the wide rich vale is closed by distant horizons of the Cleveland Hills and Pennine moors, Yorkshire's topmost height of Mickle Fell being visible on clear days. North of the river two miles beyond Croft are the Hell Kettles, a series of pools recorded to have been made by earth eruptions in 1178; anciently considered bottomless and the work of the Devil, later geologists easily accounted for their presence and found the deepest bottom at only twenty-four feet when somebody thought of dropping a plumb line. Continuing a mile from these mysterious tricks of nature leads us into Darlington.

Once remarkable for dirt, if the opinions expressed by Defoe and James I were correct, Darlington in its railway and manufacturing departments gives the impression of being rather large, nasty, and suitable for doses of spring cleaning. Distance however lends a little enchantment to the view; aspects improve as the distances from the swamps of industrialism are increased. Historically linked with Stockton, formerly a pleasant country town centred round a wide marketing High Street and Georgian town hall, Darlington also has a big and lively market square in which for many a long year natives of neighbouring villages and farms congregated to buy, sell, gossip, and where they still continue to do so. The lower end of this open space is graced with one of the county's finest churches. Tall of spire, endowed with late Norman, Early English, and other architectural features, it regularly attracts enthusiasts of ecclesiology and serves superior inhabitants for their weddings. Except for this noble building, a big block of granite in Northgate deposited during a remote glacial period, and a sprinkling of oldish houses that arrived much later, the antiquities of the town seemed to me inconspicuous, nor did I experience ecstatic moments among the Victorian dwellings and more recent additions in dull suburban roads. The praises of one local constituent however must not remain unsung; on the great road to the North resides a cook who satisfied my interior with very nice meals at the *Imperial* hotel. Since the declines of primitive man, the complicated simple life, knobby clubs for conquest, and feet for travel, leaders of the human arrangements called civilization and progress have concentrated on the quest for power. They wanted power and more power at the elbow, the cranium, and the wheel for domination with physical force, the intellect, the machine, and in the process of getting the requisites they made history with science and invention. When Matthew Boulton at Soho, in 1776, boasted to James Boswell that he had power to sell he already commanded its means of production, soon to be developed and applied by George Stephenson. The glories of the Industrial Revolution quickly burst forth prodigiously, largely made possible through advances in transportation effected by Stephenson's railways and MacAdam's roads. Hard-boiled economists therefore might consider Darlington's antiquated bits and modern appearances pale to insignificance beside the relics of portentous import exhibited on the railway station platform. Here is a museum piece, Engine No. 1, the original steam article that frightened cows in the fields when George Stephenson drove it from Stockton to Darlington along the first public railway in the world at the rate of more than ten miles an hour in the year 1825. No wonder that Sydney Smith wrote exultantly, "Man is become a bird. Time, distance and delay are abolished." As I inspected the antediluvian wheels, boiler, piston, and high chimney of the ancestral railway engine on Darlington platform the Flying Scotsman shot past, bound for Edinburgh.

"Whew! What a difference!" exclaimed a fellow observer. "We only want a pair of boots, a horse, a boneshaker, a tank, and a flying bomber overhead to complete the transport sequence up to date."

Leaving Stephenson's contribution to man's little systems of progress we return to the Tees, fresh with the eternal power of natural growth, flowing water, the everlasting hills. A few miles through the level pastoral vale, and before the uplands are reached we find Piercebridge quietly basking on the top of relics left from times of transport and conquest organised in centuries before railways were thought of. The village is attractive. A large green, shady trees, whitewashed cottages framed in leafage suggest pictures of the "Sweet Auburn" variety. Southward lines of white Georgian walls and pantile roofs bend to the high stone bridge. From the parapets you see, upstream and below, the long stretch of river winding over a rocky bed past steep wooded banks and skirting fringes of meadows. The landscape has the classic mould; its calm and serene character, full coloured on an early autumn day, made me think of visions pictured by Claude Lorrain or Richard Wilson. Straight as the crow flies the Roman road sweeps up to the Tees from Yorkshire. Still full of purpose in old age it covers the miles with direct military precision, locates a station on the west flank at Piercebridge, points for Binchester (*Vinovia*), Lanchester (*Longovicium*), and the Wall. On such a route anybody might be forgiven for expecting to meet a few Roman ghosts or tangible leavings from the Italian conquest; and though my hope of finding them at Piercebridge had been dashed by books consulted and the cheerless statement, "There is no trace of masonry," take courage, thought I, keep a sharp lookout. A few steps beyond the west side of the green led me to a first minor excitement. A series of bumps on the ground, well defined at the northern end, evidently were traces of defences thrown up by Romans for the vallum of their enclosure. My dry quest warmed up as the day grew hotter. An inn conveniently near suggested further help in the search for truth. A drink at the bar introduced me to several village natives, good specimens of those founts known for spouting local facts and knowledge not commonly found in books. My modest outlay on refreshment was quickly repaid with definite information on Roman remains, also on objects kept in the little museum across the green, to be inspected by adults for sixpence, children threepence. A good-natured farmer next led me over the green to an opening by the side of the church and said, "If you go through that farmyard of mine, turn left at the end past the cows and two lots of hay, you will see a gate leading to any amount of old stones just outside my buildings. Stop there as long as you like." Quickly I passed along, had no eyes for cows or hay in the eager moments of discovering this unexpected find of imperial masonry surviving from the second century. Though largely broken down a considerable curved section was upstanding in the well-kept surroundings of trim mown grass (248). The stonework, with the earthworks previously seen, gave the key to the plan of the station at Piercebridge, evidently a parallelogram of the usual Roman pattern, rounded at the corners and guarded by a vallum of earthen banking. More stonework obviously continued under the adjoining buildings. If the village could be knocked down and excavated—a dreadful notion!—the spade might reveal foundations of a Roman station that antiquaries cannot name with certainty. My drawing completed I took a last look round this north-east angle of the fort. But not without maudlin thoughts on things temporary and permanent, Romans, George Stephenson, scenery, weather. Once the masonry stood high and strong to serve wily conquerors in their fleeting years of power; it survives, like the Darlington railway engine, merely as a curiosity for curious people to find and gaze on. Beyond the fort continuity remained immutable, seemed likely to go on for ever; corn ripened outside the walling, colours toned the trees on the cliff above the Tees, the sun shone from a blue sky, sending fresh lights and shadows on the dead stones. With these sombre-ish ideas on certain constancy and the frailty of human contrivance I left the wreckage of a lost empire, bade good-bye to the cows, found the farmer again to thank him for his kindness, called on the friendly company at the inn to make sure that they had not passed away, then returned to the highway of the motoring age, the old road travelled by the Emperors Hadrian, Severus, and the legions before their *Britannia Magna* collapsed.

A mile or so north of Piercebridge we may leave the straight and narrow way of the Romans to find how later arrivals accommodated themselves when castles were the mode. Nearest stands Walworth, only a castle by name, for its maker built with an eye to living in peace rather than for meeting war's alarms. He developed big windows to let in the light instead of forming small openings for sending missiles out on besiegers' heads, erected ornamental towers and the picturesque outlines fashionable in the spacious Elizabethan age. Soon royalty appeared in person. Travelling south as good Scots do, King James VI of Scotland came down the Roman road to try a change of air, fortune, and a change of name to King James I on the throne of England. Calling on the way at this old home His Majesty enjoyed bed and breakfast humbly proffered by Mrs. Jenkinson, widow of the builder. King, widow, bed and breakfast had been eclipsed even as memories by the silence of emptiness and desertion when I called there. Further westward, adjoining Staindrop, Raby Castle in its park of wide acres tells a different story. It thrives to-day, has been lived in without break since the fourteenth-century Nevilles flourished and were succeeded by the Vanes. Onward from 1331, under Lord Ralph and Lord John, Raby was too domestically planned to be a military fortress of the strong castle-building period; subsequent reconstruction and mauling are obvious in the vast fortified dwelling. Yet towers, battlements and half-moat, quadrangle, stone-vaulted kitchen, and the great barons' hall can swing imagination back to the heydays of Neville pomp, to the vigilance and political intrigues of the forceful Earls of Westmorland. Outside and within the walls, by the grey stonework mirrored in the moat, it is easy to weave antique tales embroidered with waving banners, the flurry of arms, the pageantry of momentous hours long gone. Here you may mentally picture Lord Ralph riding out to victory at Neville's Cross, the sixth Earl with seven hundred Catholic knights gathered in 1569 to depose Queen Elizabeth in the Rising of the North, and end the epic with Sir Henry Vane, Parliamentarian, held at bay by Royalists during the Civil War. Characters in the scenes played at this historic house lie quiet where the silent hand of death sent them; the splendid series of effigies and memorials surrounded by architectural fineness in Staindrop church bring reality to the acts staged at Raby Castle.

On Tees-side, where we now return, the landscapes continue to show the loveliness of stream, rocks, green banks, and woods for which this river and its borderlands so notably excel. With the approach to Teesdale proper begins the finest scenery of all. Along the river's course, clear of the taint of commercial industrialism, I also found the most attractive of Durham's villages. Particularly upward from Piercebridge to Middleton-in-Teesdale do they merit finding, whether on the Durham or Yorkshire banks. Characteristically northern are the buildings. Sturdily made, honest in appearance, but inclined to be plain, they adequately fit locations where the abundant beauty of natural environment yields the greatest charm and grace. Gainford's colour-washed cottages and stone houses border a spacious green (258); secluded at the western corner is a hall of the 1600's neighboured by the church with Early English and older features. The Tees sings below the graveyard wall, rippling over stones, coloured in reflections from the trees, and no visitor should fail to discover the charming riverside walk. Over the water, in Yorkshire, a mixture of mounds, St. Lawrence's chapel in ruins, peace, quiet, and the cows I saw nibbling, locate the site of Old Richmond. Higher up the river the "woodland scene" shelters pretty Winston and pretty Wycliffe too, natal region of the Wycliffes who bred the frail, bold, unconquerable Reformer. Soon the Greta comes in to swell the stream. Rokeby woods colour the prospect. The hall, at which Walter Scott stayed with John Morritt in the early 1800's, gives a Georgian accent to its noble park. Hereabout for many a mile we remember that the Wizard of the North came this same way, finding beauty, collecting old tales, gleaning flowers and lyrics for *Rokeby*.

> Here trees to every crevice cling,

in Greta's "romantic dell." Near the confluence with the Tees the "grassy slope" still keeps the weathered walls, the carved heraldic Rokeby rooks, the courtyard of Mortham's

> battled tower and portal grey.

Tracks of Cotman, too, we can follow and find his subjects, *Greta Woods*, his lovely *Greta Bridge* at the south entrance to the park.

Past beauty vying with beauty at the river's fringes, soon are seen Abbey Bridge and Egglestone Abbey ruins in perfect settings. Next, where a tang in the air wafts down from the highlands, the view of Barnard Castle opens out, a striking group in the best romantic manner. Old worn masonry towers above the Elizabethan bridge and sparkling stream (258). Battered walls, time's curious shapes, crannies overgrown, may excite poetic ruminations on a castle in the air, pomp and state vanished. From low to high Bridgegate ascends into the bright little town of stone buildings, to the market-place, the octagonal market-house, and the *King's Head*, known to Charles Dickens when occupied with *Nicholas Nickleby*. Behind the hotel and an ancient church the castle ruins cover a wide area with a medley of courtyards, curtain walls, the gateway, and a high round tower, sometimes called the keep. Dilapidated, all in a sad sorry way, not much in the wreckage survives to glorify associations with past mighty occupants—Richard III, Nevilles, Staffords, Beauchamps, the powerful

Norman Baliols, first builders of the castle, whose name is more substantially commemorated at John de Baliol's foundation of 1260 in Broad Street, Oxford.

Roads on each side of the river lead from Barnard Castle to Middleton-in-Teesdale, ten miles away. Of these two routes my choice is the one on the Yorkshire bank for views, woods, and village pictures. Lartington charms with a collection of cottages, gardens, the squire's hall and park. Near Cotherstone, where the Balder stream meets the Tees, the tumbled-down castle of the Fitzhugh family retains the grey hoariness that attracted Walter Scott. At Romaldkirk two miles distant, Sir Henry Fitzhugh, who died in 1304, introduced himself to me with a brave armoured effigy; it lies in the church, a building notable for varied architecture and prettily surrounded by houses, cottages, and inns centred at the village green. Onward and upward past Middleton-in-Teesdale the scenery grows wilder. From crag and torrent lonely moors and fells stretch away to distant solitudes. Holwick Force hurries down, making a prelude for the river's two crowning performances. Soon is reached the magnificent spectacle at High Force, England's grandest waterfall. Currents dash along, leap past the great mass of basalt and limestone poised amidstream above the lower pool. Of nature untamed this is a sight for eye and memory. Few people witness its most imposing and turbulent appearance. When the wireless has announced depressions of bad weather, heavy rains or melting snow, no words can describe the magnificence of the Force in awesome and savage mood; only once was it my good fortune to catch the propitious day and moments. Here in good weather we may not be alone. The place has fame and popularity, is called "a beauty spot." Consequently notices request visitors not to spoil it! Further upstream, if lucky, we are far from the madding crowd. The scene is bleaker, more solitary, treeless, a likely region for meeting a Macbeth or three witches boiling lizards' legs in a cauldron. First heard, then is seen Caldron Snout hurling in wild abandon over a fall of two hundred feet. Higher yet higher the Tees brings us to the end of Durham's boundary and a view of the river's source, Cross Fell, looming nearly 3,000 feet high in Cumberland.

One of the loneliest highways I know, airy and elevated, mounts up from Middleton-in-Teesdale bound for Alston. Even higher at Killhope Pass (over 2,000 feet) is the more northerly main road down Weardale to St. John's Chapel and Stanhope. These two routes intersect open mountainous country, a wild district that generally has managed to avoid destructive handling by civilization, though scarred in places with quarrying and the old-established industry of leadmining. When I set out to explore there the locals told me, "You are going over the roof of England"; very apt their words proved to be. Continuous heights bunched together locate the Durham–Cumberland boundary (259). Sweeping lines are made by Killhope Moor, Knoutberry Hill, Lamb's Head, Dead Stones, Viewing Hill; Burnhope Seat reigns supreme at

2,452 feet. The mountains continue eastward, define Three Pikes and Fendrith Hill, branch out like the extended fingers of a hand to meet the commons of Newbiggin, Middleton, and Bollihope.

To people who no longer progress with their feet these fascinating names may convey little; they can mean much and promise thrilling sensations to tough walkers, riders on horses, expert map-readers. Never was this area troubled with much population. I found it barren of early earthworks, historic landmarks, short in supply of churches and domestic architecture because such adornments would have been redundant. But for meeting nature in the raw state, clear of man's fandoodles, embellishments, and make-up, this wild and lonely tract hardly could be excelled. It keeps stillness and quiet. The air is fine and clear. Curved backs of the mountains and wide moorland expanses display the true character of limestone scenery. Radiant sunlight and stately clouds march along, sending big shadows chasing across open miles. Wind, water, and birds tune music. Peewits call, curlews utter their plaintive cries, brooks murmur down ravines. Named to recall Scandinavian and Anglo-Saxon settlement, "becks" go south to Teesdale, "burns" run north for Weardale. The seasons bring the wild flowers. The hardy ground mulberry, locally called the knout-berry, titles Knoutberry Hill. Trees grow in more sheltered hollows, their trunks bent by wind and storm. Animate life on the ground is scarce, nor are evidences of man's doings plentiful. The total of both seen in a day's rough marching may be only a few isolated farmsteads, the black-faced sheep, by chance a shepherd and his dog. Similar configurations of land surfaces and aspects of scene continue north of Weardale to the heights overlooking the River Derwent. There, in the valley, the relic of a peel tower in Hunstanworth churchyard reminds us of Border raiding. Down the stream an old stone bridge at Blanchland leads into the next county. At this point my pages introduce

A NORTHUMBRIAN ENDING

Before pressing onward we really must look at Blanchland (259). Grey yet cheery and attractive, it is one of those oases found here and there in the North to contrast pleasantly with the prevailing austerity of stone-built villages secluded among the moors, mountain slopes, and dancing streams. These bright spots generally hint the sources of their character and individuality, suggested perhaps by the presence of the big house, signs of modern wealth, an abbey or castle probably ruined, reminders of past industry, or fragmentary relics that recall the stories, ballads, bitter warfare, and very dark deeds of the old Border life. Blanchland has an abbey church and monastic remains, a medieval gateway in the square, distinctive architecture in stone houses and cottages, Ruffside Hall for aristocratic distinction. The stream sings along under the bridge, wooded hills rise for a background. Froissart gave the village a mention, leadminers thrived in it two hundred years ago, and more recently my own thriving was at the *Crewe Arms*, a cosy hostel first made for thirteenth-century guests. Other places of this stamp in Northumberland reward the discovery and my remembrances include the following pictorial effects. Ovingham on the Tyne facing Prudhoe's Norman keep; Elsdon, gathering place of the Redesdale clans, with its peel tower now accommodating the rector; another peel tower at Rothbury erected long before Lord Armstrong built Craigside surrounded by banks of woods in the lovely Coquet valley; Etal on the Till stream prettily grouped about the mansion, the castle ruins, and the green fields of Flodden, the red Flodden of long ago, lying between the river and distant Cheviots.

Miles around Blanchland stretch the open moors, the riggs and fells, lonely, coloured bright, brown, or with heather at the right time. Burns by the score spring from the heights, bicker onward between the ridges. Over rocks, down falls in wooded valleys, the South Tyne and two Allen streams flow on to join the main Tyne River. From elevated slopes you look northward. Nearest, at the Tyne level, lie historic Hexham, Roman Corbridge. The North Tyne gap beyond encloses Chesters, Roman remains, foundations of the Roman bridge. Right and left bold ridges lead the eye along the lines on which Romans built their Wall (262), eastward to Newcastle and Wallsend, westward to Gilsland and Solway Firth. Far away wide rolling country mounts to the Cheviots. On clear days you spy into Scotland.

These sweeps of Northumberland landscape, the miles and distances visible from Blanchland Moor, Whitfield Moor, and high points all the way to the Cheviot Hills, figure like the open pages of the grim and turbulent northern story with man's landmarks of settlement, conquest, and warring to serve for the illustrations. There, picturesque on a knoll above the Tyne, stands Hexham; its tower, moot hall, the marvellous choir, transepts, and treasures inside the priory church locate St. Wilfrid's foundation of 674, ravaging by Danes, burning and bloodshed by Scots in 1296. In Corbridge, delightful to visit nowadays, only the span of time divides it from *Corstopitum*, once the busy and populous Roman military base on the highway from York to the Wall and Agricola's Dere Street into Scotland.

From east to west along the hills run the parallel courses of the Wall, vallum, and military road, traverses of imperial purpose and far-flung conquest. The tell-tale earth, broken masonry, and preserved museum collections testify to prodigious feats, immense achievements. Only to look at them makes it quite simple for imaginative souls to slip back into a Romano-British frame of mind. Forts, mile-castles, signalling turrets and rampart walks stir with life again. Out of the melancholy shades Hadrian comes, legions march, watchers keep the

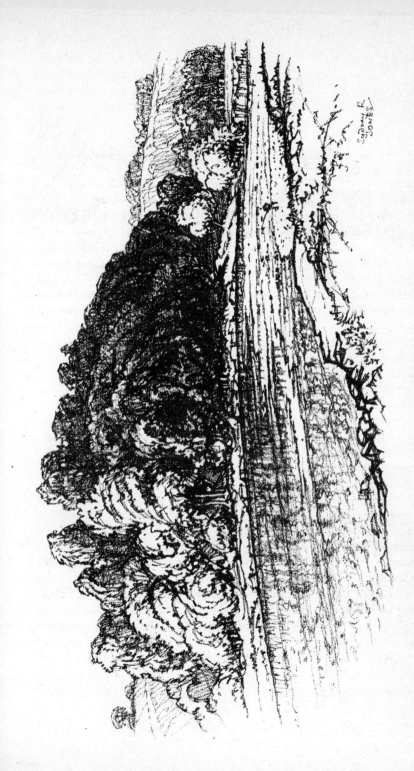

RIVER TEES *near the site of old Richmond.*

GAINFORD. *Colour-washed cottages, stone houses, and the church border a big green on the Durham side of the river where the Tees flows between wooded banks.*

BARNARD CASTLE. *"Old Barnard's towers" associated with Scott's "Rokeby." The Elizabethan bridge spans the Tees below the ruined castle first erected by the powerful Norman family of Baliol, one of whom founded Balliol College, Oxford, in 1260.*

PENNINE HIGHLANDS. *The lonely mountain stretch from which the Killhope Burn runs down to Wear Dale.*

BLANCHLAND *on the high moorlands near the source of the River Derwent. The stone-built village incorporates remains of a priory.*

THE CASTLED NORTH.

DUNSTANBURGH
Ruins of great Edwardian

BAMBURGH

WARKWORTH
dating from c. 1200
& the 15th. century tower

ALNWICK
Seat of th

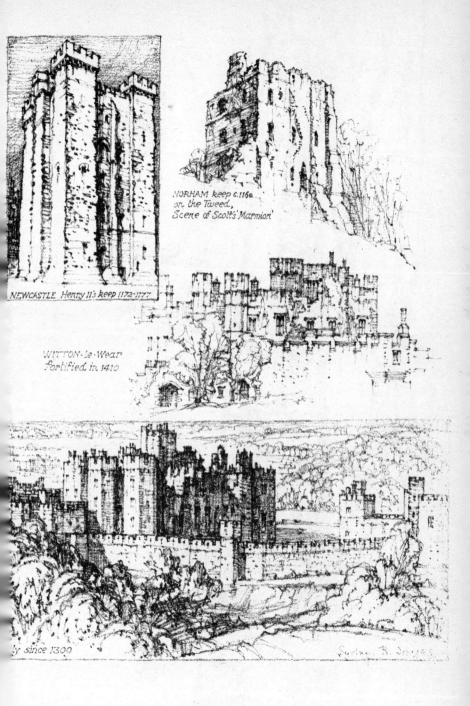

NEWCASTLE Henry II's keep 1172-1177

NORHAM keep c.1160
on the Tweed,
Scene of Scott's 'Marmion'

WITTON-le-Wear
fortified in 1410

ly since 1300

Sydney R. Jones

Sydney R. Jones
Hexham

LINE OF THE ROMAN WALL and North Tyne gap beyond Hexham town and abbey. Distant hills lead to the Cheviot range.

MORPETH *on the River Wansbeck. A ruined medieval bridge, old houses, great mounds, and relics of an ancient castle group by the stream.*

LINDISFARNE. *Remains of the priory on Holy Island. Here St. Aidan brought Christianity to Northumbria in 635 A.D. and St. Cuthbert ministered as prior fifty years later.*

THE CHEVIOT (*2,676 feet*) *and foothills from the Till valley near Wooler.*

ceaseless vigil towards the north. Barbarians pierce the line. Victorious Severus scatters the foes, rebuilds the Wall. Once more Picts break through. Again the Wall is rebuilt by Constantius in 296 A.D., by Count Theodosius in 367 A.D. Finally watchers face south, depart, never to return. The Wall ceases to function, falls, decays, serves only for a quarry to build churches, peel towers, farmhouses. Over silent miles its very place disappears under the ploughshare. But wreckage remains, bigger in meaning than for the sights it shows. To follow the course from Limestone Bank, Carrawburgh fort and the excavated shrine of the god Mithras, past Housesteads (*Borcovicus*), along the cliffs high above the loughs, up and down to the dramatic clefts at the Nine Nicks of Thirlwall, and onward to Carvoran (*Magna*) at the junction of the Maiden Way—here across Northumberland is more than enough to fire the imagination at this monument of the Roman name and fame that for two hundred and fifty years formed the northern bulwark of a great empire's authority and dominion.

Roman power faded and gone, the gloom of the Dark Ages descended with fire, sword, and raiding. Light pierced the darkness in 635 from Lindisfarne's Holy Island. St. Aidan and St. Cuthbert spread the Celtic Christianity through the troubled Northumberland country. After the Synod of Whitby the Church of Rome followed in their wake. To-day the sacred monuments of those times call us to Hexham, Lindisfarne ruins (263), to monastic remains at Newminster or Brinkburn, both in lovely valley settings. Nevertheless from medieval years until the beginning of the eighteenth century incorrigible man persisted in bad ways, plundered, spoiled, slaughtered, left gruesome pages for history and epics for Border minstrelsy. In this safer age we can think of the old tales, the family feuds, marauding Scots, moss troopers, the Redesdale and Tynedale borderers, and quite forget all about the rapine, mourning, violated shrines at Lambley or Hepple. Pleasant peaceful ways lead us to battle points at Humbleton Hill, Hedgeley Moor, to Otterburn where Douglas fell to Percy's sword at Chevy Chase, to the Flodden grave-fields of Scotland's nobility. As for fortified buildings, grim survivals from times of trouble and death, intact or ruined they stand more closely packed than I have seen elsewhere in England. There are castles by the dozen, some of which are represented by my drawings on pages 260–1. Far more than a score of peel towers hold tight in many places, from Staward Pele and Belsay in the south to the northern Doddington Bastle. Still emblematic of the old spirit of the North they lead to exciting discoveries, stern thick walls, crumbled masonry, and may summon quite frightening ruminations on dreadful ancient stories linked with such names as Wallace, Douglas, Ivar the Strider, Evers and Lonkin, Robert the Devil.

Following the decline of the terrorist and freebooting vocations the Industrial Revolution brought another kind of raiding to the south-eastern face of the county and low coastline. Coalmining, shipbuilding and manufacturing developed their own distinctive and smoky landmarks. It is not within my province to attempt descriptions of the results or to indicate where to find them. They are particularly obvious to all who wish to inspect monuments accumulated during two centuries of progress. Seaton Delaval, Vanbrugh's masterpiece, became undermined and deserted. The ancient city, Newcastle, expanded round the Norman keep, Black Gate, the stately church, the old houses at the deep ravine of the Tyne.

Fixed, defiant to humanity's bickering and changes, the hills ruled in the west. Wild, remote, austere, they seem likely to stand fast for ever. Northward from the Roman Wall their names exactly fit the bleak impressiveness of the scenes—Black Fell, Naked Man, Rough Pike, Hungry Law, Windygate Hill. The flat-topped Cheviot, reared to 2,676 feet, mounts over the loveliness of Harthope Valley, Hen Hole, and College Glen. Grand walking country is this. You find the Kielder Stone, of bloody traditions, dividing England from Scotland. A medieval way crosses the Border at Knox Knowe. Roman camps are crowded together in the solitudes of Chew Green. When mists float away from ridges and moors big clouds chase across blue skies. The sun shines through. The eye travels over broad landscapes to distant horizons. Streams run down, find the valleys, wind away to Percy's proud towers at Alnwick (261), to the wooded glens of the Coquet, to Morpeth on the Wansbeck (263). Near and far from the heights the sweeps of scene encircle villages, churches, country towns, highroads, trackways, camps, primitive earthworks, relics of wars, emblems of faith and peace, tokens of long-settled life, each set out like landmarks in a dumb procession of the centuries. Down from the hills and within sight of The Cheviot (264) I reach old Wooler, there to end my travels through *England East, England West* and *England South.*

Roman Wall near Haltwhistle Burn

LIST OF ILLUSTRATIONS

MAPS

INDEX